FOUNDATIONS FOR
CHRISTIAN EDUCATION

FOUNDATIONS FOR
CHRISTIAN EDUCATION

Co-editors:
Eleanor A. Daniel & John W. Wade

COLLEGE PRESS PUBLISHING
JOPLIN, MISSOURI

Cover Design: Brett Lyerla

Library of Congress Cataloging-in-Publication Data

Foundations for Christian education / co-editors, Eleanor A. Daniel,
  John W. Wade
     p.   cm.
   Includes bibliographical references and index.
   ISBN 0-89900-855-0 (pbk.)
   1. Christian education. I. Daniel, Eleanor Ann. II. Wade, John
William, 1924–   .
BV1471.2.F673 1999
268—dc21   99-32265
                                        CIP

Foundations for Christian Education:
TABLE OF CONTENTS

Foreword   7
Preface   9
Contributors   10

Part One: Foundation Stones

Chapter One
     Biblical-Theological Foundations of Christian Education   13
     Dr. James Estep, Great Lakes Christian College

Chapter Two
     Philosophical-Historical Foundations of Christian Education   34
     Dr. James Estep

Chapter Three
     Psychological Foundations of Christian Education   60
     Dr. Eleanor Daniel, Emmanuel School of Religion

Chapter Four
     Sociological Trends: The Church's Response   79
     Ruth Picker, Minnesota Bible College

Chapter Five
     Curricular Foundations of Christian Education   96
     Dr. Eleanor Daniel

Part Two: Teaching/Learning Encounter

Chapter Six
     The Teacher/Learner Encounter   115
     Dr. Alvin Kuest, Great Lakes Christian College

Chapter Seven
     The Church's Ministry to Young Children   138
     Sherry Parrott, Ozark Christian College

Chapter Eight
     The Church's Ministry to Elementary School Children   160
     Virginia Beddow, Manhattan Christian College

Chapter Nine
     The Church's Ministry to Teenagers   178
     Rick Chromey, Saint Louis Christian College

Chapter Ten
     The Church's Ministry to Adults   194
     Dr. Eleanor Daniel

Chapter Eleven
        Providing Christian Education for Persons with Disabilities   213
        Dr. Jim Pierson, Christian Church Foundation for the Handicapped
Chapter Twelve
        Using Media and Technology in Teaching   233
        Dr. Christine Templar, Johnson Bible College
Chapter Thirteen
        The Church's Ministry to Families   250
        Ken Greene, Minnesota Bible College

Part Three: Planning

Chapter Fourteen
        Planning for Christian Education   271
        Dr. Ronald L. Oakes, Saint Louis Christian College
Chapter Fifteen
        Developing a Balanced Christian Education Program   291
        Dr. Alvin Kuest
Chapter Sixteen
        Recruiting, Training, and Keeping Volunteer Leaders   311
        Dr. Eleanor Daniel
Chapter Seventeen
        Legal Issues Related to Christian Education   321
        John W. Wade, Atlanta Christian College
Chapter Eighteen
        Evaluating the Effectiveness of Christian Education   338
        John W. Wade
Chapter Nineteen
        The Minister and Christian Education   359
        Dr. J. Michael Shannon, First Christian Church, Johnson City,
        Tennessee
Chapter Twenty
        The Professional Christian Educator   368
        Dr. Eleanor Daniel

Appendix: Resources for Christian Educators   381
        Rick Chromey
Indexes: Names, Subjects, Scripture References   393

FOREWORD

The Christian Church movement has developed a strong group of Bible colleges in the population centers of the United States, particularly in the South and Midwest. For fifty years these have formed a concerted effort to lift the level of academic expertise of these schools. However, the most significant strength of these institutions has been the power of the practical dimensions of local church ministry. The professors of preaching, educational administration, and above all, Christian education, have been marked by this penchant for excellence, and the identification of those individuals whose local church efforts have been stellar. Achievement in the trenches has won them a place to teach. Earning doctoral degrees has not been the *sine qua non* of these teachers and writers even though seven of the 13 have gained them and an increasing level of academic reputation has been attained.

Giving leadership to this competent contingent is Dr. Eleanor Daniel, the distinguished Dean and Professor of Christian Education at Emmanuel School of Religion in Tennessee. Her personal contribution to the discipline of Christian education has very few equals. Her co-editor, John W. Wade, has a splendid record in writing and church ministry as well. They have brought some of their finest colleagues together in this salute to reality in the church. Quickly you will sense their dedication to the task of the church.

This is a valuable contribution to the field of Christian education. It is written by veteran persons in the field as well as employing the fresh-thinking of creative younger professors in the discipline. It is a delight to recommend this volume. It will serve as a fine textbook for undergraduate programs in particular but also in many graduate courses as well.

Warren S. Benson, Ph.D.
Vice President of Professional Doctoral Programs
Professor of Christian Education
Trinity Evangelical Divinity School

PREFACE

Christian education is at the heart of ministry. The New Testament clearly instructs believers and the church to teach, baptize, then teach some more. Through the centuries Christian education has taken on many different forms and has been accomplished by the church in a variety of ways. When the church has been faithful to the task of Christian education, then it has been strong. But when the church has failed in its mission to teach, it has been weak.

This book, produced by Chistian educators in a variety of colleges and settings, is designed to assist the church in this educational mission as we confront the new millennium. The book is divided into three parts. Part I examines the foundations of Christian education—biblical and theological, historical and philosophical, psychological, sociological, and curricular.

Part II applies the foundations to specific age groups in the church. This section begins with a look at the teacher and learner encounter, followed by a description of that encounter with preschool children, elementary school children, teenagers, adults, and families. Additional chapters examine the use of media in teaching and the challenges of teaching the disabled.

Part III deals with organzational and administrative issues: planning, achieving a balanced program, recruiting and training staff, legal issues, evaluating, the work of the Christian education professional, and the minister and Christian education. The book concludes with an appendix providing helpful resources for the Christian educator.

Whatever form it takes, Christian education is still the heart of the ministry of the church. It is the desire of the authors that this book will provide helpful principles and tools to enable the church to accomplish the mission of teaching, baptizing, and teaching in the 21st century.

CONTRIBUTORS

Virginia Beddow is Associate Professor of Educational Ministries at Manhattan Christian College, 1415 Anderson Ave., Manhattan, KS 66502.

Rick Chromey is Professor of Christian Education and Youth Ministry at St. Louis Christian College, 1360 Grandview Drive, Florissant, MO 63033.

Dr. Eleanor A. Daniel is Dean and Professor of Christian Education at Emmanuel School of Religion, One Walker Drive, Johnson City, TN 37601.

Dr. James R. Estep is Academic Dean at Great Lakes Christian College, 6211 W. Willow Highway, Lansing, MI 48917.

Kendall S. Greene is Professor of Youth and Family Ministries at Minnesota Bible College, 920 Mayowood Road SW, Rochester, MN 55902.

Dr. Alvin Kuest is Professor of Christian Education at Great Lakes Christian College, 6211 W. Willow Highway, Lansing, MI 48917.

Dr. Ron Oakes is Dean and Professor of Christian Education at St. Louis Christian College, 1360 Grandview Drive, Florissant, MO 63033.

Sherry Y. Parrott is Professor of Christian Education at Ozark Christian College, 1111 N. Main Street, Joplin, MO 64801.

Ruth Picker is Professor of English, Communications, and Christian Education at Minnesota Bible College, 920 Mayowood Road SW, Rochester, MN 55902.

Dr. Jim Pierson is Director of the Christian Church Foundation for the Handicapped, PO Box 9869, 134G Maryville Pike, Knoxville, TN 37940.

Dr. J. Michael Shannon is Minister at First Christian Church, 2011 Sherwood Drive, Johnson City, TN 37601, and an adjunct preaching professor at Milligan College.

Dr. Chris Templar is Chairman of the Department of Teacher Education at Johnson Bible College, 7900 Johnson Drive, Knoxville, TN 37998.

John W. Wade is Professor of Christian Education at Atlanta Christian College, 2605 Ben Hill Road, East Point, GA 30344.

PART ONE

FOUNDATION STONES

CHAPTER 1
BIBLICAL-THEOLOGICAL
FOUNDATIONS OF CHRISTIAN EDUCATION

Chapter One Summary
- ☑ Scriptural exhortations to educate
- ☑ Biblical models of education
- ☑ Old and New Testament chart of Scriptures dealing with education
- ☑ Educational significance of the Bible
- ☑ The role of theology in education

"Jesus loves me; this I know, for the Bible tells me so." It is a simple, yet profound lyric. The Bible is the center of the Christian faith. We do not worship the Bible, but it is through the Bible that we know Whom to worship (cf. 2 Tim 3:15).

The Bible serves as the primary textbook for Christian education. Not only does it supply the content of Christian instruction, but also provides direction, models of education, methodology, and a rationale for Christian education. It serves as the cornerstone of theological foundations and the prolegomena of the historical foundations for Christian education. As such, Scripture is the primary lens through which the Christian educator perceives and prescribes the character of education in the church.

The prime reason for regarding Scripture as foundational to Christian education is its claims of revelation and inspiration (cf. 1 Cor 2:10-13; 1 Tim 3:15-17; 1 Pet 1:10-12,21; 2 Pet 1:20-21; 3:2,15-16). The Christian educator is compelled to formulate a model of Christian education that is consistent with God's expressed design. The apostle Paul contends that the Scriptures "were given for our instruction" (Rom 15:4; 1 Cor 10:5-11; 2 Tim 3:15-17). Likewise, D. Campbell Wyckoff comments that "the theological enterprise [in Christian education] is necessary because of the fact of revelation" (1995, 12).

The prime reason for regarding Scripture as foundational to Christian education is its claims of revelation and inspiration.

However, a far more fundamental issue remains: What makes education Christian? Education is Christian when its theory and practices are rooted in biblical understandings. The Scriptures provide the imperative for education, and even culturally relevant models to fulfill it. Theology, as a systematic reflection of the Bible's teaching, provides a conceptual framework through which to form a distinctively Christian approach to education. Theology serves as the Christian educator's philosophy of education, from which educational particulars are derived. It provides a philosophical foundation in which education is transformed into ministry. Wyckoff defined Christian education as "a theological discipline that draws upon the behavioral sciences" (1995, 12).

Biblical Mandate and Models for Education

The Scriptures are saturated with educational imperatives and implications. The promotion and preservation of both personal and community faith is a common theme throughout the Scriptures. However, within this lies a caution: Some models of education in the Scriptures are by nature culturally specific models that cannot simply be mimicked or transplanted into the contemporary era.

While the biblical principles are undeniably essential to Christian education, the specific methods must be assessed in light of their relevance and effectiveness. It is the realization of the mandate that is essential for Christian education, not the preservation of specific methods as being "divinely established." For example, throughout the New Testament the synagogue is the center for Jewish religious education and worship, yet we have no record or reference to its inception or formation in the Old Testament. Was the synagogue initiated by God or by human design? The synagogue was a human endeavor to accomplish the educational mandate of the Old Testament, one in which Jesus himself even participated. While methodology must indeed be consistent with the biblical imperative and implications for instruction, the Christian educator is not limited to only those methods contained in the Scriptures.

Education in the Old Testament

Teaching in the Old Testament was primarily designed to equip the individual and community for faithful living (Deut 11:19; 20:18). This was a continual theme throughout the Old Testament, especially after the Exile when education assumed the task of restoring the faith of Israel and Judah (2 Chr 17:7-9; 34:29-30). Education was accomplished primarily through socialization (i.e., learning through encounter with the culture and community) and nonformal means, with few formal examples of education, e.g., schools or institutes.

Teaching in the Old Testament was primarily designed to equip the individual and community for faithful living.

Significant Passages: Numerous passages relate the biblical mandate to the community of faith throughout the Old Testament. Table 1.1 contains a list of such passages with accompanying commentary regarding their educational implications.

Teachers in the Old Testament: Educational endeavors innately include instruction, which implies the necessity of instructors or

Table 1.1: Significant Old Testament Passages

Passage	Content	Educational Implications
Deuteronomy 6:1-9	The family is responsible for childhood instruction through teaching and community life.	Both the content and context of Christian instruction are essential. Create teachable moments.
Deuteronomy 30:11-20	The nation of Israel, having been instructed, must choose between faithfulness and rejection of God.	Instruction must lead students toward making a personal decision of faith.
Deuteronomy. 31:9-13	Priests are to read the law to the assembly of people (Hebrew and resident aliens), including children, so they can know and obey the law.	Christian education is meant for both those of the community of faith and those outside of it. All are compelled to acknowledge God and live in obedience to Him.
Psalm 78	The passage recounts the intervention of God on Israel's behalf, noting that these should be taught to the children by their families.	Christian education includes the passing down of history and traditions, and as such becomes an intergenerational affair.
Nehemiah 8:1-9	Nehemiah has Ezra read the Mosaic Law to an assembly of people, with the Levites providing commentary and further instruction on the meaning of the text.	Christian education must be concerned with communicating the contents of the Bible, but must also provide commentary aiding students in understanding the meaning of the Scriptures.
Ezra 7:10-11	Teachers assume four roles: Devotee ("heart") Student ("know") Disciple ("observe") Instructor ("teach")	The teacher's spirituality must be holistic in nature, not merely intellectual, but also developing in the affective and volitional domains.
Wisdom Literature (Proverbs)	Three kinds of teaching: Wisdom (1:20; 8:1-36; 9:1) Instruction (2:17) Correction (13:24; 17:20; 22:15; 29:25-27	Christian education must seek to maintain the tradition of "wisdom," not as the mere accumulation of knowledge, but the ability to make suitable application of biblical text to life.
Prophetic Literature	Pazmiño (1997) comments that the prophets were addressing the nation to remind the people of their accountability to God, both individually and socially.	Christian education must not only focus on personal needs, but also those of the faith community and the society. God's sovereignty applies to every aspect of life, including the necessity of justice.

teachers. It is paradoxical to attempt a study of Old Testament education without identifying the primary element of all educational systems: the teacher. Throughout the history of the Old Testament, teachers played a critical role in forming the faith of God's people and community. Who were Israel/Judah's teachers?

Teachers of the Old Testament
God
Family
Community
Prophets
Priests
Sages/Wisemen
Scribes

God was Israel's first "teacher" (Isa 3:8; Job 36:22; Exod 35:34). Throughout the Old Testament God's revelatory acts, both in deed and word, demonstrate His place as the Teacher of the faith community. This fact explains the centrality of God within the life of the nation (Exod 20:1-7; Judg 2:10-15). Perhaps the most significant act of verbal revelation was the giving of the Torah (literally translated "instruction," but referring to the first five books of the Old Testament) to Moses, which was used by all the Old Testament teachers.

Educational responsibility was located primarily in the Hebrew family (Exod 12:26-27; 20:4-12; Deut 4:9-10; 6:6-7; 11:19-20; 29:9; Ps 78:3-6; Prov 6:20). Both parents were to be involved in the instruction of their children (Prov 1:8), as well as other family members, making education within the family an intergenerational matter (Deut 4:9-11; 11:19-20; Exod 12:26-27; Ps 78:3-6).

God was Israel's first "teacher."

The prophets constitute perhaps the most vocal and obvious teachers in the Old Testament (Jer 8:8; 9:13; 16:11; Micah 6:8; Isa 8:3-16; 42:21-24; Zech 7:12; Hos 1:3-9). Moses served as the paradigm for future prophets (Exod 18:20; 24:12; Deut 4:14; 6:1; 31:19). The prophets did indeed make use of the Mosaic law in their instruction (Isa 8:16; 42:21, 24; Jer 9:13, 16:11; Zech 7:12). The "School of the Prophets" (2 Kgs 2:3-5; 4:38; 6:1; 1 Sam 10:10; 19:20) should not be understood as a modern formal educational institution. The actual phrase is "sons [Hebrew *ben*] of the prophets," not "school" as the KJV mistranslates, indicating a discipling or nonformal approach to instruction rather than a formal institutional one.

Priests not only received formal education, but provided instruction to the community (Deut 22; Ps 27:31; 40:8; Hag 2:11; Mal 2:6-9, 3:11). As with the prophets, the priests used the Torah in their instruction (Ps 37:31; 40:8; Hag 2:11; Mal 2:6-9). In fact, Deuteronomy 31:9-14 indicates that the priests were to read the Torah for the instruction of the Hebrew nation, including "aliens living in your towns."

Sages or wisemen, not to be confused with the Persian magi, constitute another body of teachers in the Old Testament (Judg 14:12-14; 2 Sam 13:1-22; Prov 3:3-11; 10:8; 12:15; 13:14; 14:2; 28:4-9). These men were knowledgeable of the Torah and able to make practical application of its instruction (Prov 13:14; 28:4-9).

Scribes emerge near the close of the Old Testament (Neh 8; Jer 8:8), but are frequently mentioned in the New Testament as scribes, rabbis, and/or doctors of the law. Ezra is described as a teacher-scribe and serves as a model for this category of teacher (Ezra 7:10-11).

As a theocracy the nation reflected within its very culture a sense of spirituality and religious devotion.

Often neglected as an "instructor" of Israel/Judah is the community itself. As a theocracy the nation reflected within its very culture a sense of spirituality and religious devotion. The community itself was a teacher. Tidwell calls this "public instructions," because religious socialization occurred as one encountered the culture of God's people (Price, 1932). For example, the reason for festivals, placement of worship sites, activities of public assemblies all had educational significance (Deut 4:14; 6:1; 26:1ff; 31:39; Josh 8:30-35; 2 Kgs 2:3; 4:38; 5:22; 2 Chr 17:7-19).

Education in
the New Testament

The ministry of Jesus, teachings of the apostles, writings of Paul and other New Testament authors, and the practices of the early Christian community provide a vivid and vibrant portrait of education in the first-century church. While the preservation of faith is indeed a theme within the New Testament, as it was with the Old Testament, the added dimensions of conversion and growth toward Christlikeness, both individually and corporately, typify the education ministry of the early church.

Significant Passages: The New Testament contains many references to the educational endeavors of the early Christian community. Table 1.2 highlights several of the more significant passages and their educational implications.

Table 1.2: Significant New Testament Passages

Passage	Content	Educational Implications
Matthew 28:18-20	Jesus' commission to His disciples to continue His disciple-making endeavors, which innately included teaching.	Christian education must maintain the focus of making disciples of Christ, which does not simply end with conversion, but requires continuing instruction.
Luke 24:13-35	Jesus' teaching method: Discussion (v. 14) Inquiry (v. 17) Correction (vv. 25-27) Modeling (vv. 30-31) Response (vv. 33-35)	Pazmiño (1997, 38) comments that Jesus' teaching had three parts: Question, Listen, and Exhort. Teachers must engage their students to think and reflect, not merely mimic. Jesus provides a process model of education.
Acts	Acts refers to both the nonformal (5:42) and socialization of the Christian community (2:42).	Christian education is an essential aspect of congregational life. Instruction, both teaching and community encounter, is part of God's design to form both the Christian and the church.
1 Corinthians 2:6-16	The activity of the Spirit in applying the truth of Scripture to the believer's life is emphasized. The spiritually mature are better able to discern spiritual truth.	Teaching must allow for the activity of the Holy Spirit and encourage reflection of the Bible to life. Christian education must encourage the praxis of the Spirit and the human spirit.

Passage	Content	Educational Implications
Ephesians 4:7-16	Pastor-teachers are described as being gifts of Christ to the church. Their purpose is the completion and maturity of the church, individually and corporately.	Christian education must not only teach for personal edification, but must include the skills and talents necessary for the maturing of the congregation.
Pastorals (Titus and 1&2 Timothy)	Hayes (1991, 37-38) notes six aspects of education in 1&2 Timothy: Handling God's Word Soundness of faith Harmony in families Required of leaders Spiritual formation Perpetuation of the faith Titus 2:1-15 for instructional groups within the church.	Christian education has a variety of facets and is not given simply for one reason, one format, or one particular group in the church. Rather, Christian education is multidimensional, able to respond to the needs ranging from those of the individual to those of the Christian community. Instruction must be tailored to the needs of the specific group or age level.
Hebrews 5:11–6:3	Spiritual formation is the result of Christian instruction. The author of Hebrews employs the metaphor of growth from infancy to maturity.	Christian education must provide graded levels of instruction for those of different levels of spiritual formation and developmental levels.

Teachers in the New Testament

God

Jesus

Church

Apostles (Paul)

Pastor-Elders

Teachers in the New Testament. As in the Old Testament, God is described as teaching the community of faith (Titus 2:11-12; 2 Cor 6:1; 1 Tim 2:3-4). It is through His acts of grace and revelation that God instructs the Christian community. In the New Testament, the Holy Spirit is further described as a "guide" (Rom 8:1-27; Gal 5:16-26).

While He was addressed by many titles, Jesus was frequently called "teacher." As Mark 10:1 describes, it was Jesus' "custom" to teach. The gospel writers utilize a variety of titles to describe Jesus' instructional activity: *didaskalos* (Greek "teacher," 35 times), *rabbi* (Hebrew "teacher," 13 times), *rabboni* ("honored teacher," 2 times), "master" is used seven times, and "leader" is once used in regard to Jesus' educational endeavors (Zuck 1995, 25).

Jesus did bear some similarity to His contemporaries. For example, the metaphor of the "yoke" in Matthew 2:28-29 was used to describe the relation of a teacher to his pupil in rabbinic Judaism (cf. Sirach, Ecclesiasticus 51.25). Similarly, the phrase "Come after me" (Mark 1:17) was frequently employed by both Greek philosophers and Hebrew sages to their pupils.

Regarding the format through which Jesus instructed His followers, it is important to make one note: Jesus never opened a school. Discipleship was His instructional context and method, with His followers learning through socialization and nonformal teaching. The term "disciple" is used 142 times in the Synoptics (Matthew, Mark, and Luke), adequately demonstrating this fact (cf. Matt 28:20; Mark 6:30; Luke 12:12).

> **Discipleship was His instructional context and method, with His followers learning through socialization and nonformal teaching.**

As in the Old Testament, the community of faith itself was instructional. The church's body life introduced and reinforced the formation of faith through exposure and involvement in the community (Acts 2:42-47). Likewise, the place and function of the teacher was regarded as a gift of God to the church (Rom 12:3-8; 1 Cor 12:27-31; Eph 4:7-13,29-32; 5:15-20; 1 Pet 4:10-11).

Jesus' former pupils, the apostles, assumed the task of teaching, through instruction, preaching, and writing. Acts depicts the apostles as completing Jesus' mission (Acts 1:1) by making disciples for Christ (Acts 14:21). Doctrine assumes a crucial role in the church through their instruction (Acts 2:42; 5:28; 13:2; 17:19). The apostle Paul was perhaps the most prolific educator among the apostles, particularly through his correspondences and established missionary endeavors, e.g., Corinth and Ephesus.

Similarly, pastor-elders, appointed by the apostles, assumed teaching roles in the church. Elders were obviously more than teachers; however, among their qualifications their only ability listed is being "able to teach" (1 Tim 3:2; Titus 1:9). Teaching is an essential aspect of leadership and a qualification for the eldership. The pastor-teacher of Ephesians 4:11 would exemplify this task.

Teaching is an essential aspect of leadership and a qualification for the eldership.

Biblical Implications for Contemporary Education

Several themes emerge from the biblical material in regard to Christian education. As previously noted at the opening of this chapter, it is the biblical principles that must be preserved and maintained—the mandate, not simply the methodology. What are these biblical principles of education?

✎ Instruction is essential and obligatory upon the Christian community. Education is not an option, it is a necessity. In fact, it is a divine imperative, a command. At every level of the faith community, in both Testaments, from the family unit to the congregation to the nation as a whole, the essential task of instruction is impressed upon the faithful (Deut 6:6-9; Matt 28:16-20). Christian education is the fulfillment of a divine imperative. The church that fails to accept the task of educational ministry is neither functioning by the pattern of a New Testament congregation, nor fulfilling the Great Commission to make disciples.

✎ Faith is learned in and through the faith community. Learning requires an appropriate context, and in turn that context influences learning. The socialization of the faithful is accomplished through exposure to and involvement in the faith community. Through the church we become aware of the teachings and traditions of the faith. This is particularly relevant to the education of children, e.g., a child sees adults participating in worship and begins asking what is being done and why. Christian educators must address the issue of how one's exposure and encounter with a congregation shapes and influences the faith of the individual.

✎ Teachers are heterogeneous within the church. In both Testaments no one group or individual was the instructor. While all teachers may have accepted the educational imperative of the Scripture, they were by no means identical. A plurality of teaching contexts, emphases, and styles is maintained because of the heterogeneous nature of God's people. Hence, teachers are a diverse element within the faith community designed to reach the diverse constituents within the church.

A plurality of teaching contexts, emphases, and styles is maintained because of the heterogeneous nature of God's people.

✎ Educational formats are holistic. Education occurs in three formats: (a) formal, wherein instruction is intentional and a student studies to advance through an institution, e.g., schools and colleges, (b) nonformal in which intentional instruction is given, but not part of an institutional setting, e.g., workshops or seminars, and (c) socialization, which is the learning that occurs through community or cultural encounter, e.g., experience. In the Scriptures, all three formats are present. However, the latter two formats (nonformal and socialization) are the most frequent, with formal education being rarely mentioned or even implied.

✎ Instructional methodologies were divergent based on the individual and situation. Instruction in the Bible occurred in many forms. Jesus' teaching style alone demonstrates numerous methods which were commonly employed by the rabbis of the first century A.D., and yet on other occasions He diverged from the methods of His contemporaries (Zuck, 1995). Each method employed was obviously geared to reach and influence different individuals in a given situation. Hence, instruction must take into account the learner and the context in which the instruction will occur.

✎ Finally, education is for conversion and spiritual formation, both personally and corporately. The purpose of biblical instruction is the spiritual formation of the individual and the faith community. While it may be expressed in devotion, knowledge, relationship, service, and obedience, a holistic faith is the primary goal of Christian education. This goal is intended not only for the individual Christian, but the maturing of the Christian community as the bride and body of Christ.

The purpose of biblical instruction is the spiritual formation of the individual and the faith community.

Instruction was also given to lead one to make a personal commitment. While this is quite evident in the New Testament (Matt 28:18-20), even in the Old Testament the resident "alien" was to participate regularly in the community's instruction (Deut 31:12; 1 Kgs 8:41-43). The beginning of spiritual formation is conversion, and the educational imperative of the church is fulfilled by evangelism and education toward discipleship.

Theological Perspective on Education

The formation of a theological framework for education is essential for several reasons. First, faith is theological and requires a theological understanding of its object and function in the Christian life. Second, theology serves as the educational philosophy in Christian education. It provides a distinctive perspective through which an educational theory and practice can be formulated that is consistent with Christian belief. Finally, theology should influence both the content and methodology of Christian instruction. If theology is absent from education, it ceases to be Christian.

If theology is absent from education, it ceases to be Christian.

Relationship of Theology and Education

Education is derived from the social sciences. As previously noted, the pertinent question for the Christian educator is "What makes education Christian?" The merger and integration of theological perspective and the social sciences is a critical issue for Christian education in formulating an approach to education that is distinctively Christian. What, then, is the relationship between theology and the social sciences? While responses may differ in intensity or degree, the Christian educator must have an understanding of how theological and social foundations inform their educational theory and practice.

Sara Little (1990, 649-651) identifies five possible relationships between theology and the social sciences as a means of formulating an approach to education that is Christian. While the proposed relationships are sometimes contradictory, they are not mutually exclusive in every instance. Each one emphasizes a different aspect of theology and the social sciences, each contributing to the total formulation of a distinctively Christian education. The five relationships are as follows:

> **Theology and Social Science**
> **Theology as Source**
> **Theology as Resource**
> **Theology as Norm**
> **"Doing Theology"**
> **Theology and Education as Interactive**

- ✎ Theology as Source—theology is the sole contributor to content of instruction, relegating the formation of theory and practice of education to the social sciences.
- ✎ Theology as Resource—theology provides the student a perspective or lens through which to address life's questions, minimizing the content role of theology, but the social sciences shape the theory and practice.
- ✎ Theology as Norm—theology serves as a filter for educational content, theory and practice. The social sciences are utilized only when they are in agreement with theological convictions.
- ✎ "Doing Theology" as Educating—otherwise known as "theologizing" or "theological reflection," this approach focuses on the process of integrating theology with experience.

Primacy is given to the student's experience, with theology being influenced by it. Hence, educational practice yields personal theology.

✎ Theology and Education as Interactive—theology and the social sciences are described as being in dialog with one another. In this approach the different natures of theology and the social sciences are acknowledged, with each drawing on the other's academic disciplines. In this instance, theology is changing or developmental for the church, since integration is a continual process.

Each of these possible positions identified by Little not only reflects a view of theological-social science relationship, but also understandings of theology. These understandings of theology range from its being simply the content of propositional creedal statements, with little concern for the process by which the content was derived, to being the process whereby individuals interpret their life experiences, with little attention given to the content of faith. However, regardless of the emphasis, Christian educators must address the relationship between theology and the social sciences if their vocation is to be both Christian and educational.

Contemporary Theologies of Education

Within the past hundred years, four major theological movements have impacted and influenced education within American Christianity. First, classical liberalism entered the theological scene at the turn of the 20th century, with its educational endeavors spearheaded by George Albert Coe and his protégé Harrison Elliott. The advent of classical liberalism gave rise to religious education, that argued against the exclusivity of Christian education, favoring the dominant influence of the social sciences in education rather than that of theology.

Second, neoorthodoxy challenged the theological tenets of classical liberalism beginning around 1940. Rooted in the writings of Karl Barth and Rudolph Bultmann, neoorthodoxy appeared to be more conservative than its predecessor and soon gave rise to an educational agenda. Such contributors as E.G. Homrighausen, H. Sheldon Smith, and Paul H. Veith constructed a neoorthodox approach to education for the church.

The third major theological shift Wcykoff classifies as "affirmations of evangelical theology," shortly following World War II (1995, 19). Such educators as Frank E. Gaebelein, Kenneth Gangel, Lawrence O. Richards, and, most recently, Robert W. Pazmiño contribute to the evangelical theological perspective on what can be properly called Christian education.

The fourth theological development in 20th-century church education was that of process theology, which devalued the content of education, emphasizing the supposed changing nature of truth. Randolph Crump Miller and Nels F.S. Ferré would constitute the leading proponents of a process perspective on both theology and education. While other theological frameworks have indeed entered the church's educational scene during this century, e.g., liberation theology or congregational theology, their influence has either been limited or short-lived. Every theological shift within this century has been accompanied by a shift in the educational endeavors of the church. Hence, the Christian education arena is theologically diverse, leading to divergent theories and practices among education in the church.

Every theological shift within this century has been accompanied by a shift in the educational endeavors of the church.

How does the "theological landscape" in Christian education appear today? Mary E. Boys' *Educating in Faith* (1989) theologically analyzed contemporary educational approaches in the church. Using such criteria as the nature of revelation, conversion, relationship of faith and the Bible, theology's significance in education, the relationship of faith and culture, and the goal of education, she developed a "matrix" consisting of four distinct approaches to education within contemporary Christianity:

✎ Evangelism, which is consistent with the fundamentalist or revivalist tradition.

✎ Religious education, which is derived from the theologies of classical liberalism, neoorthodoxy, and Whitehead's process philosophy.

✎ Christian education, which is attributed to the evangelical theological tradition.

✎ Catholic education, which she regards as being separate from the previous three in content, theory, and practice.

Toward a Biblical Theology of Education

The concept of God is foundational to any theological framework, with other doctrines being reflective of the Christian understanding of God. As in any Christian endeavor, the aim of Christian education is to bring glory to God. Hence, the doctrines of revelation, church, humanity, and salvation are extensions of the Christian doctrine of God.

God as Educator: The God of Scripture is the Creator, Lord, and Redeemer of humanity. The trinitarian concept of God can be understood as educational metaphor: God the Father as Revealer, Jesus as Exemplar, and the Holy Spirit as Tutor (cf. Ferré, 1967). In so doing, God is depicted as the ultimate Educator, as the Teacher of humanity. Through both word and deed God is interactive with humanity for the purpose of instructing and forming them into His people. It is for this reason that education in the Bible is God-centered.

God has assumed an educational role through a variety of means. According to Ferré (1967, 168-171), God teaches through nature and history, Christian community, theological heritage,

> **Biblical Theology of Education**
>
> **God as Educator**
> **Revelation as Curriculum**
> **Community of Faith as Educational Context**
> **Humanity as Learners**
> **Salvation as Turning Point and Transformation**

imitation of the past [tradition], creative discovery, and participation in the life of the spirit. These parallel the four aforementioned doctrines of revelation, church, humanity, and salvation as means of instructing and enlightening individuals toward Christlikeness.

Revelation as Curriculum: From Augustine to Adler, the affirmation that "All truth is God's truth" is the hallmark of evangelical theology, since all truth ultimately originates with God as Revealer. Revelation is the act of self-disclosure, or the disclosure of truth that was otherwise humanly unknowable. God's revelatory acts have been described in regard to its content and means of delivery as being both special, e.g., the word revelation of Scripture, and general, e.g., the non-verbal revelation of nature. Because of the nature of the Scriptures as a special revelation, the Bible should dominate the Christian education curriculum.

Because of the nature of the Scriptures as a special revelation, the Bible should dominate the Christian education curriculum.

Christian educators must be concerned about the Bible as content and as process. For example, 2 Timothy 3:15-17 describes both the content of Scripture ("All Scripture is God-breathed") and the process of making use of God's revelation ("able to make you wise for salvation" . . . "useful . . . so that the man of God may be thoroughly equipped for every good work"). Scripture is not only considered a revelation of God, but inspired by the Holy Spirit, referring to God's special provision and oversight in the writing of Scripture. Only when both the content of Scripture and the proper use of Scripture are equally emphasized is education genuinely Christian. Hence, the Scriptures serve as the only sufficient rule for faith and practice within the Christian life and community not only because of the revealed-inspired nature of the biblical text, but also because of the relevance the Scriptures have for today.

Community of Faith as Educational Context: Maria Harris calls the church "a people with an educational vocation" (1989, 38).

How does the church fulfill this mission? E.V. Hill identified five aspects of the church which have educational implications: worship (which he regarded as central to the life of the congregation), fellowship, evangelism, kingdom consciousness, and service (Pazmiño 1992, 44-53). Each of these aspects not only identifies the specific context for Christian education, but also the context wherein instruction and socialization can occur.

As previously noted, the socialization approach to education is present within the community of faith in both Testaments; hence the nature and function of the church is essential to establishing an environment conducive to education, not to mention a context in which instruction can be given. Through the church we become aware of the teachings and traditions of the faith. This is particularly true of children who ask questions as they participate with their parents in worship and congregational life.

**Through the church we become aware of
the teachings and traditions of the faith.**

Humans as Learners: Humanity holds a special place among the creative acts of God. Humanity is unique due to the *imago dei*, the image of God, which is equally shared by both male and female (Gen 1:27). While this image may be described in a multitude of dimensions, it must obviously include the fact that humanity was created to be in communion with God as its Creator. In Genesis 1–3 this image was created innocent, broken by sin, and given the promise of restoration in a coming Savior, Christ.

Ronald Habermas (1993, 90-91) identifies three "practical dimensions" of the *imago dei*: (1) "transformed attitude" toward others, (2) "transformed behaviors," and (3) "greater appreciation for diversity" among humanity. For the Christian educator, students (natural, carnal, or spiritual) are possessors of the *imago dei* and hence deserving of a respectful relationship and to be treated with dignity by the teacher, regardless of their spiritual status.

The student is always in a state of process.

Students possess the capacity to exercise their free will in accordance with the guidance of God through His Holy Spirit, or to adhere to their bias toward rebellion against God as a result of the Fall; to have faith or to reject it. In short, the student is always in a state of process. This process is both in regard to the student as an individual and to humans as developmental beings, e.g., Jesus in Luke 2:40,52. Spiritual formation, as an aim of Christian education, is not automatic nor is it ever complete. God does not change; He is not in process. But we, as finite created beings, are always in a state of process. Christian educators must engage the learning process appropriately in order to facilitate this transformation.

Salvation as Turning Point and Transformation: The term "religion" refers to humanity's effort to appease and attain a relationship with God. Christianity, on the other hand, proposes that it is God Himself who initiated this relationship, and that it is His desire that humanity be saved (2 Pet 3:9).

Ephesians 2:1-10 describes a three phase change in the life of the Christian: conversion (v. 1-3) from the old self to the saved or new self (vv. 4-8) to the disciple or spiritual (vv. 9-10), and all this by God's mercy and grace, not human effort or design. Lewis Sperry Chafer (1967, 17-22), in his study of 1 Corinthians 2, defines these stages as the natural/sinful state, the carnal state (saved, but infantile), and the spiritual state (mature Christian). Hence, spiritual formation or transformation is a process. Conversion is indeed a point, but it is a point upon a continuum of spiritual formation, the path to Christian maturity. As Peter writes, "Like newborn babies, crave pure spiritual milk, so that by it you may grow up in your salvation" (1 Pet 2:2). The Christian life is both punctilar (conversion) and process (sanctification) in nature. The Christian educator, while indeed concerned about leading the individual to Christ, must understand that "leading" is a process that does not end with conversion, but begins prior to conversion and continues throughout the life of the individual.

Summary of Theological
Implications for Education

How does theology inform the process of Christian education? First, all Christian education is ultimately God-centered, since God gives us human existence, faith, community, and revelation. Second, theology informs us about the true nature of humanity, especially the spiritual dimension, which is beyond the reach of the social sciences. Third, theology allows us to understand the process of conversion and growth within humanity as one experiences spiritual formation. Fourth, church becomes the context of faith-nurture, as well as a corporate identity for the individual Christian. Finally, and most importantly, "God has spoken." The fact of revelation cannot be ignored or regarded as irrelevant by the Christian educator (cf. Little, 1961). While each of us may be in a state of process in our spiritual formation, this formation is influenced and shaped as we encounter God's revelation in Scripture and are enlightened by the Holy Spirit (1 Cor 2:6-16). It is through the integration of biblical and theological insights such as these with the social sciences that education genuinely becomes Christian.

The fact of revelation cannot be ignored or regarded as irrelevant by the Christian educator

---

p r o j e c t

✮ Choose one of the Bible passages dealing with education. Prepare a lesson method outline for teaching in that passage's setting or manner. ✮

For Further Reading

Mary Elizabeth Boys
Educating in Faith. New York: Harper and Row, 1989.

Lewis Sperry Chafer
He That Is Spiritual. Grand Rapids: Zondervan, 1967.

Nels F.S. Ferré
A Theology for Christian Education. Philadelphia: Westminister Press, 1967.

Ronald T. Habermas
"Practical Dimensions of the *Imago Dei*." *Christian Education Journal* (XIII:2): 83-92.

Maria Harris
Fashion Me a People. Louisville: Westminster/John Knox Press, 1989.

Edward L. Hayes
"Establishing Biblical Foundations." *Christian Education Foundations for the Future*, Robert E. Anthony et al. Chicago: Moody Press, 1991.

Sara Little
"Theology and Education." *Harper's Encyclopedia of Religious Education*. New York: Harper and Row, 1990.

The Role of the Bible in Contemporary Christian Education. Richmond, VA: John Knox Press, 1961.

Robert W. Pazmiño
Foundational Issues in Christian Education. 2nd ed. Grand Rapids: Baker, 1997.

J.M. Price, ed.
Introduction to Religious Education. New York: Macmillan Company, 1932.

D. Campbell Wyckoff
"Theology and Education in the Twentieth Century." *Christian Education Journal* (XV.3): 12-26.

Roy B. Zuck
Teaching as Jesus Taught. Grand Rapids: Baker, 1995.
Teaching as Paul Taught. Grand Rapids: Baker, 1998.

CHAPTER 2
PHILOSOPHICAL-HISTORICAL
FOUNDATIONS OF CHRISTIAN EDUCATION

Chapter Two Summary
- ☑ Metaphysical, epistemological, and axiological philosophy
- ☑ Classical philosophical roots of modern education
- ☑ Developing an educational philosophy
- ☑ Christian education philosophical perspective
- ☑ Highlights of Christian education history
- ☑ Modern American Christian education

Students walk into the college classroom at 8:00 a.m. They see chairs and tables set up in rows facing a podium, chalkboard, and overhead projector. Immediately they may assume that the professor will lecture to the class. The aim is to convey the content of his or her notes; the professor desires to see students intently taking notes, expecting them to be the receptacles of his knowledge. At 9:00 a.m,, these same students walk across the hall. No podium is seen in this classroom, but a table with handouts and various other items of interest is at the front of the room. Chairs are arranged in small circles. On the chalkboard are four open-ended questions. Students immediately assume that this class is going to be different from their earlier one. The professor obviously has a different expectation for the student, and methods will likewise differ from the earlier class. Why?

Instructional methods can differ for many reasons, but usually they are tied to theories of learning, the instructor's abilities, subject matter, or academic and cultural expectations.

Ultimately, instructional practices are a reflection of one's worldview or philosophy which shapes values and aims.

Philosophy is neither optional nor academic. On the contrary, it is both natural and essential to Christian education. One critical fact often escapes us as educators: *Everyone has a philosophy of education.* Whether we are aware of its presence, philosophy is the ever-present companion of the educator. Philosophy provides the assumptions and rationale for educational theory, policy, and practice. When teachers are asked to explain "why" a particular action or method of instruction was used in the classroom, they begin to access the philosophical center of their educational paradigm. Hence, philosophy is preeminently influential to our educational task, but for the most part remains unnoticed or unacknowledged. The more we as educators are consciously aware of our philosophy of education and able to articulate it, the better equipped we are to design, develop, and practice sound education according to a philosophy that is consistent with the Christian faith.

One critical fact often escapes us as educators:
Everyone has a philosophy of education.

But what about history? The study of the history of education is not primarily concerned with dates, events, or even persons; rather it is about ideas. History is philosophy in practice. History provides the trajectory of the modern education's development as educators interacted with particular philosophical perspectives in a social-cultural context.

Christian educators have a legacy of faithful instruction, with both beneficial and detrimental developments. Christian education cannot be regarded as stagnant, isolated, or one dimensional. Rather, the history of Christian education reflects a diverse, interactive, and innovating discipline within the Christian community and even the society. The study of the history and philosophy of education is foundational to understanding our task as Christian educators.

The study of the history and philosophy of education is foundational to understanding our task as Christian educators.

Primary Philosophical
Roots of Modern Education

Philosophy is the broadest category of human thought. It examines the macro-issues of a worldview and the human condition: What is real (metaphysics)? How can I know truth (epistemology)? Wherein lies worth, both in the sense of ethics and aesthetics (axiology)? These three basic philosophical inquiries (metaphysics, epistemology, and axiology) combine into a unified portrait of our perception of life. These questions are no less relevant for educators who are Christian because we too must respond to these primary human concerns. The Apostle Paul admonished the Colossian congregation, "See to it that no one takes you captive through hollow and deceptive philosophy, which depends on human tradition and the basic principles of this world rather than on Christ" (Col 2:8). Such an admonition is not a prohibition of philosophical inquiry, but rather a challenge to formulate a philosophy that is dependent upon Christ, and hence beneficial to Christian education.

Christian Faith and
Educational Philosophies

As previously noted, philosophy provides the foundational rationale for educational practice, policy, and paradigms. When educators' philosophy changes, their ed-

> **Five Classical Philosophies of Education**
>
> **Idealism** (essentialism)
> **Realism** (essentialism, positivism)
> **Thomism** (neo-Thomism, perennialism)
> **Pragmatism** (experientialism, progressivism, Social constructivism)
> **Existentialism** (phenomenology, deconstructionism)

Table 2.1: Classical Philosophical Roots of Modern Education

Philosophy	Philosophical Assumptions	Evaluation and Critique
Idealism Plato (Essentialism)	Reality is spiritual or mental. The physical is problematic and distracts from the mental disciplines. Truth is eternally consistent, accessible through reason and reflective meditation alone. Ethics is a reflection of ideal humanity. Aesthetics reflects the ideal.	Idealism acknowledges many of the tenets of Christian philosophy (acknowledgement of the affirmation of eternal truth and values). However, it does not give credence to the value of science or personal experience as a means of discovering truth. Its overemphasis on reason also restricts education to the cognitive, rather than being holistic.
Realism Aristotle (Essentialism, Positivism)	Reality is the material world. The physical exists independently of the mind or reason. Truth resides in the material world and can be discovered through observation and reason. Ethics are reflections of nature or natural law. Similarly, aesthetics are expressions of the natural world.	Realism provides an adequate basis for the scientific investigation of nature, but it fails at the point of spiritual reality. Truth, while rationally understood, is affirmed in nature, but it is limited to the cognitive realm. Truth, while rationally understood, is affirmed in nature and does not seek "eternal truth" beyond natural revelation. It cannot call humanity to any higher standard than what nature or science may provide.
Thomism Thomas Aquinas (Neo-Thomism, Perennialism)	Reality is both spiritual and material and can be known through reason and reflection. Truth is eternal, coming through revelation (both special and natural), reason, and the Catholic Church or other human authorities. Ethics are the acts of rational individuals based on eternal truths. Beauty is expressed through reason.	Of all the classical philosophies, this one shares the closest resemblance to evangelical thought. However, it once again imposes limitations on the educational scope. Primarily cognitive, it does not acknowledge the value of the affective domain. However, Thomas Aquinas did include the intuitive rooted in the spiritual. It shares historical roots with Aristotelian realism. It does affirm revelation, which is absent from all other philosophies. It also affirms many Christian tenets. However, it fails to place sufficient experience in the process of discovering truth.

Philosophy	Philosophical Assumptions	Evaluation and Critique
Pragmatism John Dewey (Experimentalism, Progressivism, Social Reconstructionism)	Change is the only absolute in reality. Reality is always in process, known through experience. Truth is situational, pragmatic (i.e., "Whatever works"), and temporal; determined by individuals and/or society. Ethics are the acts of rational individuals based on eternal truths; beauty is expressed primarily through reason.	This philosophy lacks the concreteness of the Christian philosophy of metaphysics and, in fact, lacks a metaphysical dimension. Similarly, reason is replaced with experience as the means of discerning truth. Truth is not constant, lacking an eternal source of authority. Similarly, with experience as a basis, ethics is also transient. The philosophy does remind educators that methodology must be flexible and that experience must be considered. However, it emphasizes it to a fallacious extreme. Historically, pragmatism has proven to be a fatal flaw for both individuals and educational systems.
Existentialism Kant, Kierkegaard (Phenomenology, Deconstructionism)	Reality is created by the individual's subjective experience. Perception is reality. Truth is determined by individual choice and created internally by the individual. Any liberating idea or principle is considered ethical. Aesthetics is in the eye of the beholder.	This philosophy is perhaps the most distant from Christian philosophy. One contribution is to remind the educator that to an extent reality is in each individual's mind. However, the extremism of advocating the absolute legitimacy of an individual and experience-based reality is beyond the tolerance of biblical Christianity, since this would legitimize any and all beliefs, religions, and customs. The concept of multiple realities based on each individual perception can only lead to skepticism and nihilism, which are contrary to a God-centered, revelation-based emphasis of Christianity. With the loss of educational content for instruction, it provides insufficient basis for the lives of individuals and congregations.

ucational aim and values change accordingly. While it is the concern of this chapter to present a brief sketch of a Christian philosophy of education, it is critical to note that other philosophies of education do exist, each with its own agenda. The five main philosophical roots of modern western education are Idealism, Realism, Thomism, Pragmatism, and Existentialism, each with its own modern equivalents or derivatives. Table 2.1

contains a brief overview and critique of these five main philosophies of education.

How does Christian education relate to these philosophies? Some religious or Christian educators have simply opted to accept a particular philosophy of education and adapt its use to Christian education. This approach to integrating Christian education and philosophy minimizes the Christian distinctive in education, allowing the philosophy to address the macro-issues, and in essence to shape Christian education into its paradigm, rather than formulating a paradigm reflective of Christian concepts.

These philosophies, with the possible exception of Thomism, are primarily based on general revelation, human reflection and inquiry into the natural world, and human experience, with *no* attention given to special revelation. Christian educators can find some value in these philosophies, but usually find them to err on the side of extremism, lacking holistic perspective because of an overemphasis of a specific point. Since Christian educators make use of Scripture, God's special revelation, as well as general revelation, a more holistic view toward education can be formulated which avoids the extremism of traditional educational philosophies and provides a more balanced philosophy and approach to education. Hence, Christian educators can benefit from and make use of these educational philosophies: for example, Idealism and Realism's commitment to the importance of content in education, Pragmatism and Existentialism's regard for the student's learning process and perspective, and Thomism's regard for revelation and faith.

Toward a Christian Philosophy of Education

Every philosophy, even a Christian one, must address three main categories of concern: metaphysics, epistemology, and axiology. A Christian philosophy of education addresses these concerns from a perspective consistent with Scripture and Christian theology and draws educational implications from it. Perhaps the most critical implications for Christian educators are those affecting our understanding of human nature and its spiritual condition. This section of the chapter will attempt to provide a brief sketch of such a philosophy of education.

Perhaps the most critical implications for Christian educators are those affecting our understanding of human nature and its spiritual condition.

Metaphysics (Reality): Christianity maintains that reality exists on two levels—uncreated and created. God exists in a reality all His own as the only *uncreated*, *eternal* spirit-being. The created realm is contingent on God, and consists of two parts: (a) the spiritual realm, e.g., heaven, hell, angelic beings, and (b) the physical or natural realm, e.g., the universe. God is Creator, Sovereign, and Sustainer of *all* creation, both spiritual and physical. The spiritual and physical are equally real as created realities by an eternal God, and hence Christian education must concern itself with both the spiritual *and* physical realities in which humanity exists.

Epistemology (Truth/Knowledge): The Christian basis of knowledge and truth is *revelation*, through which God has made Himself known to humanity. "All truth is God's truth," since all truth is ultimately derived from God's revelations. Since truth is based on the revelatory acts of an eternal and unchanging God, truth itself is regarded as eternal and unchanging. Romans 1–3 mentions two sources of revelation through which God has revealed Himself to humanity: Creation (1:18-25) and most importantly, Scripture (3:1-4), a special source of revelation as opposed to a natural/general source.

Truth is available, but how is it known by humanity? Truth is knowable because of God's desire to be known, because His revealing actions are intentional, and because of humanity's ability to inquire into God's revelatory sources. For example, theology is the human endeavor to discern the truth revealed in Scripture. Science endeavors to understand God's creation and even the liberal arts endeavor to explore and provide perspective on the human condition in both its fallen and restored states.

The figure below illustrates this.

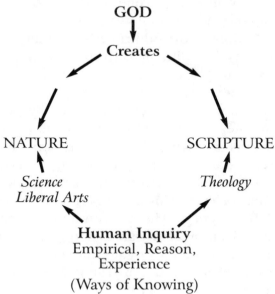

Christian Epistemology

GOD

Creates

NATURE   SCRIPTURE

Science   *Theology*
Liberal Arts

Human Inquiry
Empirical, Reason,
Experience

(Ways of Knowing)

Our ability to "know" the truth is dependent on the means of human inquiry. *How do we "know" what we claim to "know"?* The source of truth, God's revelation, has already been identified, but how do we make use of them? Christian educators have historically maintained three means of knowing: (a) empirical, e.g., scientific inquiry, measurement, experimentation; (b) reason, e.g., logic, induction-deduction; and (c) experience, e.g., intuition, conscience, internal testimony. Hence, when we make a statement about "knowledge," it is typically a statement based on one or all of these ways of knowing.

Knowledge, however, is never enough; one must have *faith* in order to maintain any degree of certainty.

Knowledge, however, is never enough; one must have *faith* in order to maintain any degree of certainty. Faith is an aspect of

Christian epistemology often absent or rejected from other philosophies. While faith and knowledge are *not* synonymous, they are likewise *not* mutually exclusive. Faith and knowledge are related, complementary to one another. We usually place our trust (faith) in our means of knowing, and hence to some degree knowledge requires faith. Additionally, our means of inquiry may provide facts, but without faith the facts have no meaning. As Anselm stated: "I believe in order to understand." Faith makes sense of the facts.

Axiology: Issues of "worth," either ethically or aesthetically, rest on the nature of God. God's holiness and righteousness are the basis for ours, as exemplified in Jesus Christ as "the author and perfecter of faith" (Heb 12:2). Ethics is based on God's revealed will in creation and Scripture and is applicable to both individuals and societies. Similarly, aesthetics is for the glorification of God, as it reflects His creation and works. Perhaps the passage best reflecting Christian axiology is Philippians 4:8, "Whatever is true, honorable, right, pure, lovely, of good repute, if there is any excellence and if anything worthy of praise, dwell on these things."

Humanity is uniquely placed within the spiritual-physical created reality, being physical, but possessing a spiritual dimension and potential as well.

A critical aspect of the human condition is the brokenness of humanity and the distortion of ethical perception accompanying it. Humanity is uniquely placed within the spiritual-physical created reality, being physical, but possessing a spiritual dimension and potential as well. Having been created in God's image (*imago dei*), humanity is composed of body-soul-spirit (1 Thess 5:23), and is not physical *or* spiritual, but both/and. However, the human condition is not ideal, since the wholeness of creation was shattered by sin, and hence humanity is not in its ideal form.

Educational Implications: The ultimate *aim* of Christian education, as with anything Christian, is to glorify God. As affirmed in the theological foundations chapter, education must be God-centered. More specifically, Christian education is primarily concerned with the transformation and restoration of humanity, both individually and corporately. This does not simply mean salvation, but the formation of the individual's spiritual life and social consciousness, and, as such, Christian education is a tangible reflection of the process of sanctification.

Christian education is primarily concerned with the transformation and restoration of humanity, both individually and corporately.

Christian education must address the *imago dei* in all its facets, attempting to restore humanity's relationship with God (spiritual aspects), one another (communal/social/interpersonal aspects), and individuals toward themselves (personal/internal aspects). In short, the aim of Christian education is the transformation of the entire student into spiritual maturity, beginning with reconciliation of the individual to God and to one another in society, and restoring the wholeness of the individual by finding his or her identity in God and living to His glory.

The curriculum of Christian education reflects the epistemological considerations previously mentioned. Perhaps the most critical focus of Christian education is on Scripture. Unique to Christian education is the attention given to the Bible and other Christian interests related to biblical studies (e.g., theology or apologetics). George Knight identifies three general approaches to using the Bible in curriculum:

❶ The Bible is the sole curriculum, which denies the relevance and importance of general revelation.

❷ The Bible is one part of the curriculum, with other parts being sought separately from it, which yields a lack of integration

❸ The Bible is a separate study, but is used in the instruction of other subjects (Knight 1989, 208-210).

The third approach would be the most advantageous in permitting the Bible's integration into other fields of inquiry.

While some Christian educators focus their attention exclusively on Scripture, a perfectly acceptable focus in the case of the Sunday school or church-based small groups, other forms of Christian education such as colleges or schools need not do so. Christian education should endeavor to provide a Christian perspective on the totality of life, including science as the study of God's creation and the liberal arts as they exhibit and explore the human condition. It has been Christian educators' lack of attention to these areas that has led to the idea that Christianity is irrelevant, not addressing concerns, queries, and issues posed from God's natural revelation.

The teacher-learner relationship is central to the educational process and reflects the aim of education. One educator has asked, "Do we teach the Bible or students?" The correct response is "Yes," but content often overrides the concern for the student, and the teacher focuses on the "what" rather than the "who" in the instructional process. A proper understanding of learners is essential to an effective philosophy of education. For Christian educators, learners are possessors of the *imago dei*, regardless of their spiritual status, and deserving of a respectful relationship with the teacher.

Transformation, the aim of Christian education, is not automatic, nor is it ever complete.

Human beings possess the capacity to exercise free will and are in a state of *process*. Transformation, the aim of Christian education, is *not* automatic, nor is it ever complete. God does not change; He is *not* in process. But, we, as finite beings, are *always* in a state of process. The student is a processing mechanism, inquiring into God's revelation as a source of truth. Allow for an illustration: while the contents and meaning of Ephesians 5:21–6:4 remains the same, the message has changed with me as I have grown. As a child, the message was "Children, obey your parents in the Lord" (6:1). When I married, the message became "Husbands, love your wives . . ." (5:25). And now, when we had adopted Dylan, the message became "Fathers do not exasperate your children" (6:4). What changed? Not the biblical text or meaning, but it became more applicable to different aspects of my life because my life had changed. *We are all in process.* We may all agree what the Bible *means*, but it may *say* something different to each of us depending on our life situation.

Christian education is by nature paradoxical. On the one hand, you have the concern for content in the instructional task, e.g., the Bible, theology, apologetics, etc. On the other hand is the concern for the process of learning, e.g., students finding application and relevance for truth. While other philosophies of education place emphasis on one of the two, Christian education affirms the equal concern for both. Christian education is not an either/or, but a both/and.

Several implications specifically involve teachers:

- Teachers must be Christians themselves, since faith cannot be learned from the faithless. Christian maturity is necessary on the part of teachers.

- Teachers are guides and nurturers of faith. Faith cannot simply be imparted through the *content* of instruction, but requires also affective and volitional aspects, as previously noted. Teachers provide intentional instruction for the enhancement of their faith as well as a nurturing relationship and environment. Faith must not be just a profession, but a possession of the student.

- Teachers must be "experienced teachers." This is *not* referring to their teaching experience, but rather their own Christian experience, so as to serve as a model and example. A developed and balanced faith should assist teachers in their task. It enables them to have greater insight into Scripture, wisdom for Christian living, and sensitivity toward the students they teach.

- Teachers are responsible managers of learning. Because God has revealed Himself to humanity, the teacher must be responsible in inquiring and examining God's revealed truth. Christian teachers also assume the responsibility to fashion a learning environment that is conducive to the formation of faith. Being a teacher means more than just engaging in formal instruction.

What methods of instruction are available to the teacher? Teachers should honor the developmental level of their students, seek to utilize teaching methods that facilitate relationships between the teacher and student, and foster a cooperative environment, not just a competitive one. Teaching should be appropriate for the developmental level of the students, relevant to their life experience, as well as spiritually challenging and enhancing. While Christian education is frequently typified as indoctrination, utilizing lecture as the primary means of instruction, this is not necessary nor is it the most beneficial method for the student. The use of instructional methods that encourage students to discover and express the revealed truth of Scripture for themselves are far more desirable. Not only do such methods aid in students' processing of God's revelation, but they provide life contexts, increasing the likelihood of immediate relevance and application of biblical truth to the student's life.

Summary

- Christian education is holistic, concerning itself with every dimension of humanity, e.g., personal, social, spiritual.
- Christian education is concerned with the cognitive, affective, and volitional dimensions of human learning.
- The philosophy of Christian education is rooted in biblical and theological foundations, as well as the social sciences, as a study of God's revelation in creation.
- Christian education is paradoxical, simultaneously affirming both the necessity of content and learning-by-process in the curriculum.
- In regard to faith and knowledge, Christian education seeks their integration into a holistic perception of reality.
- Christian education seeks to glorify God by the transformation of humanity and culture into His image through theological integration, the combining of faith and knowledge.

Historical Developments within Christian Education

The rise of Christian education in the Western world is one of challenge and innovation. History preserves for us a legacy of faithful instruction that provides Christian educators ground upon which to stand and understanding of the progression of education through the centuries. This section will be able only to summarize and provide the highlights of the history of Christian education and ministry within the Christian community. However, such a survey of history provides educators the opportunity to appreciate the Christian community's endeavors to "guard the good deposit ["sound teaching with faith"] that was entrusted to you . . ." (2 Tim 1:14a).

Pre-Christian Antecedents: The immediate predecessors to Christian education are the Hebrew-Jewish and Greco-Roman educational systems. Each of these antecedents contributed to the formation of Christian education in the early history of the church.

Early Hebrew education was centered upon home, with few formal institutions of education. (See Chapter 1.) It was not until the postexilic period, with the advent of Judaism, that educational endeavors reached their zenith with the rise of the scribes, schools, and especially the synagogue. This led to a high level of literacy among the population of Israel/Judah by the fourth-century B.C.

> ## History of Education
> ### Pre-Christian Antecedents
> (Hebrew, Greek, & Roman)
> ### Apostolic and Early Church
> ### Medieval Church
> ### Reformation and Counter Reformation
> ### Enlightenment and the Modern Era
> ### Education in the 20th Century

Perhaps the most obvious and influential advancement in the educational endeavors of Judaism was the formation of the synagogue. While the beginning of the synagogue has been attributed to the time of Ezekiel (possibly based on Jer 29:7), the synagogue did not reach its full stature within Judaism until the intertestamental period (Josephus, *Ant.* 2.25.632; 4.8.15), when the faith community contended with changes in geography, language, canon, and culture. Called *Bet hasseper* ("House of the Book"), with the *Beth hamidrash* ("House of Study") typically adjacent to it, the synagogue became the locale for education within Judaism. With the advent of the synagogue, the Jewish community provided public instruction to all its members.

**Perhaps the most obvious and influential advancement
in the educational endeavors of Judaism
was the formation of the synagogue.**

The Greeks had an educational heritage dating to the time of Homer. The most influential Greek educators were Plato, Aristotle, and Isocrates. (Isocrates was a student of Socrates and a teacher of oratory.) The main Hellenistic contributions to the development of education were (1) the formation of philosophical bases for educational practice, i.e., idealism and realism, and (2) the formal curriculum which later came to be known as the seven liberal arts. However, education was still elitist, unavailable to most of the population.

The education of Rome's aristocratic class was generally accomplished by Greek tutors, brought to Rome as slaves. Two leading Roman educators were Cicero (106-43 B.C.) and Quintillian (A.D. 35-96) who successfully enculturated the Greek heritage into Roman culture. The contributions of Roman education to the rise of Western culture include an emphasis on training civic leaders, focus on practical application of the theoretical, and development of formalized schooling for the aristocracy. Many of these concerns were later reflected in Christian education.

Apostolic Church (1st cent. A.D): Education in the New Testament was primarily through socialization and nonformal means, such as discipleship or mentoring. (See Chapter 1.) Perhaps the aim of education during this period can best be summarized by Paul's comment, "We proclaim him, admonishing and teaching everyone with all wisdom, so that we may present everyone perfect in Christ" (Col 1:28). The content of instruction in the Christian community included (1) content and Messianic interpretation of the Old Testament, (2) the life of Christ, particularly the crucifixion and resurrection, (3) the sayings or teachings of Jesus, and (4) instruction for Christian living (cf. Sherrill, 1944, 152). It was from these simple beginnings Christian education advanced and flourished.

Early Church (c. A.D. 100-500): Christians in the early church had a choice between specialized religious education and the classical education provided by Roman schools. While Tertullian and Basil the Great of Caesarea warned about the paganism facing Christian students in Roman schools, they encouraged Christians to attend Roman schools so as to provide a balanced education. In so doing, the evangelistic potential of the church was enhanced, and by the fourth century A.D. Christians were well entrenched into the classical education system, being both teachers and schoolmasters.

> **Christians in the early church had a choice between specialized religious education and the classical education provided by Roman schools.**

Perhaps the most obvious development in Christian education from the Apostolic period was its formalization, i.e., schooling. This development constitutes a fundamental shift in the nature of Christian education from the Apostolic period. During this period of early church history, the Christian community initiated six kinds of schools to provide instruction of various forms: catechumenal, catechetical, cathedral, parish, monastic, choir, and bishop schools. Formal education dominated the educational landscape of early Christianity, despite its virtual absence in the Apostolic age.

Such developments were the result of the contributions of men such as Clement of Alexandria (c. A.D. 150-215), Origen (A.D. 185-254), Jerome (A.D. 331-421), Ambrose (A.D. 340-397), and John Chrysostom (A.D. 344-407). While educational leaders in the early church were numerous, all of them attempted to interpret Greco-Roman culture in respect to Christian thought and integrate the two. This also permitted Greek educational philosophies to enter the Christian education community. Hence, the aim of Christian education focused on the intellectual development of students as they related to their pagan context.

Medieval Church (c. A.D. 600-12th century): The rise of the Middle Ages represents the fusion of Greco-Roman culture, Catholic Christianity, and feudalism from the Germanic Teutonic heritage. It was an era in which the Roman Catholic Church reigned supreme, both ecclesiastically and politically. Roman Catholicism, serving as both church and state, was positioned to govern virtually every educational development during this period.

The Middle Ages was an era in which the Roman Catholic Church reigned supreme, both ecclesiastically and politically. Education was diverse, but for the most part restricted from the general population.

Christian education in the Medieval period was diverse, but for the most part restricted from the general population. Four approaches to education dominated this period:

❶ Monasticism, which provided formal instruction and emphasis on the spiritual disciplines for the clergy.

❷ The "Chivalry of Feudalism," which provided social and military instruction.

❸ Scholasticism, which was formulated during the latter part of the Medieval period by St. Thomas Aquinas.

❹ "Christian mysticism," which emphasized personal spiritual experience (cf. Reed and Prevost 1993, 154-155).

Late in the Medieval period a new form of education arose: the university. The university model for education had two prototypes: (1) the University of Bologna in Italy and (2) the University of Paris in France (Reed and Prevost 1993, 145) which differed in curriculum design. Despite the popular conception, education during the Medieval period was neither stagnant nor unilateral; however, access was limited to the political and ecclesiastical elite.

Early contributors to Medieval education were made by such as Boethius (480-525), Benedict (480-546), and the highly regarded Cassiodorus (480-575). Other contributions were made by Augustine (354-430), who formed monastic schools and libraries, and wrote three educational texts. Alcuin served as the leading educator under Charlemagne (742-814), first emperor of the Holy Roman Empire. Alcuin established a system of education and libraries throughout the Holy Roman Empire, provided for the publication and distribution of Bibles to these libraries, as well as formulated a system of information retrieval (categorization of knowledge) which lasted for the next thousand years.

Perhaps the most recognized educator and theologian of the late Medieval period was Thomas Aquinas. His Scholastic approach to education sought to combine Aristotelian realism with Christian theology and lead to a faith based on revelation as perceived from Aristotelian realism, i.e., Thomism. The popularity of this philosophy persisted well into the Renaissance and even today as Neo-Thomism.

Perhaps the most recognized educator and theologian of the late Medieval period was Thomas Aquinas.

Reformation and Counter Reformation (13-17th century): The roots of the Protestant reformation are deeply embedded in the Renaissance. The Renaissance signaled the demise of Roman Catholic dominance in Europe, politically and culturally. Sparked by Arabic learning (e.g., science, mathematics and ancient western literature), brought to the West by returning Crusaders and Christians fleeing the Islamic threat, the culture of the West transferred its attentions from an ecclesiastical-religious focus to a humanistic-natural focus. This gave rise to classical humanism wherein attention was reassigned to nature rather than grace (which is the traditional categorizing of the shift) which revered human rational thought, classical Greco-Roman literature, the advancement of science, and the exploration of the natural world and human culture. Educators such as Erasmus, Groote, de Feltre, and Rabelais advocated curricula which were far less restrictive than was present in the Medieval period.

From the spirit of the Renaissance, the Protestant Reformation arose and the Catholic Counter Reformation in response to it, each with its own educational systems. The sixteenth-century Protestant reformation had two key leaders: Martin Luther (1483-1546) and John Calvin (1509-1564), each with his own educational agenda, but with the same conviction that the "priesthood of believers" made public education a necessity. Luther frequently emphasized the spiritual, material, and political benefits of tax-supported formal public education to children in Germany. However, it was Luther's close associate Phillip Melanchthon (1497-1560) who most fully implemented his educational ideals. Melanchthon not only developed a model for childhood education, but also developed curricula for public education and higher education, all consistent with Lutheran theological convictions. Calvin similarly favored public education as a means of glorifying God and equipping the believers, but he was less successful than Luther in fulfilling his educational objectives.

The Catholic response to the Protestant Reformation was not only theological and political, but educational as well.

The Catholic response to the Protestant Reformation was not only theological and political, but educational as well. The Jesuits, or Society of Jesus, have been the most influential Roman Catholic educators from the Reformation to the present. While their counter-reformation efforts were more than educational, the Jesuits' educational efforts proved to be the most effective tool for Roman Catholic survival in an age of reform.

The Jesuits' educational agenda included the instruction of European royalty and aristocracy, as well as the establishment of universities. However, unlike their Protestant counterparts, public education and religious instruction of the population was not a critical consideration.

Education in the Enlightenment and Modern Era (1650-   ): Educators during this period were preoccupied with the nature of the learner and the scientific basis for educational theory and practice. Was the learner depraved/sinful or innately good? In previous eras, the former was the assumption, but the latter became the prevailing convention for educators, both Christian and non-Christian, after 1650.

Educators reflected this new assessment of the human condition. The "Father of Modern Education," John Amos Comenius (1497-1560), regarded learning to be natural and advocated instruction that worked with children's natural inclination to learn. John Locke (1632-1704), perhaps the most influential educator of the Enlightenment, conceptualized the child as a *tabula rasa* or "blank slate," rejecting the depravity concept of human nature. Jean Rousseau (1712-1778) was the most radical of this period's educators. He presented a fictitious model of education in his *Emile*, which entailed the instruction of a child by a teacher in a garden setting. In it Rousseau rejected the notion of formal instruction and curriculum for children, recommending a tutorial relationship based on the child's own self-directed interests. Rousseau's educational approach never found expression in the nonfiction world, and in fact he sent his own children to school. However, his educational ideals were to influence Johann Pestalozzi (1746-1827), who opened a number of schools for children in Germany (Prussia), and perhaps most notably Friedrich Wilhelm August Froebel (1782-1852) who founded the "Children's Garden" or *kindergarten*. The Enlightenment's educational legacy includes:

✎ The notion that learning is measurable.

✎ The value of experience as an instructional mode.

✎ The potential of human intelligence, particularly through the sciences.

✎ The reassessment of human nature as being good or neutral, as opposed to depraved.

Education has continued to enter the public sector.

Perhaps the most significant development during this period was the formation of the Sunday school.

Perhaps the most significant development within Christian education during this period was the formation of the Sunday school. Robert Raikes (1736-1811) founded the first Sunday school in Gloucester, England, in 1780. The Sunday school was designed to address the social conditions plaguing England at the time and was a tool for reform. Not only did it teach Scripture, but sought to increase literacy, hygiene, and moral behavior among the poverty-stricken masses. While opposed by the clergy, who interpreted it as a threat to clerical authority, the Sunday school progressed. From this simple beginning the Sunday school became a movement and spread throughout England and the United States, with its presence being world wide. Once considered a radical endeavor in Christian education, the Sunday school is now regarded as ordinary.

Education in the Twentieth Century: Building on the legacy of the Enlightenment, the modern era of educational endeavor is marked by the desire for a scientific basis for education, pragmatic approaches, and socially-oriented curriculum. With the rapid advance of scientific discovery, and especially the advent of Darwin's theory of natural selection in *Origin of the Species* (1859), education became the domain of the social sciences, particularly psychology and sociology. Educational approaches, even those professing to be Christian, were no longer rooted in revelation or casual experience and observation of children, as in previous generations of educators, but rather in experimentation and social science theories. For example, Johann Herbart (1776-1841) developed an approach to education based on "Associationistic Psychology" while Herbert Spencer, a social Darwinist, used an evolutionary view of social development to frame and advance his educational theory. Similarly, Jean Piaget (1886-1980), developed a model of cognitive development which is acknowledged throughout educational theory, earning him the label "Genetic Epistemologist."

The social focus of education gave rise to pragmatic approaches in education, with its chief contributor being the American educator John Dewey (1859-1952). Dewey, perhaps the most influential educator of the twentieth century, was the father of "Progressive Education," which was firmly rooted in pragmatic philosophy. His five-step method of instruction, called "problem solving," advocated an experiential form of learning designed to develop in students critical thinking skills. However, his pragmatic approach inevitably met with critical reactions. For example, Dewey's pragmatic approach was countered by essentialism and perennialism, both favoring a more traditional approach to education, and utilitarianism, favoring a more task-oriented or vocational training approach to education. However, Dewey's progressivism became the most influential philosophy in twentieth century American education.

Modern Church Education in America

The history of modern Christian education is in fact a biographical sketch of the nineteenth and twentieth centuries. The undisputed "Father of Modern Christian Education" was Horace Bushnell (1802-1876). His *Christian Nurture* (1846) challenged New England Calvinism's revivalistic focus and provided an approach to childhood education in the church which emphasized the family's role in education. His basic tenets were "The child is to grow up a Christian, and never know himself as being otherwise" and 1 Timothy 3:4 ("He must manage his own family well and see that his children obey him with proper respect"). Contrary to traditional Calvinism, Bushnell nullified the idea of childhood depravity and hence the necessity of a childhood conversion experience, favoring a gradual conversion process through education. Hence, Christian education in the nineteenth century was divided into two categories: Nurture/

Bushnell vs. Conversion/Calvinists. To some degree, these categories persist even today among Christian educators, though church education has become far more diverse than ever before.

Church education has become far more diverse than ever before.

What is Christian education like at the close of the twentieth-century? Numerous responses could be given to such a broad question, since church education has encountered a vast spectrum of influences in the twentieth century and diversified accordingly. However, categories of responses have been produced based on either Christian education practice or its theoretical basis, each with their own proponents.

In regard to the practice of Christian education, Jack Seymour's *Mapping Christian Education* (1997) identified four approaches:

❶ Transformation, which emphasizes Christian social action.

❷ Faith Community, wherein education equips believers to live in the church as a covenant community.

❸ Spiritual Growth, which relies on a developmental approach to human nature, including faith or spiritual development.

Mapping Christian Education
(Seymour 1997)
Transformation
Faith Community
Spiritual Growth
Religious Instruction

❹ Religious Instruction, wherein education is designed to transfer the content of Scripture or a particular tradition.

Hence, the four foci of contemporary Christian education are social, communal, personal, and content.

Perhaps more insightful is identifying the theoretical basis of Christian education. Harold Burgess categorized the theoretical foundations for contemporary Christian education in his *Models of Religious Education* (1996). He identified four models of religious education in the twentieth-century:

❶ Liberal, relying on classical liberalism as its basis and advocated by George A. Coe and Harrison Elliot at the turn of the 20th-century.

❷ Mid-century Mainline, which utilized neoorthodoxy and/or process theology, and was advocated by Sheldon Smith and Randolph Crump Miller.

❸ "Evangelical/Kerygmatic." Burgess identifies this as a continuation of Christian education's historical prototype advocated by such as Frank E. Gabelein or Kenneth Gangel.

❹ Social Science, unique to James Michael Lee, which denies the relevance of theological influence on educational theory, even within Christian education.

> **20ᵗʰ Century Models of Religious Education**
> (Burgess 1996)
> **Liberal**
> **Mid-Century Mainline**
> **Evangelical/ Kerygmatic**
> **Social Science**

Both practically and theoretically Christian education at the turn of the millennium is diverse in both its doing and being.

Summary

✎ The core aim of Christian education is the transmission of God's truth.

✎ Christian education is adaptive to changing culture and societal contexts.

✎ The means of Christian education are multileveled, from the Sunday school to the rise of the university.

✎ Eras of reform and restoration have always been preceded by and maintained through new forms of Christian education.

✎ The history of Christian education underscores the need to integrate educational theory and practice with biblical/theological perspective.

p r o j e c t

★ Design your own philosophy of education. Include learning environment, outlook, methods, etc. ★

For Further Reading

William Boyd
The History of Western Education. 8th ed. New York: Barnes and Noble, 1966.

Harold W. Burgess
Models of Religious Instruction. Wheaton, IL: Victor Books, 1996.

J. Donald Butler
Four Philosophies and Their Practice in Education and Religion. New York: Harper and Brothers, 1951.

Steven M. Cahn
Classical and Contemporary Readings in the Philosophy of Education. New York: McGraw-Hill Publishers, 1997.

C. B. Eavey
History of Christian Education. Chicago: Moody Press, 1964.

Kenneth O. Gangel and Warren S. Benson
Christian Education: Its History and Philosophy. Chicago: Moody Press, 1983.

Gerald L. Gutek
Philosophical and Ideological Perspectives on Education. Boston: Allyn and Bacon, 1988.

George R. Knight
Philosophy and Education: An Introduction to Christian Perspective. 3rd ed. Berrien Spring, MI: Andrews University Press, 1998.

D. Bruce Lockerbie
A Passion for Learning: The History of Christian Thought on Education. Chicago: Moody Press, 1994.

Marlene Mayr
Modern Masters of Religious Education. Birmingham, AL: Religious Education Press, 1983.

Nel Noddings
Philosophy of Education. Boulder, CO: Westview Press, 1995.

Michael L. Peterson
Philosophy of Education: Issues and Options. Downers Grove, IL: InterVarsity Press, 1986.

James E. Reed and Ronnie Prevost
A History of Christian Education. Nashville: Broadman, 1993.

Marianne Sawicki
The Gospel in History—Portrait of a Teaching Church: The Origins of Christian Education. New York: Paulist Press, 1988.

Jack Seymour, ed.
Mapping Christian Education. Nashville: Abingdon Press, 1997.

Lewis Joseph Sherrill
The Rise of Christian Education. New York: Macmillan Company, 1944.

CHAPTER 3
PSYCHOLOGICAL
FOUNDATIONS OF CHRISTIAN EDUCATION

CHAPTER THREE SUMMARY
- ☑ The uniqueness of the human learner
- ☑ How teachers can develop internal motivation for learning in students
- ☑ Physical, psychological and cognitive stages of development
- ☑ Learners as physical, thinking, social, moral, spiritual and emotional beings and subsequent implications for teachers

Human learners are a unique creation. Scripture tells us so. Learners are developing persons, those in process, and are governed by the principles of human development. Effective educators understand both the biblical and psychological realities as they plan programs and lessons to meet the needs of learners.

The Human Learner: A Unique Creation

Human learners possess a uniqueness that must be understood by a prospective teacher. This uniqueness cannot be seen apart from Scripture. Persons are a creation of God, the crowning part of God's creative enterprise (Psalm 8). They were made in God's image (Genesis 1:27; 5:1), created to have fellowship with Him. These divinely created individuals share in God's ability to feel, to think, to express emotion, and to be able to distinguish right from wrong. They were given by God the task of managing the remainder of the creation and to subdue and use it for their own enjoyment and to honor God (Genesis 1:28-30, Psalm 8:6-8). Humans were made for relationship, to experience the full gamut of emotions, to love and be loved, to feel, to respond. They were created with the ability to choose whether or not to obey God (Genesis 2:15-16).

However, people chose to disobey God, to pursue their own devices rather than to follow God's desires for His people. The result was sin, the awful separation of God from His creation recorded in Genesis 3. And when sin entered the world, every aspect of humankind's makeup was affected. Thinking became distorted. Emotions were misused and abused (Ephesians 4:26). Right and wrong became blurred in the minds of people (Genesis 2:15-16). Humankind no longer possessed the ability to fellowship with God.

But there is a third act to the drama of human history. God, desiring that none should perish, provided the means by which persons can be restored to a right relationship with Him. He sent His Son, Jesus Christ, to pay the penalty for sin and to redeem those who would entrust their lives to God's direction (Ephesians 2:1-10). What was formerly impossible for mankind in terms of fellowship with God now became possible through the work of Christ (Romans 5:17, 19).

The restoration process is designed to restore mankind in God's image. It is what theologians call the process of sanctification or the idea of Christian growth. Whatever it is called, humankind begins once more to demonstrate the thinking, emotional, moral, and feeling capabilities of God. Bit by bit people develop into Christlikeness (Colossians 1:28).

Not every learner is at the same stage of development in the Christian growth process.

Not every learner is at the same stage of development in the Christian growth process. Some are relatively immature while others demonstrate relative maturity. It is a developmental process to be taken into account by perceptive teachers.

The three theological truths that explain the uniqueness of humankind have profound implications for Christian teaching (Dettoni). First Corinthians 3:1-9 provides insight for the Christian teacher.

> Brothers, I could not address you as spiritual but as worldly—mere infants in Christ. I gave you milk, not solid food, for you were not yet ready for it. Indeed, you are still not ready. You are still worldly. For since there is jealousy and quarreling among you, are you not worldly? Are you not acting like mere men? For when one says, "I follow Paul," and another, "I follow Apollos," are you not mere men?
>
> What, after all, is Apollos? And what is Paul? Only servants, through whom you came to believe—as the Lord has assigned to each his task. I planted the seed, Apollos watered it, but God made it grow. So neither he who plants nor he who waters is anything, but only God, who makes things grow. The man who plants and the man who waters have one purpose, and each will be rewarded according to his own labor. For we are God's fellow workers; you are God's field, God's building.

✎ Verse 1 distinguishes between the mature and the immature. This simply implies that the teacher must discern the development of the learner.

✎ Verse 2 states that it is the teacher's responsibilty to "feed" learners with "food" appropriate to their "digestive" ability, i.e., according to their development. This suggests that teachers must know learners if they are to provide input and direction on their levels. The teacher is responsible to discern learning readiness.

✎ Verses 6-9 indicate that all teachers contribute to the development of learners, but actual development is caused by God. This implies that teachers are responsible to use every means at their disposal to create a good learning environment.

✎ Verses 6-9 also suggest that development occurs from within learners, not from teachers. Teachers must then recognize that they do not control learning, although they do work to create the conditions by which learning may occur.

✎ Verse 9 further adds that teachers are coworkers with God. The same may be said of parents and ministers. This implies that teachers are responsible to do God's work with God, not to hinder Him. It also suggests that teachers must work with individuals at their level of development.

Dettoni also presents nine developmental assumptions for Christian educators, each of which is important to understand before teachers glean from the social sciences those understandings that will direct their teaching.

✎ Human beings are similar. Learning values and faith are similar for all people.

✎ Human beings will only be human. Human learning is of a different kind than animal learning. Though humankind does learn habitually, as the animals, the possibilities of a human being far exceed that of animals both in quality and quantity.

✎ Patterns of development are within the nature of the person. A study of the social sciences will merely demonstrate what God created.

✎ Patterns of development cannot be significantly altered. Persons are physical, mental, emotional, social, moral, and religious creatures—all of these parts interwoven—who develop along certain patterns. Teachers must then take into account the usual patterns of development.

✎ Human beings are integrated wholes. The whole person must be considered in the teaching-learning process.

✎ Externals help or hinder development, never control it. What and how teachers teach have an effect on development, but are not the only elements in the learning process.

✎ To learn is to develop to higher patterns of reasoning and behavior.

✎ Development can be thwarted or stalemated. Not everyone keeps on growing to what he/she was meant to be by God.

✎ Not to develop to the highest levels possible is to deny one's humanness. To keep on developing to the highest possible level is to become the human being God created us to be. Human beings are made to grow. Believers are made to grow into Christlikeness.

The Human Learner: A Developing Individual

Human learners are a composite of their physical, cognitive, emotional, social, and moral capabilities. It is perhaps helpful to envision the human learner as a hand: the five fingers represent the physical, cognitive, emotional, social, and moral characteristics operating at any given time. But the spirit of the person is the core of the person, akin to the palm of the hand, and provides cohesion for the human personality.

It is essential for teachers to understand the basic patterns of development in each area and what effect each has on teaching practice.

A Physical Creature

The physical component of personality at first seems unimportant to the teaching process. That may be true except in the case of exceptionalities. Biological factors have some effect on intelligence and emotional stability, both important to the teaching process.

Human learners are a composite of their physical, cognitive, emotional, social, and moral capabilities.

Between birth and ten or eleven years of age physical growth is fairly constant. Definite changes occur in body shape and proportion during this entire period, but those changes are generally gradual and predictable in nature. Alert teachers are aware of the need for physical comfort and appropriate furnishings in the classroom, of course, even though the physical needs of the learners are not unique.

However, around ten years of age, physical changes begin to occur in girls—although for some girls this will not occur before age thirteen. The physical changes of adolescence begin to occur: enlargement of the breasts, appearance of underarm hair, the growth spurt, menarche.

Individual variation is the chief characteristic of adolescent growth. Within any classroom of late elementary or junior high girls, some will have reached adolescence while others will have only begun the process.

Boys, on the other hand, commence their adolescent growth spurt at twelve or thirteen years of age, although there are again great individual differences. By the time the process is completed they will have surpassed girls in height and strength.

Both boys and girls tend to reach puberty at earlier ages now than they did in the past. The average age for each has been reduced by nearly two years during this century.

Early-maturing males have advantages over later maturing ones. They usually are given more privileges and tasks normally reserved for older children and adolescents. Later maturing boys tend to have more anxiety about their masculinity and competence. The latter need the presence of caring adult teachers and leaders.

Early-maturing girls usually do not find the advantages of early-maturing boys. They are often embarrassed to be bigger than the other children. These girls need the affirmation of caring adult leaders who can help them accept themselves as they are.

A Thinking Creature

Human development is marked by distinctive thinking modes at various stages of development. The way learners process information determines what information is taught and how it is presented. Perhaps the two most important areas to Christian teachers are how the learner processes information and his language skill.

Development of Thinking Skills

Jean Piaget, the eminent Swiss psychologist, provided helpful insight into the thinking structures of human learners. He contended that certain schemas (patterns of behavior) characterize each level of human thinking. Learning requires modifying those schema to incorporate new information, understandings, or skills. Piaget believed that there is a fixed sequence of stages in the growth of thought, and that thinking at one stage is qualitatively different than that at another. The ages at which children move from one stage to the other differ because of their own genetic endowment, educational backgrounds, cultural experiences, and degree of intellectual stimulation.

Sensorimotor Stage. The first stage of thinking is the sensori-motor stage. Infants possess only innate reflex capacity which allow only "trial and error" behavior. But children begin to discriminate about what works and what does not, providing the origins of thinking. As they learn to discriminate, children begin to repeat certain behaviors, often coordinating between one action and another. They begin to exert influence on their environment, e.g., dropping the spoon to see someone pick it up, or shaking a rattle to hear the sound.

By eighteen months or so babies pursue a sort of experimentation in the search for new things in their external environment. They even move to the point of simple problem solving, using two independent actions they have previously learned.

**Children progress from instinctual reflexive action
to symbolic activities and to the ability to separate
themselves from objects in their environment.**

In summary, it can be said that children progress from instinctual reflexive action to symbolic activities and to the ability to separate themselves from objects in their environment. They develop limited capabilities to anticipate the consequences of actions.

Preoperational Stage. The second stage, beginning at about age two and lasting to about age seven, is the preoperational stage. The onset of language is essential to progress to this stage. Once children have acquired language, a word can signify a thought, an object, an event.

Between the ages of two and four, children build up a repertoire of representational activity and also begin to differentiate the image and language on the one hand from action and reality on the other. They make many reasoning errors at this time because they reason from particular to particular, e.g., Mommy is combing her hair because she is going out; she went out last time she combed her hair. This is a time of preconceptual thinking in which children deal with each thing individually, but are unable to group objects.

At about the age of four a child begins to be able to examine and set about a specific task and apply his intelligence to it. However, children still make many reasoning errors. For one reason, they center on some striking feature of an object to the exclusion of other relevant aspects. They have no idea that two objects with different shapes can be equal in size, volume, or weight. Their thinking cannot move readily back and forth from beginning point to an intermediate point back to the beginning point. Piaget calls this intuitive thought: children can be readily fooled by what they see. Though their reasoning capacity is better, they are still bound to the here-and-now in thinking.

Concrete Operational. Children move to concrete operational thinking at age seven or so. This period usually lasts until approximately age twelve. Children begin to understand that two items can be different shapes, yet equal. They can envision reversible possibilities. They can classify objects into hierarchical groups. They learn with understanding. They can build a series. Their ability to relate time and space also matures during this time. By the end of the period, they are ready to do formal thinking.

Students still require objects, events, or actions for logical reasoning.

Students still require objects, events, or actions for logical reasoning. They also need clear, sequential directions for long and/or detailed projects.

Formal Operational. The fourth stage of thinking is called formal operational by Piaget. Children become better at organizing and structuring data. They can do systematic problem solving. They can establish hypotheses and seek to support or reject them on the basis of sound evidence. They are able to function largely or wholly on a symbolic, abstract level.

At this stage students are aware of inconsistencies and mistakes due to the use of mental checks and balances. They can also establish their own plans for long and/or detailed projects if given aims and goals for completion. The emergence of this stage seems to be directly linked to cultural patterns and the need for formal thinking in certain settings. Many researchers now believe that there is a later formal thinking period not clearly identified by Piaget. Some believe that this later period does not emerge until a person has reached the mid-twenties.

Language Development

Language acquisition proceeds on a fairly consistent basis from the time babies begin to talk and all through life—if they are in a stimulating environment. The largest increases in vocabulary occur during the preschool years when language capability literally explodes. For example, children's vocabulary increases from an average of three words at age one to nearly 300 at age two. By the time children go to first grade their vocabulary has increased to 2500+ words. But human learners at all ages recognize either aurally or visually far more words than they can use. Teachers need to keep this in mind.

Implications for Teachers

The cognitive development of learners has profound implications for the teacher and curriculum designer. Understandable biblical concepts should be taught at the time of prime understanding for the learners. Concepts should be taught in ways that are most understandable to each learner.

Teaching methods vary according to the concepts to be taught and those to whom they are being taught. Preschool and early elementary age children require many concrete experiences and media to learn Bible concepts. Teachers may use role playing and a wide variety of other techniques to stimulate older learners to assimilate and apply Bible truth.

A Social Being

Every society has to socialize its young, i.e., it must teach children to behave in ways appropriate to their place in that society. This is usually done without formal teaching, although it is certainly not left to chance.

Perhaps the most important socializing factor for children is the child-rearing practices of their parents. Certain child-rearing practices tend to produce predictable personality traits. For example, *permissive* parents (those who are nonpunitive, acceptant, disorganized, and make few attempts to shape behavior) tend to produce dependent, immature, aggressive, anxious children who have difficulty exercising self-control.

Authoritarian parents are those who have absolute standards, practice punitive techniques, and are not very affectionate to the children. Children of these parents tend to be somewhat discontented, insecure, and hostile when under stress.

Warm, nurturing parents who exercise firm control, but provide some explanation for restrictions may be characterized as *authoritative.* They tend to produce children who can exercise self-control and are socialized, assertive, competent, and appropriately independent.

Perhaps the most important socializing factor for children is the child-rearing practices of their parents.

Play is also a valuable socialization device for preschool children. Infants and toddlers pursue solitary play, perhaps playing alongside another child, but with no interaction. By the time children reach age four, they become involved in cooperative play which is organized. However children play, though, they tend to imitate the behavior of adults around them. Repetitive play tends to establish social patterns that exist long after the play is over.

Play provides a major way for children to explore their world and themselves. It also stimulates them to solve problems. It is a lab in which real life situations may be rehearsed. In every way, it is children's work, allowing them to learn to concentrate and satisfy curiosity.

Elementary children begin to develop friendships, usually based on proximity. These friendships allow the child to extend himself beyond the family and develop a sense of competence in social situations.

Teens are almost totally gregarious creatures. Their choices are affected by what others think. Though youngsters need to distance themselves some from parents, they still need the security of a group. The issue of peer pressure is real and intense for adolescents.

Gerald Tiffin (1987-88) observes that the term "social generation" has joined the traditional term "biological generation" as an everyday working concept. He observes what this means to teachers:

> New generations are created by common historical experiences (Depression, Vietnam War, post-World War II difference etc.) and pass more quickly than biological generations. Most of today's parents of late adolescents are from two to four generations distanced from their children. The youth are often just as far removed from their teachers in generational terms. Such is the impact of accelerated change. This requires careful and sensitive planning and strategy as "adults" attempt to communicate with generations several social generations removed from theirs. While the young are not responsible for how quickly life changes, teachers are responsible for teaching effectively across social generations.

Implications for Teachers

David Elkind in *All Grown Up and No Place to Go* provides six actions that teachers and parents can do to help children and teenagers to grow into independent, relatively mature individuals.
- Learn to say no when it is appropriate.
- Be persistent in dealing with youngsters.

- Deal with young people at the time that it is needed.
- Don't understand too much. In other words, hold out positive expectations and standards for them to achieve.
- Talk. Don't worry so much about open communication with teens who may choose not to communicate at all. But do talk.
- Reduce class and group sizes when dealing with children and teens.

An Emotional Person

Children are born with no capability for emotional response other than distress. But they begin early to develop a set of responses appropriate for various situations. During the first year of life, children develop the capacity for delight, joy, jealousy, and anger. From these can develop the emotional responses of love and hate.

Although temperament has a strong genetic link, to a large extent children are dependent upon role models and effective child-rearing practices to learn how to handle their emotional responses appropriately.

One way of viewing psychosocial development (certainly not the only way, but rather a satisfactory way from a Christian perspective) is to understand the work of Erik Erikson. He suggested that personality is shaped by an epigenetic cycle that is made up of eight episodes. Each person has a ground plan that emerges from inheritance and gene code plus environment and the interaction of these factors. This interaction produces feelings about life. The result is character. Models serve as basic building blocks at various steps along the way.

Erikson suggests that each step in the cycle is composed of a tension that must be resolved. Positive resolution results in a positive building block in the personality and emotional structure. Negative resolution creates a glitch in the personality that must one day be compensated for (with great effort)—or it results in long-standing deficits.

Trust vs. Mistrust (Birth to 1½). The significant person is the mother or primary caregiver, especially in warmth and consistency of response to the needs of the child. The development of trust is largely dependent upon the quality, not the amount of warm nurturance, although both are factors.

Autonomy vs. Shame and Doubt (1½ to 4). The significant relationships are both parents. Children need to come to feel good about their environment. The issue is developing the ability to control the world and environment appropriately. Obviously, disciplinary styles are critical in resolving this issue.

Initiative vs. Guilt (4 to 6). Parents still form the significant relationships for children. The issue is for them to learn to plan their own activities and organize directions for routing energy in acceptable ways. By accepting the feeling tones of others, especially parents as they nurture and discipline, into feelings about themselves, children decide whether they can exercise influence in their environment or whether they are permanently guilty of inability to do so.

By accepting the feeling tones of others, children decide whether they can exercise influence in their environment or not.

Industry vs. Inferiority (6 to 12). The significant relationship shifts to the school, both to teachers and peers. Children are involved in determining their personal competence in the completion of assigned tasks and the acquisition of tools necessary to get along in his culture.

Identity vs. Role Diffusion (12 to 18). Peers and adult models become extremely important in the lives of adolescents. Models are internalized by warm relationships. Hostile ones are rejected. The models become important building blocks of personality. Adolescents must integrate their previous experiences in order to create commitment and direction for life.

Intimacy vs. Isolation (18 to 40). Young adults are particularly affected by peers and close friends or a spouse. The important issue at this stage is learning to fuse one's identity with another without losing personal identity. One must learn to commit to affiliations and partnerships.

Generativity vs. Stagnation (40 to 60 or 65). Generativity is the sense of transmitting something to the next generation. This is frequently done through parenting, but need not be accomplished only in that way. Middle adults must decide to renew themselves because they are contributing to the next generation.

Ego Integrity vs. Despair (65+). Ego integrity involves bringing closure to life, assessing it as having been satisfactory, even if not perfect. When ego integrity has been reached, individuals no longer fear death.

Implications for Teachers

Alert teachers will be aware of where the learners are in their personality development. They will provide some experiences that will help them to grow in appropriate ways. Much of this is done through personal relationships with learners, but can also be enhanced with appropriate application of curriculum content and selection of teaching methods.

A Moral Character

Morality is defined in *Webster's New Collegiate Dictionary* as "moral character; virtue" or alternatively, "the quality of that which conforms to right ideals or principles of human conduct." Moral is also defined as "characterized by excellence in what pertains to practice or conduct; right and proper." Moral choice and behavior involves three factors: (1) a capability of discerning right and wrong, (2) affective response to the objective principles of right and wrong, and (3) a felt obligation to act in accordance with this knowledge."

Studies in moral development began as early as 1925 when Macauley and Watkins published the results of their work among 3000 children in England. They concluded that (1) children build up a value system by the acceptance of social conventions and (2) there appears to be a pattern of development in this growth.

In 1949, Havighurst and Taba studied the character development of children, ten and sixteen years of age, in Morris,

Illinois. They concluded that (1) moral character is controlled by social expectation and (2) moral character is controlled by moral ideas. Arnold Gesell and associates studied fifty children from 1946 to 1956 and concluded that moral growth was in a sequential pattern.

Jean Piaget contributed to the study of moral development early in his research. He concluded in a 1932 study that moral autonomy follows heteronomy, i.e., determination of moral behavior proceeds from an external source to an internal source. The heteronomous person is characterized by believing that (1) rules are timeless and emanate from God, (2) goodness comes by respecting those in authority, and (3) the consequences of behavior determine what is good or bad. The autonomous person, on the other hand, respects rules, and very well may acknowledge his ultimate source as God, but these rules have become self-chosen and internalized. He no longer makes the choices he makes because he has to, but because he wants to. The autonomous style should be well formed by the age of eleven or twelve.

The autonomous person makes the choices he makes not because he has to but because he wants to.

The application of Piaget's ideas has been carried out by Lawrence Kohlberg of Harvard. He has concluded that moral judgment and behavior develops in two major stages.

✎ Dependence. Individuals are concerned with external consequences. They seek either to avoid punishment or to benefit themselves. They may behave morally because of social expectations. It is obvious that disciplinary style and the input of moral content is important at this time, but so is the internal development of the conscience to allow the person to move to the stage of independence. (Conscience development is affected by warmth and nurturance from parents, the presence of effective models, and consistent discipline.)

✎ Independence. The focus moves to internal commitment. It begins with a desire to maintain the social order, but should proceed to decisions of behavior based on valid ethical principles. It is at this point that individuals may allow their conscience to be their guide.

Implications for Teachers

How can teachers help to develop morality? Certainly the home is a critical factor, but so are appropriate models in the classroom and youth group. Children must have consistent discipline by parents, caregivers, and teachers. Realistic stories can be used to provide the content of faith and moral behavior and to show how others have struggled with making moral choices.

Another helpful teaching strategy is to create moral dilemmas in which students must select their course of action, explaining why they chose as they did. Role playing is another effective teaching tool because it allows learners the opportunity to try out their moral choices in a real life situation, yet one that is not irreversible. Teachers must develop good listening skills to find out why students choose as they do in the strategies mentioned in the previous paragraph. Then they can raise additional questions to help individuals clarify their behavior and how that fits into stated principles.

A Person of Faith

Faith development is critically linked to all of the previous components of personality. Thinking capability is an important factor. Trust and the ability to experience healthy guilt are essential for faith. The capacity to act consistently with cognitive decisions is a contributor to faith development. It is difficult, then, to speak of faith without speaking of a thinking, feeling, social, moral person.

James Fowler is perhaps the foremost researcher in faith development. He describes the faith of early childhood as undifferentiated, that is, it is not identifiable. That is not to say that children have no idea of God, for they do. However, God is described in the experiences children can understand, i.e., anthropomorphically. God lives in heaven or in the church building. He made things. Children may even ask to see Him.

**Faith development is critically linked to all
of the previous components of personality.**

In the later period of early childhood, from about four to age seven, children's faith is described as intuitive-projective by Fowler. It is a fantasy-rich, imitative phase during which the child can be permanently influenced by examples, moods, actions, and stories of the faith of adults. Children still seek to locate God: He is in the sky or inside of children. Their thinking about God is limited to the concrete (as is their thinking about other matters as well).

The richest resource for teaching for faith is stories—stories from both the Bible and of the church that emphasize God's loving care and power. A second important factor is loving, consistent care from those who teach about faith.

Somewhere between the ages of five and seven, children begin to develop a concept of causality and coherence of the world. Conscience becomes permanent. Questions of fairness become urgent. Shortly thereafter, perhaps at eight or so, children move to a mystic-literal faith. At this stage they begin to take on for themselves the stories, beliefs, and observances that symbolize belonging to their community. God is still seen anthropomorphically, but He is increasingly described by attributes such as all-powerful, all-knowing, creator as the period progresses.

Stories should be used throughout this period. But teachers should also allow, even encourage, children to read from the Scriptures themselves. They should plan for participation in every aspect of class. Music can be used powerfully. Most of all, teachers must be warm models of the Christian faith, giving children a demonstration of Christlikeness.

Fowler suggests that most adolescents are in a synthetic-conventional faith mode. Faith begins to synthesize values and information to provide a basis for identity, and it is structured in interpersonal terms. This is a conformist stage in that it is attuned to the expectations and judgments of significant others. These persons have a generally consistent clustering of values and beliefs, but they have not objectively examined them.

The two most important things that can happen to assist faith development in youth are to provide a trustworthy congregational environment and to support youth classes and groups that allow those involved to test the limits of belief. Youth in the church also need adult guidance in exploring faith issues, but never adult control and manipulation. In addition, they need opportunity to contribute to the life of the church.

Adults, if they progress in faith development at all, move to an individuative-reflective faith. It often does not appear before the mid-30s, however. The movement is often triggered by contradictions in values and beliefs or by experiencing marked changes by officially sanctioned leaders of policies or practices deemed previously to be official.

Young adults need the opportunity to test a way of life if they are to develop productively in their faith. Service opportunities need to be plentiful. Teachers must allow questioning. They need to be taught as adults rather than as children.

Fowler speaks of one more stage of faith, which seldom emerges before middle adulthood. Conjunctive faith integrates into self not only what one has always believed, but also new points of view. Although Fowler does not say so, it stands to reason from a biblical perspective that these new points of view must be weighed against biblical teaching.

Finally, older persons must determine whether life has had meaning or not. Faith is a powerful aid to developing this kind of integrity.

Effective teachers of older adults deal directly with their faith.

The effective teacher of older adults deals directly with their faith, how it provides integrity, purpose, and a future. He will confront the issues of change, death, and hope with a sense of hope and continued growth. The issue of faith development should not be confused with the idea of conversion. Faith development refers to changes in the ways of knowing and valuing the biblical information we possess. Conversion refers to a change in the content of faith and/or a significant intensification of commitment. Conversion, then, often occurs at times of transition in faith development.

Conclusion

This chapter has examined the various components of the human personality, how these develop, and some implications for teaching. Teachers will, then, do all that can be done to make instructional plans that take into account the developmental levels and/or needs of the students.

---

p r o j e c t s

☆ Observe a learner (you choose the age) for an hour. What characteristics mentioned in this chapter did you observe? What did you observe that wasn't mentioned in the chapter? ☆

☆ On note cards, develop lesson-related student projects for each of the following learner types: auditory, visual, kinesic. ☆

For Further Reading

James Fowler
Stages of Faith. San Francisco: Harper and Row, 1981.

Robert J. Havighurst
Developmental Tasks and Education. New York: David McKay Company, 1948.

Robert W. Pazmiño
Foundational Issues in Christian Education. Grand Rapids: Baker, 1988.

CHAPTER 4
SOCIOLOGICAL TRENDS:
THE CHURCH'S RESPONSE TO A RAPIDLY CHANGING WORLD

Chapter Four Summary
- ☑ Current demographic trends
- ☑ Single, prison and age population statistics
- ☑ Consumerism, technological advances and other trends' effects on education
- ☑ Five types of Christian education outreach

Population and information continue to mushroom world-wide as we enter the 21st century. Generally, the social climate reflects rampant technology and consumerism. As Christian educators, it is hopeless to seek to stem tides of change. Instead, we must purposefully anchor to the timeless truth of Scripture. Setting relevancy in motion takes too long. The next wave has swept us under long before we have begun to implement the most innovative of visions, leaving the church ten years behind. Relevance and relativity forever shift under our feet. But in the midst of a "super highway" and many slippery slopes, there is still that constancy in the absolute truth of Jesus Christ that has always dumped the world upside down. As Christian educators, we have the only stable information for every audience, even in the 21st century. We must bend society into the truth, rather than bending the truth to fit our world. Transforming lives is still our goal. Even today, the gospel can convert all of the bleak realities of our world. We can use these myriad technologies and people groups to make our goal a reality.

**As Christian educators, we have the only stable information
for every audience, even in the 21st century.**

It makes sense to consider demographics and social trends in order to understand our current audience. The following statistics will ironically be somewhat outdated before they can be printed. Being able to accept that these facts do not provide a formula is the key. Hopefully, they will demonstrate one way to assess an audience. That skill must then be constantly reapplied so that we always meet our audience head on.

Demographic Trends

In 1992, the world's population was 5.4 billion. The population is projected to climb to between 8-10 billion by the year 2020 and then to stabilize around 8-12 billion by 2050. This doubled increase will come primarily from countries still in the process of industrialization (often called Third World Countries). In European countries, Japan, and the United States, birthrates do not replace death rates at this time (*World Reference Atlas*, 1994). The population decline in industrialized nations is due largely to the advent of legalized abortion, birth control, and the choice of many to have small families or no children at all.

The church's staggering task is further complicated by the fact that the majority of births will take place in countries already largely unchristianized. These countries are known in mission terms as the 10-40 Window because of their latitudinal location. The most populated and fastest-growing cities of the world are within this window of opportunity.

If we ignore these demographic shifts, we will always be running to catch up. If we accept the challenge to adapt immediately to the places of largest population, we could live to see the greatest numbers of conversions ever noted.

In the United States, the population booms despite the decreased birthrate amongst citizens. This increase comes primarily from immigration (legal and illegal) and longer life expectancy. About 10 million immigrants settled in the United States in the 1980s—more than in any other decade (*World Reference Atlas*, 1994). Immigrants continue to arrive year by year, changing the ethnic mix and ratio. Every imaginable ethnic background seeks temporary entrance into colleges and universities in the United States.

The United States population contains 84% Caucasians currently. By 2050 whites will comprise only 65% of the total population (*World Reference Atlas*, 1994). Once again we are reminded how important it is for us to choose the right strategy for discipling our world. We must go to all nations and meet them when they come to us.

Single Population

Another population phenomenon that the church faces is the growing numbers of singles. Divorce rocks our world. Today nearly twice as many people land in divorce court in the United States as did in 1960. Worldwide the divorce trend is also significant.

As contributory as divorce is to the picture of singleness, the even greater change involves those who have never married. Presently almost half of the population is not married. Within that unmarried population, significantly more women than men are single. Because the life span of women is currently about seven years longer than that of men, many of these women are elderly widows. But the majority of those now single have never married. People are waiting longer to marry even if that is their ultimate choice. The average age of first-time marriage has risen nearly five years since 1950 (from 20 to 24.5).

**Many who grew up in unstable homes
fear the commitment of marriage.**

Many who grew up in unstable homes fear the commitment of marriage, choosing rather to live together even though not married. Because of materialism, many choose more convenient economic arrangements than they believe marriage provides. Anymore, few espouse the old adage, "Two can live together as cheaply as one." Many want to complete a college education before marriage. Others choose to "shop around" endlessly, looking for the perfect mate. In the midst of all these options, promiscuity and disease rage at epidemic proportions. The trend toward singleness spawns a continuum of response, from loneliness and alienation to freedom and independence.

Prison Population

Another growing segment of the population (largely overlooked by the church) is the prison population. Sadly enough, it is large enough to be considered a demographic entity. Every ethnic background finds this a growing concern. The Lindesmith Institute reports that between 1970 and 1998, the total population sentenced to prison jumped from 20,686 to 94,113. In 1970, 16.3% were drug offenders (1998). By June of 1998, 59.1% were drug offenders. The notion that the bad drug years were left back in the '70s is obviously a myth.

It currently costs taxpayers $5,421 per year to educate a child. That same year for one inmate costs $20,804.

It currently costs taxpayers $5,421 per year to educate a child. That same year for one inmate costs $20,804. In California alone, 21 prisons were constructed between 1984 and 1996, while only one university was built. Over 1.6 million people are presently incarcerated in the United States alone. The tough-on-crime political agenda seemingly has had questionable results. The church must obey the command of Christ to visit the prisoner.

Age Population

Equally imprisoned in generational ideals stand the Builders, Boomers, Busters and Xers. These names, assigned by pollster/demographers such as George Barna and Gary McIntosh, describe the philosophies of the living generations in the United States.

The first Builders were born just before 1925. They joined organizations and built institutions. They give well to appeals and care about the church and her history, educational institutions, denominational affiliation, and service clubs. They hold the sanctuary of the church building in holy reverence. They minister out of duty.

The first Boomers were born in 1945 at the close of WWII. They distrust institutions and resist joining them. They are committed to relationships and support causes rather than programs. They are loyal to people, not institutions, and want to experience their faith. They minister out of personal satisfaction.

The first Busters were born in 1965. They are committed to family. They expect up-to-date technology. They desire a place that meets their needs. They want stress to be relieved and problems to be fixed. They are often not ready to minister until they are "fixed." They minister out of a sense of caring about someone's problems.

The first generation Xers were born in 1977. It is the second largest generation in the history of the United States, promising a long and large impact on the future. They are unimpressed by experts. In all events they expect professional excellence that competes with the best in entertainment. They are not easily motivated to action. They like variety in music and electronic learning. Yet they are passive learners, for the most part, a result of the inability to interact with electronic teachers. They have short attention spans. Because reality may not be as gripping as virtual possibilities, they are not very moved by crisis or urgency. They have little global concern. They want to take care of immediate, visible local needs. They minister with short-term, hands-on models in realms they have personally seen.

It remains to be seen how the Millennial Generation will react to their parents' generation.

The children being born to Generation Xer's will be characterized by such names as Millennial, Bridgers, or Blasters. It remains to be seen how they will react to their parents' generation.

In days gone by people seldom lived to see their own grandchildren reach adulthood. Now a number of families could be found for a five-generation picture (if they could ever be gathered together in a mutual event). Nearly one-fifth of the United States population will be over 65 by the year 2020 (*World Reference Atlas*, 1994). Such persons may live nearly as many years retired as they were employed. Perhaps, such persons might be widowed as long or longer than they were married. A person not marrying until age 40 could celebrate a 50th wedding anniversary. As one can see, Christian education for a church containing a cross-section of America is no easy task.

Social Trends

Just as these demographic issues make the task of Christian education so challenging, so does the frenetic social climate. Jesus' healing touch has never been more needed.

Consumerism

Consumerism is a worldwide urgency. Phrases like "shop until you drop," "menu," "fast food," and "smorgasbord" permeate vocabulary and advertising in all arenas. Most Americans are sunk deeply into debt because of the need to have more. Walk-in closets, garages, storage sheds and second seasonal homes store all the newest (or the most antique) treasures. Name brands are known by the smallest of children. Bigger and better malls and supermarkets appear every year. Hundreds of restaurants sit side by side on any main street or exit with signs posted next to them announcing yet another to open.

**We can always find more things that we want.
We hero worship those who get rich.**

The rest of the world is not exempt. McDonalds can be found in all but the remotest corners of the earth. In order to have more material benefits, immigrants sometimes attempt to stay in industrialized nations by marrying a citizen. Probably dozens, if not hundreds, of individuals far outdistance Solomon's wealth. Yet, all but a small percentage spend their money any way but personally. The frantic search for more, and more variety, continues to escalate. We can always find more things that we want. We hero worship those who get rich.

Technology

Technology has also taken on a life of its own. Radio and television satellite programming spans the globe. Laptop computers make communication possible anywhere in the world, even en route to the destination. People can see a video about Jesus in the most primitive jungle. Knowledge doubles before our eyes. People can access any book in the world on-line, not to mention any kind of pornography. Software becomes obsolete as we carry it home to install. Cars practically drive themselves, with climate control on both halves of the same seat. A person can go anywhere in the world on the Internet without moving from her desk. The Jetsons begin to look old-fashioned.

Medical technology provides opportunity for creation of life. Women can now conceive after menopause by artificial means. Fertility can be induced in those who do not conceive naturally. And most recently, the idea of cloning without use of any human anatomy other than a little DNA and a lab boggles our minds.

Gangs

The need for God can get pushed farther and farther away as humankind begins to feel all-powerful with their technological pursuits. On the other hand, technology can be used to advance the gospel to the ends of the Earth.

All the goods and information we can imagine are at our fingertips. Yet, in the midst of the bounty, dissatisfaction and emptiness remains. Young people are forming gangs. Every city over 50,000 (and many smaller cities) contains notable gang activity. Violent crime has been on the rise for over twenty years. On the surface it would seem these youth are attempting to have more money and power. In actuality, they may be merely attempting to escape painful alienation and to find a place to belong. Many of these gang members will eventually be incarcerated, where they will be yet more alone. Few churches make the needs of this type of youth a priority.

Termination of Life

Comfort, undoubtedly, tops the list as the most wanted commodity in this postmodern age. People leave churches for softer pews and better sound systems or worship bands. Add to this need for comfort, the need to escape loneliness, guilt, or pain, and termination of life becomes the natural consequence.

Comfort, undoubtedly, tops the list as the most wanted commodity in this postmodern age.

Since 1973, developing humans have been aborted by the millions at all stages of pregnancy and by any age mother. Even the legalization of partial birth abortion in 1998 barely caused a protest in Congress.

At the other end of the spectrum, euthanasia has also become acceptable by a large segment of the population. Jack Kevorkian, a physician who helps the terminally ill to die, is a household name. Anyone made uncomfortable by personal illness or by a relative's illness can find ways to get rid of that situation permanently. Relativism, the philosophy of this age, has made the distinction between taking a life and kindness very hazy.

"The right to die" is a phrase heard commonly today. Some believe any reason for self-inflicted death is a matter of personal decision. The National Center for Injury Prevention and Control [NCIPC] reports that more people die from suicide than homicide: 31,235 Americans took their own lives in 1995. Suicide is the ninth leading cause of death by all Americans and the third by those between 15-24 years of age. Ninety percent of these deaths are among Whites and mostly among males. The rates are rising dramatically among Native Americans and Blacks as well (NCIPC, 1998). People are frequently deciding to end lives of quiet desperation.

Homelessness

Not all troubled people join gangs or take their own lives. Some roam the streets, eking out an existence. Many homeless are young people on the run, escaping from or rebelling against parental guidance or unhappy home lives. Some are mentally ill or otherwise disabled. Many are chemical users. Some are families. Some are unemployed or unemployable. Some do not ever intend to work. Most are cold at times, nutritionally impoverished, and spiritually unhealthy. Few believe they have adequate alternatives. The homeless in many countries are the result of nationwide poverty. That the numbers are on the rise in such a wealthy country as the United States, with its low unemployment rate and entrepreneurial possibilities, calls into question the worldview of society at large. The church must be more willing to offer her alternative.

Addictions

Another coping (or perhaps noncoping) mechanism in a troubled society is that of addictive behavior. People obsess over alcohol, drugs, food, gambling, television, working out at health clubs, shopping, sex, video and computer games, pornography, and fun. Perhaps, addiction is the logical extreme of consumerism. The more people have, the more they seem to want, and the more they get at any cost. The clientele of the counseling world never runs dry. Some people are even addicted to counseling sessions.

Leisure

Still others are addicted to leisure activity. Leisure (or at least rest) is a biblical concept. The Builder generation faces leisure with guilt and fear of the Devil's idleness. They often work for the sake of being busy. Since that generation, the focus has shifted toward frenetic pleasure. People are working so hard at leisure that they are exhausted and sometimes bankrupt by their fun. Pleasure motives rule behavior and salary in every arena of life. In the business world, the largest salaries and the highest honors are awarded to those in sports, music, and acting careers. The worth of something is judged by whether it is fun.

Illiteracy

Perhaps because reading is an activity of the mind rather than the body and perhaps because it is not technologically diverse, its popularity is waning in this generation. Reading levels are falling annually. Even college students resist buying textbooks. Building resource libraries is a lost art. Dangers of getting information off the revered Net lie in the lack of quality control or simple verification. Anyone can publish. No one edits. How does one check competence or honesty without a clearinghouse?

Unless reading is connected with leisure or pleasure, few read daily or avidly.

Unless reading is connected with leisure or pleasure (sports magazines and pornography are the most lucrative print businesses), few read daily or avidly. This is the first generation illiterate by choice. The church must ponder where that phenomenon will leave the Holy Scriptures. Perhaps, the destruction of reading is Satan's most crafty ploy to date. Public education is beginning to see the parallel between illiteracy and at-risk children. Such programs as Kids Hope joins volunteer tutors with an elementary school child in order to improve literacy and give relational support simultaneously. The church must be equally innovative in developing ways to reintroduce the joy of reading, particularly the Bible, among her members.

Lifelong Learning

Despite the decline in reading ability and interest, all races, sexes, and ages are granted access to education. In the past, higher education was provided for the middle and upper class person in his or her late teens and twenties. Now colleges and universities enroll a gamut of races and ages. Furthermore, education is no longer a terminal event. Continuing education is mandated by many employers and often funded by them. Annual programs for the elderly on campus are a common occurrence. No one is disallowed if he or she can meet the standards. Buildings are handicapped accessible and services for learners with disabilities are prevalent. Hope for a better society rests in the ongoing search for the truth.

Teamwork

A century of sentiment for the individual is shifting toward the group or team. The role of an individual authority figure or expert is no longer highly regarded. The group working together to ascertain majority view is common. At times this has a downside. If there is no expert, then anarchy is a possibility. Even a carefully thoughtful majority can be wrong or evil. A ship without a captain, no matter how able the crew, can run aground. Even a small group studying the Bible may do little more than pool ignorance. Leadership is a biblical concept.

A century of sentiment for the individual is shifting toward the group or team.

At other times, the idea of teamwork has real merit. At the Mayo Clinic in Rochester, Minnesota, a patient is seen by a team of specialists. No part of the body is overlooked. The possibility of diagnosis based on a one-track mind is almost impossible.

However, sometimes, it is frustrating when no one takes charge. Little relationship can be established between doctor and patient since a different consultant is assigned each visit. Consequently, many resident patients seek other less world-known facilities in order to feel like someone is in charge of their case.

The current cultural trend is for a team of doctors, engineers, architects, teachers, sales forces, or ministers to work together as a body. As long as we do not become obsessed with this swing of the pendulum, this is a trend we can capitalize on biblically.

Implications and Innovations for Christian Education

Because of the societal trends toward consumerism and instant gratification, constant change and variety is deemed necessary by the public. Many churches are returning to weeknight Christian education programs. Even though Wednesday night services were an unquestioned tradition thirty years ago, the Busters and Xers find it an innovation. If there is a diverse and activity-based children's component, coupled with food, people flock to participate. A smorgasbord of Sunday school electives appeals to the younger generations as well.

The hottest debate nationwide surrounds worship style. Most churches offer the olive branch of several worship options. Contemporary, traditional, and blended music appeases most people. The majority can find a style they enjoy. Megachurches abound, giving credence to approval of such variety.

How does the church teach the sacrifice of praise if one never worships outside his own preference?

One serious consideration, unfortunately, finds little debate. How does the church teach the sacrifice of praise if one never worships outside his own preference? Is the concept of "God's" pleasure being lost? How does the church teach the whole of Scripture if learners pick and choose content? How does the Body function together when it is most often fragmented into its place of choice? How does the Body learn from and fellowship with members not homogeneous? Is there a danger of offering a menu rather than a sequenced curriculum? Is the mission of the church to satisfy people?

Distance Learning

Technological trends provide the possibility of taking classes on nearly any subject anywhere in the world. Missionaries can be refreshed and updated daily. Ministers on the field can obtain advanced degrees without leaving their position. New Christians in areas of the world without Christian colleges and seminaries can be trained on-the-spot for leadership. Immediate access allows for encouragement and accommodation of brothers and sisters in Christ worldwide. Networking between Christian agencies can eliminate duplicative services, information, or expense. Even medical advice can be sent to remote regions at a moment's notice. Economic, governmental, and time constraints can be minimized with ever-expanding telecommunication abilities. Quick-change options and storage enhance biblical translation. Certainly, these aspects are all positive. Getting the Word out to as many people as possible is the Great Commission.

Are there any negative aspects to such helpful options? Perhaps at least one. Technology cannot offer the personal touch. In a world already lonely and alienated, this kind of learning can only happen in one dimension. Gentle touch or meaningful eye contact cannot be used to encourage or relate to the learner. Notably, Jesus did not send His ministry to us via satellite or video. The struggle to be simultaneously current and an incarnation of Christ to the world remains problematic.

Small Groups and Task Forces

In light of the teamwork trend, study and service groups are very popular. Inductive learning flourishes. Individual creativity compounds. Efforts multiply. This format provides necessary identity and support for group members and many needed services to unreached peoples. Short-term mission trips and local ministry outreach are examples of these joint efforts of the Body of Christ.

Many groups for seekers also exist within the Church with the purpose of biblical instruction and relationship. Such groups sometimes provide basic counseling services in a less threatening or costly fashion.

Some churches, seeking to combine the best of small group dynamics with a foundational, comprehensive understanding of the Bible, have begun a program called Core Curriculum. These basic, short-term classes with limited enrollment, introduce small groups to a survey of the Bible, the Church's mission, and a Christian worldview. The culmination of the study group is a task force in which each student chooses to actively participate in a ministry. Some even include a mentorship component, training group members to teach the course another time it is offered.

Table 4.1 A Core Curriculum Model

Courses (Each course lasts six weeks) The Nature of the Church Christian Worldview Overview of the Bible Reliability of the Bible Nature and Ministry of the Holy Spirit	Mentoring of Learners to Become Teachers Graduation Certificate of Preparation to Teach and Serve Task Force Ministry Options Ongoing Group and Service Identity

The implications of such a model are far-reaching. These classes, in small doses, stretch the thinking of a fast-paced, ever-changing society toward lifetime preparation, purpose, and commitment. The mentoring aspect appeals to those who are lonely, biblically illiterate, and hungry for spiritual growth. This approach also serves as built-in, nonthreatening teacher training. The small group approach and the quick closure of each element of the curriculum allow for enough comfort to attract the 21st-century learner.

Women Volunteerism

The advent of single moms who must work springs from the rise in divorce. But, even beyond that, the majority of women are working regardless of their marital status. Economic pressures, escalating taxes, and better education, along with women's rights have made it either necessary or desirable for women to work. This poses a problem in the area of volunteerism in the church. In bygone days, many women gave the equivalent hours of a full-time job to the church as a volunteer. Add to their job constraints the need for volunteerism in all segments of society, and giving so much time to the church is no longer an option for most women. Sheer logistics, not to mention exhaustion, prevent that method from operating well any longer. The church could creatively integrate the growing retirement population into volunteer positions. Christian colleges must consider adding ministry specialties for the senior years.

Tentmaking

Because of the societal trend away from giving to causes or appeals, new ways of doing missions are being found. Most developed countries reflect postmodern pluralism, thereby making their governments resistant to traditional missionaries. In order to be creative, the present day missionary must not be dependent on local fundraising nor foreign governmental cooperation.

One way to circumvent current fundraising downturns is to find a career that provides employment internationally. Teachers of ESL (English as Second Language), nurses, doctors, engineers, electricians, computer specialists, bilingualists, and carpenters are granted access almost anywhere in the world.

Another positive aspect of these innovations is time effectiveness. No longer must missionaries spend one of four years frantically searching for reluctant supporters. No longer do they have to wait until governments change hands to penetrate a region now hostile to the gospel. One of the best things about Generation Xers is that they do not know or care how things were done traditionally. Because of their motto of "working to live" rather than "living to work," they are very willing to support themselves as they go. This is a perfect combination with societal trends. Each generation has strengths to offer evangelism. The church must encourage education for those who "go into all the world" (Matthew 28:18-20) within the tentmaker model.

Sometimes going into our world means going next door.

Community Outreach

Sometimes going into our world means going next door. The brokenness of our world demands that the church offer grief/loss training to church staffs and support groups for people within the church grieving over divorce, teen pregnancy, death, addiction, abuse, and violence.

The church needs chaplaincy, tutorial, and hospice services for the incarcerated, the at-risk child, the hospitalized, and the terminally ill. Jesus reminded us that it is the sick who need a physician (Luke 5:31). We cannot afford to wait for those who come to us. We must not relegate such training to professionals alone. The task is too great. The church must be out front in offering healing to those who are on the brink of disaster.

Conclusion

A generation that thrives on impulsive, risk-taking decisions has great potential for breaking out of current apathy and inertia. Christian educators must purposefully guide it toward renewed interest in saving the lost, looking past themselves, and seeking the truth of Scripture. The Great Commission is more captivating than any virtual reality and takes more ingenuity to accomplish than any computer game. The Holy Spirit is more powerful than any computer drive. He reaches to the single parent, the working mom, the homeless, the imprisoned, even the bored teen. The church must invoke the Spirit's presence to change the 21st century for the glory of the Father and His Son, Jesus Christ.

p r o j e c t

★ Plan a quarter's worth of Sunday school studies (topics) for all age groups utilizing the five types of Christian education outreach. ★

For Further Reading

M. Anthony, ed.
Foundations of Ministry: An Introduction to Christian Education for a New Generation. Wheaton, IL: A Bridge Point Book, 1992.

E.J. Elliston & S.E. Burris, eds.
Completing the Task: Reaching the World for Christ. Joplin, MO: College Press, 1995.

A. Goldstone, ed.
World Reference Atlas. New York: Dorling Kindersley, 1994.

A.Y. Hsu
Singles at the Cross-Roads. Downers Grove, IL: InterVarsity Press, 1997.

S.P. Kachur, L.B. Potter, S.P. James, & K.E. Powell
Suicide in the United States, 1980–1992. Atlanta: Centers for Disease Control and Prevention, National Center for Injury Prevention and Control, 1995.

The Lindesmith Center
Prison Population, Criminal Justice Quickfacts, 1995. http://www.lindesmith.org/quick/prison2html.

National Center for Injury Prevention and Control
Suicide in the United States, 1998. http://www.cdc.gov/ncipc/dvp/suifacts.htm.

P. Wagner, S. Peters, & Mark Wilson, eds.
Praying Through 100 Gateway Cities of the 10/40 Window. Seattle: YWAM Publishing, 1995.

CHAPTER 5
CURRICULAR
FOUNDATIONS OF CHRISTIAN EDUCATION

Chapter Five Summary
☑ Curriculum defined
☑ Principles of:

context	sequence
scope	design
balance	process

in education

Curriculum—a big word often misspelled and sometimes misunderstood. Curriculum—a frequently used educational term. So what do we mean when we use the word curriculum?

Curriculum in its basic form literally means "race course." Used in education, it refers to all that happens to the learner—not merely formal instruction. Applied to Christian education, it looks beyond formal classroom instruction to the community life of the church and the relational climate of the classroom.

Curriculum in its basic form literally means "race course."

Used more narrowly, the word curriculum sometimes describes a course of study—all of the classes and experiences woven together to achieve certain specified outcomes. It includes, of course, formal instruction, but also other experiences designed for the student.

An even more focused use of the word curriculum refers to teaching materials—the teachers' guides, pupils' books, audiovisual packets, all that teachers are given to develop lessons for students. This may be the most common use of the word, at least in Christian education.

All three definitions are applicable to the church. Though good teaching materials provide a strong foundation for the teaching ministry of the church, materials alone cannot accomplish effective Christian education. (Effective Christian education may be achieved with few or no teaching materials.) Materials must be chosen carefully because they fit together to accomplish the goal of developing Christlikeness in every learner. Materials are merely tools, one aspect of the total curriculum of church life.

Christian educators cannot control every aspect of the curriculum of the church. They can, however, choose materials carefully and purposefully and help teachers to use effectively the materials they have. This chapter, then, focuses on the two definitions that can be more readily planned and directed. But Christian educators must remember that the total life of the community is a kind of hidden curriculum, often affecting outcomes as much as the planned and overt curriculum.

Principles for Curriculum Planning

Imagine Eric and Lauren entering kindergarten for the first time. Stretching ahead of them are at least thirteen years of formal education. Imagine further that the kindergarten teacher is a purposeful person who wants both to be well prepared for college and professional training. The teacher begins by teaching algebra—never mind that they have not yet learned the basics of adding, multiplying, subtracting, and dividing. At the beginning they are given a copy of the works of C.S. Lewis with the expectation that they will read aloud from the book by December. Never mind that they have not yet learned letters and sounds. The teacher, ambitious as she is, decides also to begin formal chemistry instruction. They are taught cursive writing. At the end of the year, they, their parents, and their teachers wonder why they failed to learn all that the teacher thought they should or would.

Next year they somehow advance to first grade. The first grade teacher is concerned that these children have a proper understanding of social studies and science, but has little concern about math. She pays little heed to what Eric and Lauren have already learned (or failed to learn). This year they are introduced to the American governmental system and expected to memorize the entire list of American presidents. They learn about astronomy and physics. Again, they, their parents, and their teachers are frustrated when they seemed to learn only a part of what was presented—and remember almost nothing from what they covered in kindergarten.

Each year brings a similar scenario. Each teacher along the way has his or her own agenda for learning, with little regard for what Eric and Lauren have previously learned. At last, they graduate from high school, so frustrated with their so-called education that they vow never again to enroll in a formal education experience. Teachers cannot understand what happened. Nor do parents.

Ridiculous, you say! Of course, it is. Schools plan curricula carefully. Children are expected to learn certain content and skills in kindergarten, then progress to new skills and content in each succeeding grade. When children fail to learn, the results are carefully scrutinized and strategies are developed to correct the problem. Though schools are not perfect nor do they always achieve the intended results with every student, school leaders, for the most part, take seriously their responsibility to plan, provide resources, and teach. (The remarkable public school debate of the 1980s and 1990s regarding American schools demonstrates this truth.)

If the scenario is ridiculous for the school, why should it be accepted in Christian education? How can a congregation make sense out of curriculum?

Perhaps the most basic principle for curriculum development is context.

Principle of Context

Perhaps the most basic principle for curriculum development, aside from the overall purpose of developing mature disciples, is context. Teaching never occurs in a vacuum; it is always carried out within an environment, which also shapes the outcomes. It is difficult to teach people to love one another if a congregation is embroiled in a dispute over the color of the carpet in the sanctuary, the kind of music chosen for worship, or any one of the many arguments that can arise within a congregation. Christian educators cannot control all these events, of course, but neither can they ignore them. Sometimes curriculum topics are chosen to meet an overt need.

Beyond the larger congregational context, educators must give attention to the specific program context. This requires analysis and planning by the Christian education leadership team. Some specific questions must be considered:

- ✎ What is the purpose of this program? Ostensibly, Sunday school, children's church, youth groups, vacation Bible school, and any other Christian education program should exist to make disciples. Yet, each should have a particular niche to fill: programs should not be clones of each other. Churches may answer the purpose question differently in regard to a particular program. But each must know why a program exists, its particular function in developing disciples, and how it differs from and is complementary to other programs.
- ✎ Given the purpose of this program, who is the audience? Is this program designed for all age groups? If not, who is the audience?
- ✎ Understanding the purpose and defining the audience, what curriculum topics and experiences are most appropriate?
- ✎ What materials would best aid in developing this program?

Principle of Scope

A second principle is scope. What should be taught? The context helps to provide an answer to this question. We may determine, for example, that Sunday school is the place we intend to provide basic Bible information. In that case, we determine what biblical content should be included for each age level.

Christian education leaders must decide how content is the same or varies from one context to another. Do you, for example, want to pursue three different topics each Sunday for preschool children—one for Sunday school, another for children's church, and yet a third for the evening program? Or do you want to choose one theme, perhaps even one section of Scripture, to develop in all three programs? The same decision must be made for each age group in light of the various settings in which it meets each week.

Must content be limited only to biblical materials? The answer depends in part on the context and the age level. For young children, the choice may consist only of biblical topics and stories. But we may want to include a missionary education program or a musical expression program for elementary children, in addition to the biblical teaching times. The curriculum for older learners will almost certainly include leadership development topics and skills as well as service and missionary themes. Church history, Bible survey, hermeneutics, ethics, and apologetics are topical studies valuable at certain age levels.

Must content be limited only to biblical materials? The answer depends in part on the context and the age level.

In the end, the Christian education leadership team must make informed decisions to develop curriculum. Many topics could be included. But what is best included if the goal is to develop mature disciples?

Principle of Balance

An effective Christian education curriculum is balanced. Not all study is done in the New Testament to the exclusion of the Old Testament, or vice versa. Not all studies are topical, giving little or no attention to expository studies, Bible survey, and doctrinal themes. Some types of topics may be better for one program than the other. The leadership team should make decisions that assure keeping a balanced curriculum.

Principle of Sequence

The principle of sequence suggests that some order should guide the development of the curriculum. What is best learned first? Second? At succeeding levels? This is a critical question. And, if the Christian education curriculum is carefully designed to move from the most basic to the more complex, how are newcomers integrated into the teaching system? How do they gain the basics? In an era of computer technology, the solution to this problem may be solved with computerized resources designed to help older learners gain the basics that would have been learned at earlier age levels.

Sequence not only refers to the progression of curriculum topics from one age level to the other, but also to the development within a given level. Should topics be introduced chronologically? Will special days and seasons be acknowledged or ignored in the curriculum?

Principle of Design

Closely akin to the sequence issue is the organizing principle of the curriculum. Four basic approaches have been chosen through the years.

- ✎ *Uniform*. Choosing a uniform curriculum means that the same topic is taught to every age level in the church. This is an appealing principle because it means that every person in a family would explore the same text each Sunday, allowing the family to discuss the lesson during the week. The problem is that not all content is equally appropriate for every age group. Using a uniform curriculum means that either topics too difficult for younger ages are selected or that the more difficult topics (such as Romans) are eliminated. The result is, in the first case, frustrated learners who cannot understand the concepts considered or, in the second case, a lack of depth for older learners.

- ✎ *Group graded*. Sometimes described as cycle-graded, this arrangement chooses curriculum topics and experiences for each age level and then organizes them appropriately. We could, for example, have a one-year curriculum for children who are one to two years of age, follow that with a two-year cycle for children two to four years of age, another two-year cycle for children four and five years old. This could then be followed by a two-year curriculum for children in grades one and two, a three-year curriculum for children in grades three through five, another three-year cycle for middle school children, and a four-year cycle for high school students. Adult curriculum could be developed on a six- or seven-year-cycle. Two or more classes could be using the same curriculum, but the topics would vary from one level to the next.

✎ *Closely graded*. Publishers for many years developed a closely graded curriculum, that is, specific topics were provided for each succeeding year of development. No two classes in the Christian education program would study the same topic at the same time. This is a worthwhile concept for large churches in which one or more classes are conducted for each age level. It is impossible for small churches where two or three grade levels must be grouped together in classes, simply because of the numbers available.

✎ *Electives*. In an elective-based curriculum, each learner chooses what he or she wants to study and enrolls and attends the appropriate class. The notion is that learners are more highly motivated when they choose their own curriculum topics. However, an elective curriculum seems particularly inappropriate for children. It may not develop learners with a breadth of knowledge since they pursue only those topics in which they are interested. Elective studies also undermine the development of fellowship and caring among learners

---

The Christian education leadership team must decide what approach—or combination of approaches—are most appropriate for each context and the intended audience for each.

The Christian education leadership team must decide what approach—or combination of approaches—are most appropriate for each context and the intended audience for each. Specific curriculum resources can then be chosen to support the purpose and design of the program.

Principle of Process

Curriculum development extends far beyond topics and materials. How will the curriculum be taught? How do various age levels learn best? What teaching methods best support the purposes for the curriculum? Curriculum materials should support the desired process. Teachers and leaders must then be recruited and trained to carry out the process.

Managing Curriculum Decisions

Every church must make curriculum decisions. Some churches do so on the basis of careful planning. Others do little planning and supervision. To choose the latter option is to abdicate responsibility as leaders to plan for the best possible Christian education for the church. It is akin to the scenario of Eric and Lauren outlined earlier in the chapter.

Every church must make curriculum decisions.

A conscientious leadership team should give careful attention to the curriculum for Christian education—not just for Sunday school, but for the total Christian education program. It may work to design a curriculum one program at a time—but over time, it should consider how curriculum for all programs fit together. It may involve teachers and professional educators in their planning process. Only after some planning has been done should actual materials be selected.

Should teachers be allowed to choose their own materials? If curriculum is planned and materials are chosen as carefully as we have outlined in this chapter, then specific materials are chosen for specific purposes. Teachers should, of course, be permitted—even encouraged—to develop each session as they deem best given the Scripture and their learners. But the actual curriculum guide provides structure, sequence, and organization for the teaching task of the church.

But may no deviations occur? It may be desirable to deviate from the planned curriculum guide at times. Perhaps a special need has arisen that should be addressed. In that case, the curriculum guide may be altered and new materials provided. Such deviations should not be common. They should be planned to meet a need and accomplish a goal. Teachers may suggest the alteration. But the change should be approved by the leadership team.

Selecting and Using Curriculum Materials

After Christian education leaders have planned an overall curriculum utilizing the principles mentioned in the previous section, they are ready to select or develop curriculum resources to put into the hands of teachers and leaders. Unless we have a clear idea of the intent of the curriculum, the context in which it will be taught, and how we should teach it, no curriculum materials will be satisfactory. Curriculum materials are merely tools and resources to carry out the curriculum plan.

Not all curriculum materials are equal, however. Christian education leaders need to select carefully. The following curriculum analysis guide may serve as a helpful resource for selecting materials.

Guidelines for Selecting Curriculum Materials

Rate the materials, with 4 being excellent, 3 good, 2 fair, and 1 poor.

Criteria	4	3	2	1	Notes
Appropriateness					
Of Bible stories or passages for the age level					
The choice of Bible version(s) for the age level					
Of the memory work for the age level					

The lectures, activities, learning centers, and other elements of the lesson plans to the developmental needs of the age group					
Lesson applications for the age level					
Lesson objectives for the age level					
The wording of the quarterly and lesson titles					
For various ethnic groups in the church					
Visuals for the age level					
Take-home paper for the age level					

Bible Content

Biblically based					
Interpretations and applications of biblical material					
Objectives and content of the lessons based solidly on Scripture					
Evangelistic emphasis					
Helps the learner to know what it means to be a part of the church					
Consistent and satisfactory explanation of alternative interpretations					
Teacher helps to understand the Scriptures					

Teachability

Adequate supplementary helps					
Clear lesson objectives					
Clear and appropriate verbal illustrations					
Clear and appropriate definitions					
Degree of learner involvement in the lesson					
Adequate explanation to tell teachers how to use materials					
Adequate introductions for each unit of lessons within a quarter					

Adequate help in developing a satisfactory room arrangement					
Teachers alerted to special advance preparations					
Teachers alerted to special materials needed					
Apparent outline of main points that are summarized and reinforced					
Activities lead to the accomplishment of the lesson objectives					
Variety of learning activities					
Teacher's book correlated with the student's book					
Adaptable to classes with only a few students					
Adaptable for large classes					
Help given to adjust for exceptionally short or exceptionally long class periods?					
Vocabulary and reading levels of the pupil's materials					
Pupils encouraged to use Bibles					
Provisions for "more advanced" and "less advanced" students					
Visuals help to accomplish the objectives for each lesson					
Effectiveness of visuals					
Take-home paper teaches biblical concepts and principles					
Students led to carry out the concepts and principles presented					
Leads pupils beyond merely parroting right answers					
Appearance					
Attractive outside appearance of the books					
Attractive inside appearance of the books					
Attractiveness of art and photographs					

Materials appear to be up-to-date					
Attractive visuals					
Attractive take-home paper					
Overall Evaluation					

Using Curriculum Materials to Develop Effective Lessons

Curriculum materials are helpful tools for teachers, but materials alone can never achieve the goal of making disciples. Teachers have responsibility to use those materials effectively. But how can a teacher use curriculum materials, with all of the details and ideas included in them, to assist students to develop in their faith? The answer lies in careful preparation for each teaching session, using good principles of lesson organization and presentation.

Materials alone can never achieve the goal of making disciples.

Effective teachers first examine their materials to gain an overview of the quarter or unit. This will help them to understand how the lessons fit together to achieve the goals for the series of lessons. But how should teachers organize their time on a week-to-week basis?

Teachers should begin their weekly preparation by developing a study plan for the lesson. Perhaps the most effective way to do this is to read the text, without consulting reference materials, and write down ideas, words, places, people, and concepts that need to be identified and understood before attempting to present the lesson. The teacher then uses this list as a guide to personal study.

Once the study is done—and this step may take some time to complete—the central idea for the session should be identified. *The central idea is a statement of the basic teaching to be considered during the session.* It should emerge naturally from the Scripture text used for the lesson, but it should also be related to pupils' needs and understanding level. It is best stated as a declarative sentence, though a concise question may sometimes be used. It could be a simple declarative sentence—"God made everything," for a study of Genesis 1 for preschoolers, for example—or a clear linking of the Bible truth with a life need—"We should tell the good news of Jesus as the shepherds did," for a study of Luke 2:1-20 with adults. The central truth is the key idea of the lesson; it is what you want the learners to remember if they forget all the details. It is the thread that holds the lesson together.

Curriculum materials sometimes have a statement of the thrust of the lesson. Even so, teachers should go through the study process to develop their own central truth. The curriculum materials may provide ideas, but materials can never know the specific needs of learners. Only the teacher can make that link.

After the central truth has been developed, teachers must then decide their teaching goals for the session. What do they want the learners to know, feel, or do at the end of the session? Again, the curriculum materials contain a statement of objectives. But teachers must determine if these objectives are appropriate for the central truth they have chosen. The teaching goals should emerge naturally from the Scripture text and the central truth chosen.

A Bible lesson is composed of four basic elements.

A Bible lesson is composed of four basic elements. Consider these building blocks for preparing a lesson. Careful development of these four elements will result in effective lessons.

The first element is the *approach.* Sometimes called the "hook," the "introduction," or any one of a number of other labels, this element is designed to gain the students' attention as they enter the classroom and begin their study. An effective approach is related to the lesson. It may be an effective question. It could be a good illustration. It could be a group activity. Whatever is chosen, it is often to engage learners in the lesson and to stimulate their thinking as the session is developed. It need not take much time—in fact, it shouldn't overshadow the remainder of the lesson—but it must be well designed.

The second element of the lesson is the *Bible study*. Sometimes called the "book" or "Bible exploration," this section is designed to examine the Bible facts. This section may be developed by lecture, discussion, storytelling, or a combination of several approaches. But however it is developed, it should lead students to an understanding of the Scripture text.

The third element is the *application*. Sometimes called the "look," this section is designed to encourage the learners to explore the relationship between the teaching of Scripture and their lives. The application helps the learners to understand the legitimacy of the study of the text. It answers the question, "What does this mean to me?"

The final element is the *response*, sometimes called the "took." This section, usually relatively brief, is designed to bring the lesson to a conclusion, asking the students to consider their response to the Scripture text. This response may encourage the students to do something. It may require a consideration of attitudes.

Teachers can consider the options presented in the materials, make careful choices, and use what is most meaningful for their class.

Most curriculum guides provide ample material to assist teachers' preparation. In fact, most guides have more materials than teachers can use in a single session. But teachers can consider the options presented in the materials, make careful choices, and use what is most meaningful for their class. Should the materials not suggest an appropriate option, teachers can then develop their own ideas for presentation. (Of course, they may prefer to do that even if the materials present good options. However, most busy teachers are more than happy to find some good suggestions to assist them in their planning and preparation.)

The lesson plan below is an example of taking a prepared curriculum, yet developing the lesson to meet the needs of learners. Notice also the form of the written lesson plan. Good teachers write out their plans in a form similar to that presented below and leave their teachers' books at home.

Title: The Visited Planet

Scripture: Luke 2:1-21

Central Truth: Jesus' visit to planet Earth, though not as we might have expected, is a demonstration of God's love for us.

Objectives:

1. Students will identify the unexpected elements of Jesus' birth as recorded in Luke 2.
2. Students will explain the significance of Jesus' birth for them personally.
3. Students will thank God for Jesus' birth and what it means to them.

Hook: (5-7 minutes)	
For you, what is most meaningful at Christmas?	Write the question on the board before class. Refer to it as the session begins.
Book: (25 minutes)	
1. If you had been in charge of planning the details and circumstances of Jesus' birth, what would you have planned?	Discussion
2. Read Luke 2:1-21	Assign readers: Narrator 1: Luke 2:1-7 Narrator 2: Luke 2:8-10a, 13, 14a, 16-21 Angel: Luke 2:10b-11 Angels: Luke 2:14 (have all the class read this) Shepherd: Luke 2:15b

3. Look again at the text. What in this account is unexpected: What would you have expected to find recorded?
    Note the careful historical details.
    Note that very little is said about the birth itself.
	Discussion

4. Why did God choose to announce the birth to shepherds? Why is that surprising?	
5. Look at 2:19. How did Luke know this?	
6. Did Mary and Joseph understand the significance of all that happened?	
Look: (8 minutes)	
1. What do we learn about God from all this?	
2. Read "The Visited Planet" from J.B. Phillips' *New Testament Christianity*.	Read dramatically
Took: (2 minutes)	
1. Galatians 4:4-5	Read
	Pray

After the lesson plan is finished, teachers are now ready to teach. They are well prepared. They know what they intend to do in the class. Yet they can alter the process if that is necessary.

After the class session is finished, good teachers reflect on what happened. What worked well? What could have been done more effectively? What needs were met? What needs were left unmet? This careful reflection helps teachers to make continual improvement as they lead learners to understand and live Scripture.

Though the amount of time consigned to each element of a lesson may vary because of the content or the age level, every element should be present in each class session. These elements are not developed sequentially with preschool learners, though all of the elements are present. But this plan, if followed carefully, helps teachers to develop fresh Bible studies aimed to lead students to think and respond to the teaching of Scripture. Clearly, materials alone cannot accomplish these goals: only well-prepared teachers can enliven that printed in a curriculum guide. The materials in the guide become beneficial resources for teaching.

p r o j e c t s

★ Go to your local Christian bookstore and compare 2 curriculum offerings for the pre-school level. Note what is appealing/not appealing about each. Grade one of them according to Daniel's chart. Grade your church's effectiveness in incorporating the six principles on a scale of 1-10. ★

★ *Alternate:* Choose a passage, parable or Bible story and prepare a lesson according to Daniel's guidelines. Make sure it is age appropriate for your target audience. ★

For Further Reading

Gary Bredfeldt and Larry Richards
Creative Bible Teaching. Chicago: Moody Press, 1998.

Howard P. Colson and Raymond M. Rigdon
Understanding Your Church's Curriculum. Nashville: Broadman, 1981.

Iris Cully
Planning and Selecting Curriculum for Christian Education. Valley Forge, PA: Judson Press, 1983.

LeRoy Ford
Design for Teaching and Training. Nashville: Broadman, 1978.

Marlene LeFever
Learning Styles. Colorado Springs: David C. Cook, 1995.

Robert Pazmiño
Foundational Issues in Christian Education. 2nd ed. Grand Rapids: Baker, 1997.

PART TWO

TEACHING / LEARNING ENCOUNTER

CHAPTER 6
THE TEACHER/LEARNER ENCOUNTER

Chapter Six Summary

- ☑ Methods Jesus used in teaching
- ☑ Suggested teacher planning methods
- ☑ Criteria for grouping by age and commonality
- ☑ Building effective discussions
- ☑ Characteristics of an effective teacher
- ☑ The impact of caring for students on the learning experience

---

Finally the temple guards went back to the chief priests and Pharisees, who asked them, "Why didn't you bring him in?"

"No one spoke the way this man does," the guards declared (John 7:45,46, NIV).

Many teachers in church education programs are frustrated. They prepare great lessons, gathering knowledge and understanding they want to impart to their students. Yet the members of their classes do not seem to respond. Perhaps the problem lies in a lack of understanding of the teacher/learner encounter. Too often students are seen as receptacles into which knowledge can be poured. This concept of education ends with discouragement for both students and teachers.

Too often students are seen as receptacles into which knowledge can be poured.

Learning is an encounter. Whenever tension is created, such as unexpectedly meeting someone you have wronged, trying to pay the bills at the end of the month, or trying to explain to your spouse why you are late again, an encounter has occurred. How that pressure is handled determines the future. In education, encounter occurs when the materials in a lesson cause students to rethink their views or come to grips with a new concept. As teachers and students encounter the Scriptures together a transformation takes place. Transformation is the change that takes place as the teachings of the Bible become a part of the lives of learners. Their way of living and thinking are turned around just as those who heard Jesus in person were changed. Teaching for encounter involves knowledge, communication, and an awareness of the students' needs. When teaching and learning are seen in this light, the potential exists to transform lives.

The ability to transform lives is an encouragement for us to examine and follow Jesus' model.

When looking at teachers, the master example is Jesus. He was the greatest of teachers, *the* master teacher and is our example as we prepare ourselves to be successful educators. The ability to transform lives is an encouragement for us to examine and follow His model. To understand His ability to transform lives, we will look at Jesus as the master teacher, one who has knowledge, is able to communicate that knowledge, and makes connection with the student through the ability to care. The teacher/learner encounter is rejuvenated when it follows Christ's model.

Jesus, the Master Teacher

In Matthew 23:10, Jesus said to His disciples, "Nor are you to be called 'teacher,' for you have one Teacher, the Christ." There is only one master teacher and He is that teacher. Wherever He appeared, crowds gathered to hear what He had to say.

As the people listened, they understood and their lives were changed, transformed as no other had ever been able to do. Without the availability of modern day teaching aids, props, or computers, He was able to grasp the attention of the people and radically change their lives forever. His methods were simple and direct, worthy of note as we prepare ourselves to teach.

Jesus the Teacher
(John 3:2)

"Never was anyone better fitted for his task than Jesus was for teaching. In qualifications, as in other respects, He was the ideal teacher. This was true whether viewed from the divine or human angle. In the fullest sense he was 'a teacher come from God'" (Price, 1946, 1).

"Read through the Gospels, and you quickly conclude that Jesus was a dynamic, remarkably effective teacher. Never boring, always stimulating, never obtuse, always clear. Never pompous or distant, always personal and lovingly concerned. No wonder people who heard him teach often addressed him as 'teacher'" (Zuck, 1995, 10)!

Whether viewed from the divine or human angle, Jesus was the ideal teacher.

As a child before the teachers in Jerusalem, Jesus' knowledge and understanding of the Scriptures held people in awe (Luke 2:46,47). Later as an adult He taught as one who had authority, not as the other teachers. Again the people were in awe (Mark 1:21,22). Of the more than forty titles given to Christ in the New Testament, the most common one (other than Jesus, Lord, and Son of God), used 45 times in the four Gospels, is that of teacher. Although Jesus had not gone through the normal process of rabbinical education, His wisdom and manner of teaching resembled that of a rabbi. Jesus proclaimed the divine law, taught in synagogues, debated with scribes and Pharisees, supported His teachings with Scripture, and settled legal disputes, all with an authority that exemplified His knowledge of the Scriptures (Stein, 1978).

In His short lifetime, Jesus was never doubted in His knowledge of the Scriptures. His knowledge was so great He was asked to read from the Scriptures in the synagogue, a position given only to those who were recognized as an authority in Scripture. When He was opposed by the priests, scribes, and Pharisees, His answers were accepted. The only time He came under attack was when He would speak of God as His Father, and Himself as the Messiah (e.g., John 8:31-59). As a teacher His knowledge of Scripture was impeccable.

Jesus was never doubted in His knowledge of the Scriptures.

Jesus used His knowledge wisely to instruct, correct, and discipline. He taught about His being the Messiah, but never utilized His knowledge to become an earthly ruler of mankind. Knowledge was used to correct or discipline those who questioned Him, but never to taunt them. Though His wisdom was far superior to those who came to learn and to question, it was used to build up, not destroy. Jesus was indeed discerning as He taught.

Jesus the Communicator

Jesus was able to teach using words and ideas the people could understand. He did not try to use academic or theological language understood only by the highly educated, nor did He speak in patois that only the uneducated knew. He spoke to the people in their native languages so that all would know His message. Those who came to hear Him speak marveled at the way He spoke and the understanding they gained. His methodology was to use the materials and methods available to Him to educate those who came to learn. His ability to communicate is indicated by the multitude who came every time He appeared. People wanted to hear more.

"He had no formal classroom. He followed no set curriculum or class schedule. He gave no course credit to his students, and they never formally graduated. He had no modern devices such as slides, films, overhead projectors, flipcharts, flannel-boards, puppets, or chalkboards. He never required any written assignments or gave written examinations" (Zuck, 1995, 13).

Yet, He communicated with those who came to learn, and He transformed their lives. Jesus did make use of the materials and methods that were available. He did not depend on any one method, but He used them all—and used them effectively. Lecture is often seen as the primary method used by Jesus, but a closer look reveals that it was used in conjunction with other methods. While lecturing, He asked questions in order to develop a discussion to draw the people into the conversation. Parables and stories are the most heralded additions to the lecture. Through these simple story truths, the audience was better able to grasp the subject presented. Similar to parables was the use of object lessons. Who can forget the withering of the fig tree as an example of what happens to a follower of Christ who does not produce fruit?

Jesus was also the master of using media, personal example, and life through the socialization process.

Jesus was also the master of using media, personal example, and life through the socialization process. He used media to enhance and strengthen His message. When teaching in the synagogues, He first read from the Scriptures to give credence to the lesson that followed. Media was incorporated into the account of the woman caught in adultery. When He stooped down and began writing in the sand, the impact was so great the crowds left the woman. He taught by personal example, exemplifying the father/son relationship. Who can forget the lesson on compassion when He wept at Lazarus' grave and again over the city of Jerusalem?

Life itself was a vital element in His teachings. Skillfully, He wove His teachings into the lives of people, and the impact of the lessons had a profound effect on their physical and spiritual futures. Socially, the people were taught to care for each other, instead of finding ways to avoid their neighbors. Jesus used every possible means to teach so that His students could understand. One method was not enough.

Jesus Cared for His Students

One of the most important aspects of education is the bell system. Students get excited when they hear a bell because that means that they can get out of class. Sadly, the same holds for some teachers. When the bell sounds, they breathe a big sigh of relief and leave. The interaction between the learner and the teacher ends with the sounding of the bell. However, this did not hold true for Jesus. His interaction with those who came to learn went beyond the lesson time; He knew that being a teacher goes beyond instruction. He became involved with them on a personal level. When students came to ask questions after a lesson, He had time for them. He spent time in their homes, visiting and eating meals. The healings that He performed were not cold dispassionate encounters; He felt their needs, listened, and fulfilled them. Jesus went beyond the classroom.

Because of His personal involvement with the people, they knew of His love for them.

Because of His personal involvement with the people, they knew of His love for them. When we consider those examples, we know that He loves us and is still personally involved. To Jesus, education was more than a lesson; it was an encounter, and the result was transformation.

Using the example of Jesus, we can see the elements that make the teacher/learner encounter a transforming experience. Lives were changed when people met Jesus. Lives can still be changed today if we will follow His example. To better understand the relevance of Jesus' example to us, we will look at three areas of His teaching that will have great impact on ours. They are teaching as knowledge, knowing the subject being taught; teaching as communication, knowing how to get students to hear and understand the lesson; and teaching as caring, becoming personally involved to help learners improve their lives.

Teaching as Knowledge

Several years ago *Group Magazine* carried an article on the subject of youth ministers as professional "Wingers." Wingers are those who show up to teach a class and do not prepare ahead of time, or only just lightly, teaching whatever comes to mind. Sadly, this is not just commentary about youth ministers. Many Sunday school teachers, youth leaders, and Bible study leaders fall into this category too. Jesus spent His lifetime preparing to teach; He knew the Scriptures and He knew how to apply them. As teachers prepare to teach, they too must be adequately prepared. Teachers and students cannot have a transformational encounter with the Word of God if proper advance preparation has not taken place.

A well-prepared instructor will be able to handle students' questions and doubts.

Merely a casual reading or a Saturday night study will not properly prepare a teacher. The lesson must be well researched so that the students will be able to understand what is taught. The backgrounds of Bible passages and their interpretations are important if the learner is to understand the message found in the passage. Bible commentaries combined with the more story-type layman's commentaries will help the instructor understand the passage. Professionally written curricula help to carry through themes and relate the Scriptures to the students. A well-prepared instructor will be able to handle students' questions and doubts. Readiness also allows the teacher to confidently make adjustments in the presentation as the need arises, for sometimes a special need presented by a student becomes more important than the original lesson. A well-equipped and knowledgeable educator can instruct with confidence, ready for class and ready for change.

An easy-to-follow study method is to read the passage or prepared lesson on Monday night, take Tuesday off, read it over again on Wednesday night and make notes about further investigation, on Thursday night read it again and make a list of the materials needed to present the lesson, on Friday collect the materials and read the lesson again, on Saturday reread the material and go to bed early, and then on Sunday night review the lesson taught and evaluate its effectiveness. This will not automatically create a master teacher; but the teacher will understand the lesson and its applications, and the students will notice a difference. When educators prepare properly, they too will have an encounter with Scripture and thus be more effective in bringing their students to an encounter.

When educators prepare properly, they too will have an encounter with Scripture.

Some learn merely to accumulate knowledge. But this should not be the focus of the teacher. Jesus always applied His lessons to the learners' lives. He taught for transformation. When the teacher is able to present a lesson to a class and inspire the learners to change, learning has occurred. At that moment when the encounter with the Bible becomes relevant, transformation can take place. Knowledge for the sake of knowledge is commendable. However, many who know the Bible do not know the author and cannot connect it with their own lives.

A teacher must be well informed about the Scriptures—not necessarily a Bible scholar—but well informed nevertheless. During the preparation process, the instructor must spend time investigating how to make connection with the students' lives. One without the other will make a weak lesson. One adult class teacher was failing miserably to make connection with his students. Finally in exasperation he remarked, "I don't know what is wrong. I read this lesson over six times, but it is not coming out right." His problem was that he was prepared for knowledge, but he did not prepare how to relate the lesson to his students. Preparation requires research and application and these become even more effective when combined with the leader's own personal life which serves as an example to the class.

Teaching as Communication

"The lecture is dead!" has become the rallying cry of many educators. Too often the lecture has been seen as the only method for communicating a lesson and it has been misused. However, there is much more to be considered in communicating a lesson and encountering Scripture than the method of oratory. To focus only on the method of delivery is to leave the student out of the learning encounter. Communication begins with understanding the students being taught. The teacher must know the age of the students and how their groupings affect learning, the lifestyles of the class members, and the personal needs of the students. These affect the methods of instruction used.

To focus only on the method of delivery is to leave the student out of the learning encounter.

LeRoy Ford, in his book *Design for Teaching and Training*, has a classic cartoon showing a man who has been assigned to teach the nursery. As the class begins, the lesson is introduced as he holds up a sign and says, "And now a word about transubstantiation" (11). We laugh as we see cartoons like that. However, there is a large grain of truth in the cartoon. Often teachers do not make connection with their students because they do not realize the learning abilities of the age group with whom they are working. Each age has its own characteristics. It would have been fabulous to have heard what Jesus had to say to the children in Mark 10:13-16 as He gathered them into His arms. His awareness of their needs is shown in that moment. The disciples wanted to run the children off, but Jesus had something to tell the children and called them to Himself. He used the situation as a learning experience for the disciples.

Just as Jesus knew the proper way to reach children, so should the teacher. Christian educators have tried to make this job simple. Books have been written that describe the different ages and their ability to learn. In the professionally prepared curricula there are sections which describe the group to be taught. These, with the inclusion of periodic training seminars, will help a teacher understand the learning abilities of class members.

The way students are grouped together will also make a difference. When educational programs are small and facilities are limited, students are placed in multiple age groupings. However, there are some groupings that make interaction difficult. Effective communication requires age groupings that are compatible, for example: 4s and 5s, 1st through 3rd grade, and 4th through 6th grade. Sometimes the ability to relate can take place in poor situations, such as junior/senior high or all of the adults in one class, but it is enhanced when the groups are separated. Teachers must be aware of the group they are teaching and develop methods appropriate for the ages represented.

Effective communication requires age groupings that are compatible.

The lifestyle of the class is another important area to address. When Jesus was in the rural areas, He used lessons and objects that were appropriate. When He was in the city, He changed the approach. One specific example is the woman at the well. If He had tried to teach her as He would a Jew, she would have turned Him away. However, He taught her as a Samaritan and transformation took place. In our mobile society, people are constantly moving to new locations. With them they bring customs and languages from different parts of our society.

This is generally not a problem until they begin to teach. They often try to teach and communicate in the manner of the culture in which they grew up. If they do not make the attempt to understand and change, then their efforts will go for naught.

One age group is a constant challenge—teenagers. Their culture is constantly changing, and the effective teacher will make the attempt to understand their lifestyles. If they are a '50s type teacher trying to teach '90s kinds of students, change has to occur or all will be lost. In order to comprehend lifestyles, it is necessary for teachers to become involved with students away from class. When working with teens, teachers can find help by reading their magazines and listening to their music. By doing this, the leader can understand and guide them, instead of standing back and appearing to attack them. Standing at a distance will provide only surface knowledge, not life change. If a teacher is honestly trying to get to know the class, its members will be genuinely impressed and develop a better awareness, resulting in a true collegiality. The instructor gains through understanding the class members and is able to better prepare lessons. The efforts result in aiding the development of a teacher/ learner encounter with Scripture.

Getting to know the class requires more than just learning their lifestyle.

Getting to know the class requires more than just learning their lifestyle. Students have personal needs with which they are having to wrestle. If the class does not bring them to an encounter, they become apathetic and leave. The evidence of this is found in comments like, "I don't feel like I am being fed" or "There is nothing that I can relate to." As the teacher and learners encounter the Bible, the Scriptures need to apply to their lives in order for transformation to take place. As the teacher interacts with students on a personal level, the needs become apparent and helps can be incorporated into the lesson. Personal interaction also allows the leader to note changes in pupil behavior during the class time. Facial expressions or twists to a question provide clues to needs and the direction of the study can be changed. Jesus had an advantage; He knew the needs of His followers. We do not have those capabilities, but we can learn to understand our students better.

Facial expressions or twists to a question provide clues to needs.

Jesus was able to communicate not only by knowing the people. His teachings were made known because He intelligently used speaking skills. As mentioned earlier, He did not have all of the communication advancements of today. Things we take for granted—audiovisual materials, chalkboards, and flannelgraph—were unknown in His time. However, He was able to teach as no other. People came for miles to hear Him speak. It is often assumed that the crowds were drawn because of His healings. However, if we note the teaching by the Sea of Galilee, the crowds were so large He was forced to teach from a boat. No miracles were recorded. Also, with the feeding of the 4,000 and 5,000, in their excitement to hear Him, the throngs forgot to bring food, and no mention of miracles is made until the food was multiplied. People came just to hear Jesus, and their spiritual and physical lives were transformed.

Teachers of today need to take note of the skills Jesus used in presenting His lessons. He did not depend on one method. The methods He chose were used with great ability. The most popular method used in teaching today is the lecture. Lessons for adults down through the nursery department are based on telling. There is nothing wrong with this approach in itself, but the problem arises when it becomes the only method. One style of teaching, especially if used improperly, cannot effectively communicate the Bible and its lessons.

Recent research has shown what Jesus already knew: different people learn in different ways. Teaching approaches such as the 4Mat system, Brain Compatible Learning, and Multiple Intelligences have been developed to understand and enhance the different ways of learning. They have shown that some people learn through various approaches: verbal (lectures, discussions, problem solving, etc.), visual stimulation (art, drama, charts, etc.), music, physical (drama, touch, dance, activity, etc.), interpersonal (research groups, small groups, discussions, field trips, etc.), and intrapersonal (independent research, memorization, reading, etc.). To assume that everyone learns from one style of teaching is a fallacy. Jesus knew this and masterfully used them all as the teacher and learner came together in an encounter with Scripture and God.

The lecture is often the most maligned method of teaching, mainly because it can be dull and one sided. However, it is not dead, for it is a valuable teaching tool when used properly. The main problem is the lack of proper preparation. Putting a lesson together requires research. A teacher can speak with authority when the background and interpretation of the material are understood. The materials must then be put together so the students understand the teaching and it is apparent that the teacher knows the material. Finally, the instructor must be aware of ways to draw the learners into the lesson. Illustrations, questions and other methods of student involvement can be used to help the members of the class comprehend the message being taught.

**The lecture is not dead, for it is
a valuable teaching tool when used properly.**

Though the lecture is the primary verbal method used in teaching, it is easily combined with other techniques that will enhance the lesson. The easiest is discussion, yet it can be the most difficult. Unless questions are well prepared in advance and properly presented, the class may sit in silence. To build discussion, questions should require more than yes and no answers, be clear and concise, allow class members freedom to seek their own answers, and allow the whole class to become involved in seeking the answers. In discussion the questions should lead to other questions as students seek solutions. Drawing the students into the lesson and involving them in the solution creates encounter and growth begins.

Other elements that work well with lecture and discussion are small groups, panels, problem solving, and role play. The lecture can stand alone, but the incorporation of other methods enhances the message conveyed. Often those who depend on lecture are uncomfortable with any other format. However, they must think beyond themselves to the students' needs and try new ways of presenting the lesson. It is easy to say, "I tried that once and it did not work." A good rule of thumb is to try a new approach at least three times before rejecting it, measuring its value by the students' response. Many teachers have found a refreshing excitement when new techniques are tried.

A good rule of thumb is to try a new approach at least three times before rejecting it.

Everyone knows an excellent storyteller. Good storytellers seem to know how to capture and hold attention while carrying out a story line. Jesus was a master storyteller. His parables are as fresh today as they were when He first spoke them. Just about every teacher wishes he or she could tell a story or develop a parable like Jesus did. The teacher may never gain that ability—His was God given—but he or she must remember that good storytellers have developed the skill over time. Educators can do the same by beginning now and gaining expertise through practice. The beauty of a story is that it captures our attention and we become involved in our own imagination as we await the ending. This mental imagery is an encounter that helps to make the Scripture lesson take on new meaning and come alive.

A fig tree, lilies, and a coin are all objects that Jesus used to teach His followers. The use of an object to teach a lesson creates a lasting impression. Long after the class session is over, students will call the message to memory every time they see the object. Children's sermons and lessons generally contain object lessons to simplify biblical truths and to relate them to the child's life. Adults and teens can and should use object lessons for the same reason. The use of an apple to explain the Trinity is a lesson that comes back many times while preparing the fruit to eat. When students can encounter the Bible by simplifying and understanding a passage of Scripture, transformation can begin to take place.

The use of media was one teaching facet of education that was not available to Jesus in great variety. But, what He had, He used, such as the printed word as He read Scripture in the synagogue, the dirt or sand as He wrote in it, and art as He used a picture of Caesar on a coin. Today a vast array of materials is available. To many, the only medium used is a chalk- or whiteboard, a flannelgraph, or bulletin boards (which too often only get changed once a year). Media is the plural form of medium; a medium is any source that is used to transmit a message, the most common being the human voice. Ours is a media-oriented society. Everywhere a person looks some type of message is being transmitted: billboards promoting a product, program, or philosophy; T-shirts and other clothing that act like billboards; television and radio with their multiple messages in advertising, programming, and news; and movies that entertain and teach. Properly used audiovisuals in the classroom expand and clarify a passage of Scripture. Pictures and writing on a whiteboard or an overhead hold students' attention much longer than speech alone. Several research projects done in this area show that people remember 5-10% of what they hear and 25-30% of what they see. The use of media helps learners retain more of what is presented in class. If teachers can help their students remember more of what they encounter, then the use of media is a valuable asset.

It is likely Jesus used music because it was prominent in the worship of the time.

Many older students at some time in their childhood or teens were told by some enterprising adult to tone down the volume on their singing or that their voice was not very good, leaving them fearful to sing in public. However, with a little encouragement and the use of songs that relate to them, they will begin to sing and love it. It is likely Jesus used music because it was prominent in the worship of the time. He used the book of Psalms, the Hebrew songbook, in His teachings; He may not have used the music that went with them, but the people knew and remembered the lessons because they sang them. Using music is a help to remembering Scripture.

Music has another advantage. It is a window to the heart and soul of the believers. As learners listen to a song, they not only hear the music, but it stirs something within them and becomes a part of them. Music is able to express and change moods more easily than mere words because of its connection to our inner beings. The use of music in the teaching/learning encounter can stir the hearts of learners like no other media.

The percentages of the amount of a lesson remembered were given earlier, but the element of personal involvement was left out. When students become personally involved in their lessons, the retention rate rises to 85-90%. If a student can encounter the Bible truths through self discovery and/or put it to work, then the transformation from the old to the new can be readily seen by both teacher and learner.

When students become personally involved in their lessons, the retention rate rises to 85-90%.

Personal involvement can be as simple as activity teaching in which students are actively involved in their own learning process. The class can start with a short lecture or Bible study, then the learners engage in a project, research assignment, discussion, etc. in which they learn further about the subject or enhance what they have just learned. Student involvement is not just for children. Adults may be hard to motivate at first, but they will find it very enjoyable. With encouragement from the teacher, adults can become involved in activities that will bring great rewards to the class members.

Mission/field trips are an excellent opportunity for students to encounter biblical teachings and to bring about transformation in their lives. Jesus' ministry was one long mission/field trip, and His disciples traveled with Him. As He ministered, they were there observing and participating in the transformation of the multitudes. As they watched and participated, their own lives were changed, and the impact has affected the world as no other nation or philosophy. When Christians today experience Christian work in the inner city or in home and foreign missions, a tension is created between their lifestyle and that of the people with whom the missionaries are working. As they resolve this conflict, the meaning of God's grace has an even greater effect on their lives. Christianity becomes more than fun and games. It becomes a lifestyle, and transformation takes place.

Long reserved for youth, these excursions are extremely valuable for adults as well. Lessons on evangelism and grace come alive when students work alongside missionaries. The impact is momentous when students see those who have nothing become everything in the eyes of God when they encounter Christ. The transformational experience happens right before their eyes, and their own lives are transformed at the same time. Preparation time will draw the students together, and the experience on the mission field draws them to Christ as no other force can. Some will complain that the money could be more effectively used in other ways, but the impact of an encounter with Christ and missionaries can never be measured in dollars and cents.

Long reserved for youth, mission/field trips are extremely valuable for adults as well.

The ability to communicate is vital to the teacher/learner encounter. If teachers do not understand their students or are unable to make known the lesson, then encounter and change will be extremely difficult. Time must be taken to comprehend the learning styles of the class being taught. Each age and group of ages offer challenges to the leader. When the teacher is able to communicate the gospel to students, then encounter can take place and transformation begins to occur.

Teaching as Caring

The trademark for Jesus is caring. He is one who truly understands and loves those with whom He comes in contact. The woman at the well had never met a man like Him nor had the woman caught in adultery. The tears He shed over the death of Lazarus are evidences of the concern He had for everyone to whom He ministered. Sometimes His caring is not pointed out, but the implication is there, such as the time He called the little children to Him. First, His very presence must have been caring because the children came to Him without any fear. Second, He gave them what they wanted most, personal attention. He had time to listen and talk to them one on one. He showed compassion for the multitudes by providing food for 4,000 and 5,000. But His greatest caring showed when He focused on individuals.

Jesus interacted with those He taught and healed, never at a distance and never healing without being asked (Matt 8:5-12; Mark 5:22-43). When He healed the servant and the child who were not with Him, the master and the father had come to Him asking for His help. Jesus' hallmark for caring was to be there, listening and helping those who needed His aid to overcome their problems.

In spite of what the Hallmark Corporation says, caring is more than sending a card. We have become a people of convenience. We want the simplest and fastest way to accomplish a task. If there is a need somewhere, we send money or a card of encouragement. When a need is presented in church, the common response is that we will pray for the person. Fathers are often seen as uncaring because they believe that cash and gifts are all that is needed to express caring. Each of these incidences shows a concern for someone, but they do not necessarily show caring.

Caring is reaching out to people in need, helping them meet that need, and then rejoicing when the problem has been overcome. Caring involves the personal touch. In teaching, it is the teacher spending time with class members, getting to know them, and going to them when they have a difficulty or concern. If educators do not spend time with class members, they will rarely know of problems that arise until it is too late to help. When needs arise, sending cards and offering to pray show concern, but when the teacher comes to the student and becomes personally involved in helping solve the dilemma, then caring has been shown and felt.

Caring is reaching out to someone in need, helping them meet that need, and then rejoicing when the problem has been overcome.

Jesus never sent one of His disciples to do His work for Him. If someone came to Him with a need, He listened and carried out the helping Himself. When a person came to Him with a concern, He did not just say, "I'll pray for you." He personally got involved. It was by the touch of His hand that we know He cared. Jesus is our example. To show caring, we have to become personally involved. If we reflect back on our own lives, we will note that those who we felt really cared for us became personally involved.

Caring is more than becoming personally involved and solving problems. Children become frustrated when they try to do something and a bigger person comes along and completes the task for them. They learn more quickly when they do it themselves with someone guiding them. When we work alongside and give help as is needed, students know that we care for them. Jesus performed miracles, but He also required people to take a part in those miracles. This is evidenced by the lepers who had to go to the high priest (Luke 17:11-19), the disciples who had to pass out the baskets of food (Matt 14:15-21), and the disciples who were required to cast their nets on the *other side* of the boat (John 21:5,6). Caring does not involve solving another's problems, but helping them find ways to overcome those concerns.

Caring goes one step further. It is allowing the one helped to reciprocate. Reciprocation often is as simple as a thank you, as the one with leprosy did. It sometimes is more elaborate, as

Mary using special perfumes on Jesus' feet (John 12:1-3). The one who has been helped must be given the opportunity to give back to the person who helped. A caring action is not to be done expecting anything in return, but when the thank you is given, it should be graciously accepted. Sometimes when the return of favor is too great, suggestions may be made, as Jesus did when the multitude wanted to make Him king. When a difficulty has been overcome, it is a time for both to share in rejoicing. It is hard to decide which is greater, experiencing the satisfaction of being the one showing care or the joy of the one receiving the help knowing that someone cares. The whole process results in celebration.

It is hard to decide which is the greater satisfaction— showing care or knowing that someone cares.

The first step in caring is getting to know the students. Sometimes that begins as simply as learning their names. It is sad when the teacher does not even know students' names. The next step is to find out where they live, locate the addresses on a map, and then go visit. Class members will be surprised and pleased when the teacher walks up to the door. You do not have to stay long, but the impression of caring has already begun. From there on, it is visits outside of class, further stops at their homes, taking them out for coffee or cokes, spending time with them, the personal touch.

During the visits, they will begin to trust the teacher's friendship and share their personal lives and needs. This is an opportunity to draw that person into an encounter with the Bible message of God's love. As their concerns become known, the situation can be applied to what God has taught and they can be helped to find ways to overcome the problem. Talking with them, encouraging them, and pointing them in the right direction result in celebration as they realize the work that God has done. Perhaps the greatest reciprocity is the joy in seeing them grow in God and Christ.

A warning is needed. Do not pry into the students' lives. Be open and let them share when they are ready. Be available. And never share that information with anyone else without permission. To pry and to gossip will destroy everything God is trying to do.

Notice that the involvement of the teacher in the caring process takes place outside of the classroom. Leaders cannot get to know students during the 45 to 60 minutes spent in class. Outside involvement is necessary to help class members overcome problems. Caring involves going into the other person's world and making yourself available. When the students feel that teachers really care, they are able to encounter the Bible in such a way that their lives are transformed. When you care enough to send the very best, you send yourself.

Reprise: The Teacher/Learner Encounter

When people encountered Jesus, their lives were changed. He produced a tension in their lives that caused them to measure themselves by the message He brought. As they considered that message, their way of thinking and lifestyle changed. That change was transformation. Jesus did not teach just to expand the knowledge of His followers; He taught so that their thoughts and lives would encounter the teachings of God. The results changed their world.

As teachers of God's word, we, too, need to teach for encounter. When our students enter the classroom, it should be with a sense of tension, a desire to understand more so that they might mature spiritually. Tension does not mean anxiety, but it is a sense of anticipation, a desire to grow and mature in Christ. The members of the class spend time both in and out of class dealing with the lesson presented, bringing their lives into harmony with Scripture, and casting aside that which does not measure up.

Encounter with the Word of God results in transformation. Lives once lived outside of Christ are changed and become centered in Him. Jesus' teaching changed His followers' lives. Our goal as educators is to allow our students to encounter Him, so He can transform their lives. Transformation is our ultimate goal.

---

p r o j e c t s

★ Do a study of the Gospels and identify the various methods and techniques demonstrated by Jesus. ★

★ Interview two or three good teachers. How do they define good teaching in a Christian education setting? ★

For Further Reading
References

L. Ford
Design for Teaching and Training. Nashville: Broadman, 1978.

J.M. Price
Jesus the Teacher. Nashville: The Sunday School Board of the Southern Baptist Convention, 1946.

R.H. Stein
The Method and Message of Jesus' Teachings. 2nd ed. Philadelphia: Westminster Press, 1994.

R.B. Zuck
Teaching as Jesus Taught. Grand Rapids: Baker, 1995.

Bible Backgrounds

W.A. Elwell and R.W. Yarbrough
Encountering the New Testament. Grand Rapids: Baker, 1998.

N.L. Geisler
A Popular Survey of the Old Testament. Grand Rapids: Baker, 1977.

R.H. Gundry
A Survey of the New Testament. Grand Rapids: Zondervan, 1994.

P.R. House
Old Testament Survey. Nashville: Broadman, 1992.

L.O. Richards
Expository Dictionary of Bible Words. Grand Rapids: Zondervan, 1985.

Communication

R. Heinich, M. Molenda, D. Russell, and S.E. Smaldino
Instructional Media and Technologies for Learning. Englewood Cliffs, NJ: Merrill, 1996.

M.S. Knowles
The Modern Practice of Adult Education: Revised and Updated. Englewood Cliffs, NJ: Cambridge, n.d.

M.D. LeFever
Creative Teaching Methods. Colorado Springs: David C. Cook, 1996.

B. McNabb and S. Mabry
Teaching the Bible Creatively: How to Awaken Your Kids to Scripture. Grand Rapids: Youth Specialties, 1990.

R.A. Sarno
Using Media in Religious Education. Birmingham, AL: Religious Education Press, 1987.

R.B. Zuck and R.E. Clark
Childhood Education in the Church. Chicago: Moody Press, 1986.

Caring

N. Noddings
The Challenge to Care in Schools: An Alternative Approach to Education. New York: Teachers College Press, 1992.

D. Spaide
Teaching Your Kids to Care. New York: Citadel Press, 1995.

CHAPTER 7
THE CHURCH'S MINISTRY TO
YOUNG CHILDREN

Chapter Seven Summary
- ☑ Key characteristics of young learners
- ☑ Addressing the needs of preschoolers
- ☑ Stages of cognitive and physical development
- ☑ The nurturing role of the nursery worker
- ☑ Methods for teaching preschoolers
- ☑ Preschool programs

A blond-headed, blue-eyed little boy comes racing down the hallway to his Sunday school class. "Good morning, Jonathan," greets Miss Kay. He takes no time to answer, but quickly races to the pile of blocks in the middle of the room. "Ha, Ha," he says, "I'm Goliath, and I've come to fight you." He pulls out an imaginary sword, ready for action.

The lives of preschoolers never want for a dull moment. They are full of energy and ready for a challenge. In just five years, they have gone from learning how to grasp a toy to writing their name. They have come from making only grunts to reciting memory verses and many other Bible songs. They now interact and play with other children and are learning they are children of God who are loved very much by parents, teachers, and most of all, by God.

How many ways have these children grown? What should teachers know in order to best respond to their growing needs? What methods should be incorporated into teaching? What programs should these children be part of?

The Growth of a Preschool Child
Physical Development

The rate of physical changes in the lives of preschoolers is greater than at any other time in life. The first two years will witness their most rapid growth. This development will then begin to slow rather quickly, settling into a more gradual pace by the time they reach six years of age.

As to physical size, the average child weighs approximately seven-and-a-half pounds and is twenty inches long at birth. At a year old, weight will have tripled, averaging 19-25 pounds, and height will have increased by a third, having grown to 28-30 inches. Between the ages of two and six, a fairly consistent rate of growth will continue with a gain of approximately nine pounds and five inches each year.

The rate of physical changes in the lives of preschoolers is greater than at any other time in life.

The skeletal frame begins as soft cartilage. In time, with the deposit of various materials, the bones harden. This process begins in the womb and extends into the teen years. As a result, young children's bones are soft and pliable, causing them to be more sensitive to sudden movements such as shaking and jerking. Therefore, careful handling of children is important, especially in the early childhood years. Without this sensitivity, soft bones can easily be dislocated from their sockets or deformities of other sorts may occur.

Another rapidly developing part of the body is the brain. The central nervous system began its development as early as the third week after conception. By the time an infant is six months old, all of the nervous system and the brain cells have been produced. From this point, the fully developed brain cells have only to enlarge to their full capacity. By the time children are two-and-a-half, the brain will have reached 75% of its adult weight. By the time they are five, it will have grown to 90%.

While the brain is increasing in its capacity, another process known as myelinization is taking place. A white corpulent substance known as myelin acts to coat the neural fibers in the brain, which enables the brain impulses to travel along appropriate fibers, reducing the random spread of brain signals. The specialization of the brain helps to improve the hemispheric activity which occurs there. The right hemisphere becomes more controlled in the areas of visual-spatial activities, emotions, musical abilities, and creativity. The left brain gains a better grasp of language skills and motor development.

One last element of growth is muscle development. Although infants are born with all of their muscle tissue in place, the muscles are rather small and limited in regard to overall size. However, these fibers will grow in length, width, and density to forty times their original size by the time infants become adults. In fact, much of children's weight gain will be in muscle tissue.

There are two basic types of motor skills that are enhanced in this time of growth. Both the gross and fine motor skills interact with each other and develop simultaneously. First, the large muscles or the gross motor skills begin to develop. These progress from head to toe and encompass the movement of the head, arms, body, legs, and feet. Large muscle skills include sitting, standing, walking, running, skipping, and jumping activities that require extensive space for preschool children.

At birth, muscle development is confined to the basics of breathing and digesting food. Over the next few months muscle development extends to lifting the head, rolling over, tracking objects and grasping for them. Infants continue muscle development by learning to sit upright, crawl, stand, and walk. Between eight and eighteen months of age, children should be walking.

During the toddler years, children spend more time developing gross motor skills. They learn to walk sideways, backward, upstairs, and down. They are also able to mark time. Proficiency in running, jumping, hopping on one foot, throwing, catching, and bouncing should be evident by the time children are five or six.

Later, as some gross motor skills have emerged, fine motor development begins its progression, moving from the center of the body to the outer limbs. In the beginning stages, infants work only at developing their sense of perception and at grasping objects. Hand preference may begin as early as infancy but fully develops by age three or four. Cutting with scissors comes approximately at age four. Working three- to five- piece puzzles is achievable by most three-year-olds and five- to seven- pieces for fours and fives. Other skills soon emerge including drawing, lacing shoes, zipping up jackets, and brushing teeth. This process of fine motor development will not be complete until into the elementary years.

Preschool children's physical abilities should affect the way teachers design and carry out lesson plans.

How do preschool children's physical abilities affect the way teachers design and carry out lesson plans?

- ✎ Preschoolers need space to move around.
- ✎ They need furnishings that correspond to their size. For instance, tables and chairs should allow for them to sit comfortably with their feet touching the floor and their arms resting comfortably at a table.
- ✎ Bulletin boards and pictures on the walls should be at their height.
- ✎ A variety of activities that provide movement and visuals during stationary times help maintain attention and accommodate muscle development, as well.
- ✎ Keep activities simple.
- ✎ Art activities should be age-appropriate, taking into consideration children's abilities to control scissors and crayons, glue, and other miscellaneous art supplies.

Cognitive Development

Closely tied to the physical development of children is the growth they experience mentally. Jean Piaget is the most noted authority in early research on intellectual development. He outlines two stages of cognitive development in the preschool years: sensorimotor (0-2 years) and preoperational (2-7 years). Both developmental cycles depend largely upon exploration by use of the child's five senses and various spontaneous interactions with the world around them.

Throughout infancy and into the beginner years, there appears to be a cycle that motivates the learning process. The more children develop in their capacity to move and grasp objects, the more they are found exploring their environment. Everything they see, hear, touch, taste, and smell becomes an adventure in exploration.

In the sensorimotor stage (0-2 years), children pass through six stages of learning development. They begin with simple reflexes and involuntary movements. Nothing else is really "known." Secondly, initial exploring techniques such as hand-mouth coordination and tracking sounds and objects from side-to-side (one to four months) begin to develop. Intentional action is the most pronounced development of the third stage (four to eight months). Infants are now able to differentiate between themselves and other objects. They are able to formulate a goal in their mind and then act upon that intention, repeating activities that are pleasurable. In the fourth stage, intentionality has progressed to the ability to predetermine the means by which they gain an object. Eight- to twelve-month-old children also begin to understand the cause and effect relationship. For instance, in the past when they could hear air in their bottle, that meant it was about empty. Now when they hear the air, they throw the bottle away, assuming that it is empty. In the fifth stage, children extend the means-end relationship to problem solving. They like to see how things "work." In this stage and into the final stage from eighteen to twenty-four months, children begin moving toward preoperational methods of cognitive development.

In the fifth stage, children extend the means–end relationship to problem solving.

Piaget divides the preoperational stage into two different stages. The first is the preconceptual stage, involving two- through four-year-olds. The second is the intuitive stage composed generally of five- through seven-year-olds.

Characteristic of the first stage is symbolic interaction with the world around them. Such a designation comes from watching children at play. For instance, they pretend objects to be what they really are not. A teddy bear will be to them a baby. Reality is still very much subjective. Their egocentric nature limits reality to be only what they perceive it to be rather than what others view it to be. For instance, if children see a living object move, they may perceive that all moving things are living (e.g., moon, clouds).

Generally two-year-olds will be able to speak fifty words and understand 300.

Language development is another of the characteristics of this stage. Words become symbols for what used to be only grunts and points of the finger. By the time children are five, they have developed a vocabulary of over 2500 words. Generally two-year-olds will be able to speak fifty words and understand 300. By the time they are three, their vocabulary ranges from 500 to 1,000 words and they speak in four- to six-word sentences. Keep in mind that language develops at different speeds and varies with each individual child. Reading to children, carrying on a conversation with them, and taking time to answer their questions will help vocabulary to develop.

The intuitive stage, lasting from five to seven, matures the symbolic thought patterns of beginner children so they can distinguish between mental and physical reality. Although children still depend a great deal on their own perceptions of reality, they have developed some awareness of other points of view.

Identifying objects and categorizing them is a vital aspect of learning for preschool children. This process brings to order the world they have just begun to explore. Unlike adults who identify objects by their properties, children, rather, identify things according to examples they have experienced before.

There are also certain basic concepts that children are best able to learn. Those may include dog, cat, trees, or flowers. It is not until children are about four that broader categories can be used to group these basic ones such as pets, plants, fish, and reptiles. Five-year-olds, then, are able to carry this one step further and use more specific concepts such as beagle, robin, or trout.

For the Christian educator two principles from this section can be gleaned.

❶ When teaching concepts to children (e.g., sharing, kindness, love, forgiveness), it is always best to use examples to illustrate them. A Bible story such as Jesus healing the ten lepers is a good example for teaching thankfulness.

❷ Concrete examples are best to use as well as basic concepts. A teacher's vocabulary must be equivalent with the level of understanding for those being taught. A preschooler must be able to see and to touch the concepts a teacher brings, if not by the words themselves, by the examples the concepts portray.

Concrete examples are best to use as well as basic concepts.

Conservation is another concept often foreign to preschoolers. Piaget's hypothesis is that conservation cannot be understood by a child until he is about seven or eight. Involved in supporting his hypothesis is a battery of tests he performed on children to see if they can distinguish between reality and appearance as different elements change shape. His most famous two are the liquid test and the pennies test. In one instance children are shown two containers of liquids, same size and same amount. One liquid is poured into another container that is taller and thinner. The children are then asked if the amounts are still the same. The second test lines up two rows of five pennies each with both rows being the same length. Then one row of pennies is spread out to make a longer row. Children are asked again if the amounts are the same. Based on Piaget's results, he demonstrated that children would choose the liquid in the taller thinner container and the pennies in the longer row as being more on the basis of appearance alone.

Application to Christian education is a little abstract. Conservation is tied to actions and behaviors rather than elements, but the same principles apply. Often Christian educators teach that they must "be a Christian" or "act in Christian conduct" in and out of the church building or with church people, even though actions change according to context. Again, by involving examples, especially present-day examples into the realm of teaching, conservation of actions can be taught. Also the use of magic and symbolic object lessons are discouraged at this level for this reason as well.

Cause and effect reasoning is an important element in cognitive development. As stated previously with infants, some basic concepts of cause and effect are understood. Even children as young as a year old know that there are certain things they should not do. When they do them, their hands may get slapped. When that does not occur, they look around to see if anyone is watching. As a side note, when discipline is needed, it should be done quickly so that children may understand the relationship between their actions and the reaction. The best indicator that cause and effect has been established in older children is when they begin to ask why. Rather than always answering the question, it would be best to let them explore to find the answer themselves.

Children as young as a year old know that there are certain things they should not do.

Involved in a similar way as cause and effect are reasons based on reversal and seriation. Seriation simply involves putting pictures in order or identifying the missing element. Reversal is simply going through the series in reverse. For instance, if a teacher tells a Bible story using a series of four pictures, the question is, can preschoolers put that series of pictures in order or identify which picture is missing? Most three- and four-year-olds can do so. Reversal is a little more difficult but still manageable by the same age group. However, when seriation and reversal is used in regard to relationships, young children find this to be more difficult. For instance, if you ask a preschool girl, "Do you have a sister?" she will say, "Yes, her name is Karysa." If you ask her if Karysa has a sister, chances are she will say no.

Time, distance, and numbers are another questionable area for preschoolers. Children understand certain times of the day, for instance morning, lunch time, snack time, and bedtime. However, they cannot measure time. The same applies to distance. In regard to numbers, the average preschooler can identify and count numbers one through twelve. As far as understanding number concepts beyond that, few have the ability.

Time, distance, and sequencing of numbers in Bible stories will be meaningless if not confusing to preschoolers. Therefore, it is not necessary to stress them in a lesson. For instance, it is not important for a child to know Jesus fed 4,000 people, but that as God's Son, He was powerful enough to feed lots of people. Concepts and themes are what is vital to a child's understanding. Important, too, is the time-related vocabulary used with children whether it be while asking them about their week, or referring to time to clean-up, or when a Bible story took place.

Social-Emotional Development

Just as important as the cognitive and physical growth of a child, is his social-emotional development. During the preschool years children are learning who loves them, whom to trust, and where they feel secure. They are learning about emotions and when to display them. They are also learning what their relationship is to others around them and how to interact with them. And they are learning what is acceptable behavior and what is not.

Important to the study of social emotional development is the research of Erik H. Erikson. The result of his work was the classification of eight stages of psychosocial development. Preschool children progress through three of these stages.

The first stage a child enters is basic trust versus basic mistrust (ages 0 to 1). A great deal of children's social development at this stage depends on the interactions of parents with them. If children receive the necessary care and affection, they develop a sense of trust. However, if they are neglected, the result is suspicion, fear, and lack of trust in their surroundings. The actions done to an infant to convey these messages include feeding, tactile stimulation (cuddling, fondling, holding), and diaper changing. Generally, the mother is responsible for providing the majority of the care.

Nursery workers are an extension, for the infants in the church, of the mother's responsibility.

Nursery workers are an extension of this responsibility for the infants in the church. Children will begin to know the church as a place where they are loved and cared for by the way they are treated in the nursery. Rocking babies, comforting them, and changing their diapers are all important ways of communicating love for them. Talking to them, singing, reading to them, and playing with them are also vital to what a nursery worker does.

By the time children reach a year old, they begin to enter the second stage of development referred to as autonomy versus shame and doubt. Once children have progressed through the infant stage, they have increasingly become aware of self separate from environment. They begin to challenge and manipulate that environment to increase independence. Parents are still considered the primary subjects of their world, as well as any siblings in the family. Interaction with others in a play environment is still limited. Toleration and supportive guidance and understanding are all things children need at this stage. They must not be allowed to roam freely to do anything they want, but they must also not be discouraged from developing an independent spirit. This is a good time to challenge them to develop abilities such as dressing themselves, using the bathroom facilities, washing their hands, and cleaning up after themselves. Praising them for their accomplishments during this stage is very important.

The last stage in preschool development is initiative versus guilt (4-6 years). Now is their chance to develop their sense of self in regard to right and wrong and how they will interact with others. This is a time of intense curiosity. They have developed the skills of play and will begin to interact with others in games and various activities. To encourage children's sense of initiative, parents and teachers should provide opportunity to enhance their physical and cognitive skills, answer their questions, and encourage their sense of imagination. Those who do not encourage these aspects are left with children who feel they are a nuisance and whose fantasies and imaginative stories are a waste of time.

Those who do not encourage initiative and imagination are left with children who feel they are a nuisance and whose fantasies and imaginative stories are a waste of time.

A teacher must be patient and kind, as well as consistent and caring, with children in these two stages of development. A variety of activities planned for the children is an excellent way for parents and teachers to foster independence, initiative, individual creativity, and interaction with others.

Accompanying the social development of preschool children are the emotional responses they are learning. From birth children are able to communicate emotional responses of distress with cries and contentment with smiles and coos. Expressions of frustration and anger soon follow when children learn to manipulate objects (four months). When they reach eight months, feelings of separation anxiety set in. At twelve months, they begin to develop fears of things such as large objects, new people, or new places.

The emotional responses of preschoolers from two to five years is one of extremes. When they are happy, they explode with excitement. They may run. They may jump. They may laugh out loud and have faces covered with huge smiles. When they are frustrated or angry, they may throw tantrums. They may stomp or yell, or they may cry. For teachers, it is important to help preschool children identify their own emotions and to identify emotions in others by facial expressions and actions. As time passes, they will gradually learn to control their responses by learning to identify them and to be guided into an understanding of how best to display those emotions by a teacher or parent.

Gender identity is also established between the ages of two and six. It is an age of curiosity. Children want to know what makes girls different from boys, why they dress differently at times, and like different toys. Adults need to address these questions in a positive manner and use correct terminology when it is applicable. Children should also be taught modesty, who is allowed to touch them, and why they are being touched. The presence of both parents or a close role model is also extremely important to children. Children learn best by imitation and example.

The word that best characterizes the social-emotional development of preschool children is the word "play." Play is the way a preschool child practices and imitates "real life." Play begins in infancy as children interact with objects. Other children become important between the ages of two and three, but only in the sense of social interaction. It is not a cooperative type of play, but rather two children playing side by side, engaging in parallel play. Not until the child is four does cooperative play emerge.

Play is the way a preschool child practices and imitates "real life."

Moral/Spiritual Development

The early childhood years are the time for creating a strong foundation for moral and spiritual development. Conscience is beginning to form, as well as a basic understanding of who God is. Most important to children's moral and spiritual development is the guidance of parents. Secondary to that is the influence of those in the church, more specifically a Sunday school teacher or nursery worker.

Lawrence Kohlberg is one of the most noted authorities on moral development. He would say this is an age of the developing conscience. During the preschool years (ages 2-5), children learn what rules are, who sets those rules, and how to act upon them. Morality is determined on the basis of what is right and wrong. Parents, teachers, and caregivers are the key to the proper development of morality.

The most important environment for proper moral development is a loving home.

The most important environment for proper moral development is a loving home. Parents must be consistent with children. Consequences for wrong behavior must also be coupled with the assurance of unconditional love. Parents must uphold their expectations of obedience and help children understand that discipline is a form of love.

Morality is not something that is developed instantaneously. Rather, it, too, is a process of exploration. Children who are two or three are beginning to establish their own independence. Therefore, they will test what is right and wrong on the basis of the reactions they get from their parents. Children this age also have trouble remembering what it is they are supposed to do. They often need to be reminded of what the rules are.

Once children are four or five, they have a good understanding of what is expected of them. They know that it is wrong to push another child. They know they should share their toys. They begin to respond to rules, not on the basis of a fear of punishment, but rather to please those in authority over them. They rarely have to be reminded of rules as long as there has been consistency in their environment. Children who have been in a variety of child care environments or have had to tolerate changes in authority may feel frustrated by what is expected of them and could be somewhat regressed in this area of moral development.

The faith of children is indeed a wonder to see develop. It is as if their belief in God comes naturally, as well as their love for Him. No wonder when the disciples were arguing among themselves as to who would be the greatest in the kingdom of heaven that Jesus called their attention to a child and said, "I tell you the truth, unless you change and become like little children, you will never enter the kingdom of heaven" (Matthew 18:3).

It is as if their belief in God comes naturally, as well as their love for Him.

James Fowler attaches two stages of faith to this age group. The first is primal faith, which is present in infancy. From birth, infants seek love and security, which translates into a sense of trust and hope. Nursery workers can convey that love and security while infants are in their care. Communication with infants should focus on telling them God loves them, cares for them, and provides for their needs. This can be done by talking to them, singing to them, reading to them, and showing them objects and pictures.

The next stage of spiritual development is called intuitive-projective faith. Children enter this stage of faith when they learn to talk. During this time, children become lost in the fantasy of the Bible stories and seek to imitate what they hear. They are influenced by examples, by the mood of the Bible stories, by the manner in which the stories are told, and by the actions of the characters. Parents and teachers alike can capitalize on the powerful images of God and of Jesus, the Son of God. Other power-packed stories that can influence the faith of a child are the stories of David and Goliath, Daniel in the Lions' Den, Moses, the Creation story, any of Jesus' miracles, and other action-packed stories.

During the preschool years is the time for preschoolers to develop positive loving attitudes toward God, Jesus, the Bible, the church, the family, and themselves. Parents are children's first introduction to the characteristics of God. They, too, are the ones children will imitate in action and attitude toward the elements of faith. Parents and teachers alike must commit themselves to provide this positive learning environment. Both groups of individuals are powerful images in a child's mind of how they should worship and love God.

The Church's Responsibility for Preschool Child

While parents are the primary caregivers of their children, the church must support parents in their endeavor. In a time when parents seem overwhelmed with their task in the midst of busy schedules, the church has become increasingly important. Attention must be given to proper programming, staffing, safety measures, and methods for teaching this particular age group.

Nursery Programming

The importance of a properly managed nursery program is vital to a growing church. Often parents of young children who are searching for a church to attend will base their decision on the quality of care and nurture they see in the church nursery and the preschool department. The purpose of the nursery is to first meet the needs of infant and toddlers. Secondly, the nursery should exist to give parents the option of care for their children while they themselves focus on worship and other adult education.

Staffing is one of the most important elements of the nursery program. A nursery worker must first of all love children and be committed to the safety and care of each child. This ministry is not limited to mothers of young children, but rather is open to fathers, grandfathers, grandmothers, college-age adults, and teenagers who have been trained in the care of infants and toddlers. The best kind of staffing is long-term. Although weekly rotations may work, they are not the best for infants and toddlers. Children this young often experience separation anxiety from their parents. It is easier for children to make a transition from parent to nursery worker if staffing is consistent. Rotations set up by the quarter or by the month work best.

Safety is an important issue when it comes to the nursery. Furnishings must meet safety standards and be age appropriate. Toys should be kept in an orderly fashion and be age appropriate as well. A regular cleaning schedule should be set up specifically for the nursery room to sanitize and wash toys, sheets and blankets, and furnishings. Cleanliness in regard to diapering and feeding is also important in caring for nursery children. Items including a fire extinguisher, smoke alarms, electrical outlet coverings, cabinet locks, and a first-aid kit must be in place and readily available to nursery workers. The arrival and departure of children must be carefully monitored. Sign-in cards are an excellent way to monitor children, the location of their parents, and any allergies and instructions a parent may have for their child as well. Finally, in regard to safety, children who are sick should not be allowed into the nursery.

The goal of Christian education for nursery children is that they understand they are loved.

The goal of Christian education for nursery children is that they understand they are loved by their families, by the church, and most of all, by God. Methods for teaching infants and toddlers include guided conversation, music, and simple activities. Activities may include looking at themselves in a mirror and telling them that God loves them and that God made them. It may include building with blocks or holding objects from nature and emphasizing God gave us hands to build things and eyes to see what He has made.

Method for Teaching Preschoolers

Utilizing learning centers is the most effective method for teaching preschoolers. Children learn best when they can explore their environment and employ all of their senses in doing so. Learning centers are activities that allow children to discover information about a Bible story. Centers encourage the application of certain behaviors and actions observed in the story (i.e., sharing, helping one another). Six to eight different centers are commonly used in the planning of a preschool lesson. Listed below is each center, its materials, and how it may be incorporated into a lesson.

Block Center should include large wooden or cardboard blocks and small wooden or plastic blocks. The center may also include trucks, cars, plastic animals, people, and various small props such as barns, play houses, schools, or churches. Children may be encouraged to build Noah's ark, the walls of Jericho, or other objects related to the lesson theme.

Homeliving Center should include a table and chairs, refrigerator, stove, doll cradle, tool table, dolls, kitchen utensils, play food, dress-up outfits, and baby items. Children may be encouraged to act out life at home, in the community, or at church.

God's Wonders Center should include items from nature, a magnifying glass, magnets, books and pictures of science and nature, live animals, plants, and a water, sand, or bean box. Children may be encouraged to name animals that God made or put in the ark. Children may care for plants or animals. They may take a nature walk and collect items for their center. Or they may manipulate objects by burying them in the sand as a squirrel would do nuts to prepare for winter.

Do not expect perfection, but praise the efforts of the children.

Art Center should include paints, fingerpaint, watercolor paint, playdough, crayons, glue, scissors, paper, construction paper, craft sticks, and a variety of other items to manipulate such as beads, buttons, wall paper, string, etc. Craft items should be simple and age appropriate. This center is an excellent one to build the self-image of a child. Do not expect perfection, but praise the efforts of the children, the colors they have chosen, and the manner in which they have chosen to do their project. Remember to allow for projects in which children are allowed to make whatever creation they choose.

Music Center should include a variety of instruments, cassette tapes/CDs, and players. Some of the best kinds of instruments can be made by the children such as drums, tambourines, shakers, and music sticks. Also recorders, kazoos (as long as they can be kept sanitary), bells, and xylophones should be included in this center. Children may be encouraged to march around the walls of Jericho or form a worship band while playing church or to play their instruments while singing songs during together time.

Puzzles and Games Center should include a variety of puzzles based on Bible stories, animals, and people in everyday life. Other materials may include simple Bible games, plastic tiles, lacing cards, and matching cards. Children may be encouraged to make an animal or a boat out of tiles or play a Bible matching game or lace a card in the shape of a sheep or a puzzle together that has to do with the story for the day.

Listening Center should include books, books-on-tape, flannel graph materials, puppets, and story cards. Books and materials should be rotated to include items appropriate to the lesson for that day. Children may be encouraged to listen to a story, act out the story with puppets, or arrange a story in order with story cards or flannelgraph.

The most important element of learning centers is guided conversation.

The most important element of learning centers is guided conversation. A teacher must be involved in helping the children discover the purpose of an activity by tying it into the lesson or story. Without guided conversation, the activity has no meaning except to entertain the children. Guided conversation may include telling the Bible story or an application story as the children build with blocks, or it may include questions for the children to answer as they paint a picture. Whatever it may be, guided conversation must exist with the activity to help the children discover the lesson behind the story.

Learning centers can be used in a room with one teacher or with multiple teachers. Centers are used during the first thirty to forty minutes of a lesson. Generally only three to four activities can be accomplished during this time frame. When only one teacher is present in the classroom, the teacher proceeds through the activities one at a time with all of the students together. When multiple teachers are present, each teacher is in charge of an activity and the students are arranged into groups which rotate to each of the centers.

Designing a Lesson

A lesson plan is essential to the success of a lesson. Included in the lesson plan are the objectives, the lesson goal, the activities, the materials, the guided conversation, and together-time songs, stories, and activities. The time allotments are also noted with each portion of the lesson to ensure good balance.

The following lesson plan has been included to demonstrate the use of learning centers, the proper flow of a preschool lesson, and the time frame for each portion. The lesson is designed for one teacher in a classroom. However, the same lesson could be used in a classroom with multiple teachers by assigning a teacher to each of the activities.

Class: Four & Five Year Olds

Title: God Cared for Noah & the Animals

Scripture: Genesis 6–9

Central Truth: God cares for you.

Objectives: The learner will be able to:
1. Identify different kinds of animals that Noah put into the ark.
2. Explain that God had Noah build the ark to keep him, his family, and the animals safe.
3. Name ways God keeps us safe.
4. Thank God for keeping us safe.

Learning Centers (30-40 minutes)
1. Art Center: Children will make animal masks.

Materials: Paper plates, markers, construction paper, glue, Guided Conversation: What kinds of animals did Noah put on the ark? Who told Noah to put the animals on the ark? Are you glad God kept the animals safe?

2. Block Center: Children will build an ark and load plastic animals
3. Homeliving Center: Children will pretend there is a storm outside and demonstrate what happens in their home when a storm comes.

Materials: Tables, chairs, blankets for beds, dolls

Guided Conversation: What happens at home when you are scared of a storm? How does God protect us from the lightning and the rain outside? Let's thank God for giving us safe, warm homes and parents to help us when we are frightened.

Together Time (10 minutes)

Sing: "Arky, Arky Song"

Story: Tell the story of Noah's Ark using the book *The Story of Noah and the Ark* from the Alice in Bible Land Series.

Application & Response (10 minutes)

Have the children identify pictures of God keeping them safe. Have the children then color the pictures. Pray together thanking God for keeping them safe.

Other Programming for Preschoolers

Mothers Day Out/ Play Groups

Mothers Day Out programs are generally one morning per week. The day is designed to be a play group for preschoolers. The focus is usually unstructured play. The program is also designed for mothers who need time during the week for running errands or to get together with other mothers in a support group ministry.

Day Care

With 56% of preschool mothers in the workforce, families need quality care for their children. A healthy place for people to turn to is the church. Buildings are generally equipped for such a program in regard to fire codes and furnishings. A caring Christian staff can be employed through church members. Parents also appreciate a Christian atmosphere for play and interaction with other children.

Preschool/Kindergarten

A growing number of churches are forming structured preschool and kindergarten programs. These programs are generally for children ages three through six and operate on a two-day, three-day or five-day program, meeting only half days. Curriculum includes a Christian emphasis in conjunction with a readiness program to prepare them for kindergarten and the first grade. The schedule usually includes learning centers, together time, snacks, and outside play.

Conclusion

Working with infants, toddlers, and preschoolers is both a challenge and a joy. Never at any other time in their life will children go through as many changes as they do in these first five years. Having the chance to be a part of this growing experience is a rewarding one. The exhortation for teachers: stay focused on the goal to draw them to Christ, remember both their limitations and what they are capable of, challenge them with activities that cause them to grow, and in the midst of it all, love them, love them, love them!

---

p r o j e c t s

★ Observe a group of preschool children. What physical, emotional, cognitive, and spiritual characteristics did you observe? ★

★ Plan a teaching session for preschool children, using Genesis 1 as your text. ★

For Further Reading

Lowell E. Brown
Sunday School Standards. Ventura, CA: Gospel Light, 1986.

Joanne Brubaker, Robert Clark, and Roy Zuck
Childhood Education in the Church. Chicago: Moody Press, 1986.

Wes Haystead
Everything You Want to Know about Teaching Young Children. Ventura, CA: Gospel Light, 1989.

Karyn Henley
Child Sensitive Teaching. Cincinnati: Standard Publishing, 1997.

Klaus Issler and Ronald Habermas
How We Learn. Grand Rapids: Baker Books, 1994.

Paul C. Reisser
Complete Book of Baby and Child Care. Wheaton, IL: Tyndale House, 1997.

Lawrence O. Richards
A Theology of Children's Ministry. Grand Rapids: Zondervan, 1983.

Jolene L. Roehlkepartain
Children's Ministry That Works! Loveland, CO: Group Publishing, 1991.

Daniel Schantz
You Can Teach with Success. Cincinnati: Standard Publishing, 1994.

CHAPTER 8
THE CHURCH'S MINISTRY TO
ELEMENTARY SCHOOL CHILDREN

Chapter Eight Summary

- ☑ How children learn
- ☑ Characteristics of elementary learners
- ☑ Designing effective learning experiences for children
- ☑ Methods for teaching elementary learners

It is Sunday morning at First Church in Anycity. A new family walks in the front door. When they are welcomed by a greeter, the mother asks, "Do you have babysitting for our children?"

If you were the greeter, how would you answer? Your answer will depend on the goals of your children's department. In some churches, the honest answer might be, "Yes, we can keep your children busy while you worship comfortably." However, an effective children's ministry enables you to answer, "Here at First Church, we offer more than babysitting. We have a children's ministry that offers Sunday school classes and children's worship sessions this morning. On Wednesday nights we offer a full program that includes children's choirs. We also help sponsor regular family events and children's support groups." (Pausing) "Rather than go on and on, let me give you this brochure that explains our goals and the programs that we offer for children. Right now, we need to take you and your children to their classrooms. Come with me."

Such an answer describes an exciting children's department. To be effective, however, not all the programs listed in this example have to be offered. A small church can also develop an effective children's ministry if the leaders understand how children learn, design effective learning experiences for them, and develop within the church's capabilities a few programs that minister to children.

Understand How Children Learn

Learn from the Bible

✎ Children were important to Jesus; they should be important to the church today. Read about Jesus' encounters with children: Mark 9:33-37; Mark 10:13-16; Matthew 18:5, 6.

✎ Parents, especially fathers, are commanded to teach their children the law: Psalm 78:5,6 and Proverbs 4:1-4.

✎ God's law is to be taught in daily life experiences with immediate application: Deuteronomy 6:4-9.

✎ Spiritual teaching involves both content and an understanding of the individual child: Proverbs 22:6.

Learn from Research into Faith Development

When and how do we develop a mature faith? Many people are exploring these questions. James Fowler traces the development of a person's faith in predictable stages much as those we see in cognitive/mental development. He suggests that persons move from one stage to another as they grow. In Fowler's theory it is possible for a person to develop through six stages. Figure 8.1 pictures the progression from stage to stage.

John Westerhoff proposes a different model. He compares the development of faith to the growth rings of a tree. Such a model means that persons retain the elements of the center ring as they add the second ring. Likewise they retain the first two when they add the third and then a fourth. Figure 8.2 pictures this.

The Search Institute in Minneapolis, Minnesota, conducted a study to discover the life experiences that had contributed to the spiritual growth of people who had mature faith. They discovered that those people had been influenced by specific

Stage Six
Universalizing Faith
(Mid-life and Beyond)

Fowler's Stages of Faith

These steps do not
grow ∧ naturally
or develope

Stage Five
Conjunctive Faith
(Mid-life and Beyond)

Stage Four
Individuative/Reflective
Faith
(Young Adulthood)

Stage Three
Synthetic/Conventional
Faith
(Adolescence and Beyond)

Stage Two
Mythic/Literal Faith
(Childhood and Beyond)

Stage One
Intuitive/Projective Faith
(Early Childhood)

Primal Faith
(Infancy)

Figure 8.1

Westerhoff's Styles of Faith

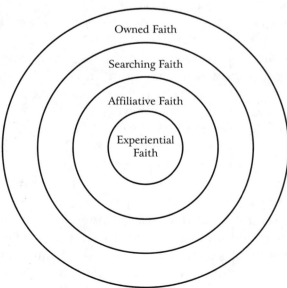

Owned Faith

Searching Faith

Affiliative Faith

Experiential
Faith

Figure 8.2

family practices and quality Christian education programs in their local churches.

More about these studies may be read in the books by Fowler, Westerhoff, and Search Institute listed in the resource list at the end of the chapter.

From the results of these three studies, we can make some general observations about helping children develop their faith.

✎ Recognize that children will display a faith that falls into a lower stage or inner ring. This does not mean that they do not have faith; it is merely appropriate to the age.

✎ Faith involves more than knowing Bible facts; it is also expressed through behavior. Christian education programs need to help people obey the truths they learn from the Bible.

✎ Westerhoff suggests that during the elementary and early adolescent years, children need to belong to and participate in a community of faith. This means that leaders need to design programs and classroom experiences that provide such participation and a sense of belonging to the church. Teachers and parents are models of Christian living and teach through their interactions with children. A ratio of one teacher for 6-8 children is imperative to develop such relationships. It also means that teachers must make a commitment to teaching for a time period that is long enough to allow them to build relationships with the children in the class.

✎ Children's leaders need to help prepare parents to teach their children. Many parents have not learned from their own parents how to teach God's Word to their children, so they need help from their church family. The children's department can develop parenting classes, offer special seminars, and provide parent support groups.

Learn from Research Done by Developmentalists

If we are to teach children God's Word and help them apply it to their lives, we need to understand how they learn and what motivates their behavior. Perry Downs (70) points out that researchers in the social sciences can help us answer that question.

How do people learn?. . .How has God created people to learn? By casting the question in the latter way, we are assuming that all truth is God's truth and that both the social sciences and theology are important for understanding human beings.

As they build relationships with children, parents and teachers immediately recognize that each one is unique. However, there are some patterns of development that have been discovered by researchers. A few of those patterns are outlined in chart 8.3.

	Developmental Characteristics	Responses of Teachers
First and Second Graders (First graders are in a period of transition from preoperational thinking to concrete thinking.)	Differ in small muscle ability, i.e., skill with scissors Awkward and uncoordinated Active—may want to run everywhere Enjoy stories Have little understanding of spatial distances Learning to read and write Want to be accepted and do well	Teach them as if all three sensory systems are dominant. Use visuals for them to "see" and plan activities that allow them to experience the concepts you want them to learn. Change the pace frequently; remember the traditional rule, "one minute attention span for each year." Let them change positions throughout the learning session. Although they like to read and write, plan carefully such opportunities so that they have time to be successful. Print in upper case and lower case letters. Allow them to express their understanding and ask questions. Give them lots of positive interaction.
Third and Fourth Graders	The preference for a sensory system is becoming more obvious. Improved eye-hand coordination They have new cognitive abilities: (1) understand that certain attributes of an object remain constant; (2) can classify items by similarities; (3) can place objects, events, and ideas in logical order (Piaget). Can now read to learn information Still think concretely; sorting out reality from make-believe Able to memorize Can work with others in a group more easily, but prefer to be with their own gender. Boys and girls are developing at different rates; boys are usually more aggressive than girls. Want everything to be "fair" Developing heroes	Avoid abstract terms unless you can give concrete, life-related examples. Help them learn the chronology and geography of the Bible. Provide clear, consistent standards. Provide opportunities for visual learners to "see" and kinesthetic learners to "do." Be a model of Christ and help children discover heroes in the Bible and history. Create a caring atmosphere; continue positive interaction.

Figure 8.3

	Developmental Characteristics	Responses of Teachers
Fifth and Sixth Graders	Fifth and sixth graders are completing the concrete operations stage and moving into abstract thinking (Piaget).	Continue to allow children to express their understanding and ask questions.
	Girls are experiencing a growth spurt; many will begin menstrual cycle; boys may feel small and awkward.	Encourage thinking; ask "why" questions. Continue to provide clear, consistent standards.
	May see themselves as "teens"	Plan social events; watch for cliques; help newcomers to become involved.
	Imitators of heroes	Continue to give positive interaction.
	Self-conscious	Emphasize forgiveness and grace.
	Trying to understand an invisible, sovereign God with their literal thinking	Continue to be a model of Christ and point students to other models.
	Can begin to understand that they have sinned against God	Some churches are calling this class/department the Preteen Department.
	Can still memorize easily	

Learn from Research Done in Learning Styles

During the last part of the twentieth century, some research has resulted in the introduction of the phrase, "learning style." or "kind of learner" to several different models. Some descriptions refer to how a person perceives and processes information—whether the person is a diverger, analytic, converger, or accommodator learner. Others talk about environmental influences—whether a person learns better sitting at a desk, in a comfortable chair, or sprawled on the floor. Still others may be talking about preferred sensory systems—whether the learners remember better what they heard, experienced, or saw. Drs. Kenneth and Rita Dunn have identified 21 elements that they believe affect a person's "style." A growing number of authors, such as Howard Gardner, write about which kind of "intelligence" a person has.

Whatever system teachers use, they are all trying to recognize that individuals are different. They recognize that no one method will successfully teach all the children in a class at the same time. Children's ministry leaders need to select one of the models or a combination of models so that they can train volunteer teachers to use a variety of methods that will meet the needs of all the learners in the classroom.

The writer of Proverbs (22:6) said that we should "train a child in the way he should go." In order to accomplish that effectively we need to consider that particular child's "style of learning."

Sensory System/Perceptual
Modalities

A helpful model to use with volunteer teachers is the sensory systems/perceptual modalities model. It explains that most of us have a preference for which of our sensory systems—hearing, doing, or seeing—we use to perceive information. We can use all of our systems, but most of us find it easier to learn new information through our strongest sensory system.

Auditory learners remember much of what they hear. That makes learning in traditional classrooms easier for them. Some researchers suggest that only about ten percent of Americans learn best through auditory avenues.

Auditory learners understand oral directions and pay attention during teacher-directed activities. They may read or think "out loud." They are easily distracted by sound and remember by auditory repetition. They may find writing notes distracting; they would rather concentrate on listening to the teacher. As they grow older, they often become adept at recognizing the importance of information by the inflections of the teacher's voice.

**Auditory learners are easily distracted by sound
and remember by auditory repetition.**

We can help them learn if we provide opportunities to hear the information through as many media as possible. We should always read aloud any instructions. We can be alert to classroom noise levels that distract these learners.

Verbal learners are auditory learners who need to hear themselves saying the information. They definitely read or process information out loud when concentrating; they enjoy listening but cannot wait to talk. They often repeat or restate the things they hear and talk problems out. They may hum or talk to themselves.

We can help them learn if we plan an activity in which they can ask questions of the teacher or discuss the facts with other classmates. We can give them listening assignments when they are going to receive new information. We want to provide an opportunity for them to explain the lesson to other learners. We can let them make up rhymes, poems, or songs about the information and its application.

Kinesthetic people learn best by being physically involved in the activity (more than writing!) and doing something with what is being learned. They can do two or more things at the same time. It is estimated that about 35 per cent of Americans are kinesthetic.

Kinesthetic learners can do two or more things at the same time.

We will recognize kinesthetic learners because they usually move body parts when concentrating. They may gesture when speaking or pace when talking or thinking. Children may sit at the front of the class and/or offer to "help" teacher; they may handle or play around with props or supplies. They often make airplanes from their papers or tear the Styrofoam cup into a hundred pieces. They use their whole bodies to express feelings. They prefer stories in which action occurs early. During periods of inactivity, they find a reason to move (i.e., go to the rest room during the sermon). To some parents' and teachers' surprise, they can concentrate for a long time if totally absorbed in an activity.

We can help them learn if we structure "real-life" situations such as field trips or service projects. We use bodily motion as much as possible to illustrate what we're saying; we can let them walk a floor map or march as the children of Israel. We point to the clock on the wall and let them know when the work study time will end; we don't ask them to sit too long, even if we merely let them move to another area in the classroom for the next activity. We add active games related to the lesson theme. We make things, offering big spaces to draw and write (wall murals or graffiti murals). We challenge them to come up with ways to move without disturbing other students, i.e., doodle, take notes, squeeze a Koosh Ball or Silly Putty. We plan activities during which the children may choose their body position as long as they do not disturb others; for example, they may choose to stand or sprawl on the floor during study, work, or discussion. We do hold them accountable for being able to relate the facts or main idea of the material. We don't expect them to stand still or maintain eye contact while reciting.

Some kinesthetic learners are tactile. They learn best when there is equipment or material they touch or feel. They need to use concrete objects as learning aids. They have difficulty learning abstract concepts at school like letters and numerals. They really face a challenge when they are expected to understand and practice love, forgiving, sharing, omnipresent God, etc. They definitely handle props and supplies in the classroom.

Tactile learners are often mistakenly called "hyperactive" by nonmedical people.

They may be classed at school as underachievers or be described by other people as children who "can't keep their hands to themselves." They need to explore their environment more than average for people their age. When spelling, they write words to determine if they "feel" right. They are often mistakenly called "hyperactive" by nonmedical people.

We can help them learn if we use pictures to help establish associations and supply concrete objects for sequencing, establishing patterns, seeing likenesses and differences, categorizing, etc. We can suggest they write notes or highlight information while listening. We will provide experiences where they handle objects whenever possible. We need to plan times for mobility and give them "elbow" space to cut down physical contacts with other pupils. When singing, we provide rhythm instruments to play in beat with the songs.

Visual learners need to see something to learn it. Approximately forty-five per cent of Americans are visual. They maintain eye contact during conversations or the story. They find details easily in visual material; they are distracted by visual disorder or movement. They may become impatient when they have to listen for a long time with no visual stimulus, so they find something to watch out the window, in the classroom, or on the activity sheet. They have vivid imaginations and think in pictures, so when reading they may pause to imagine a scene. They write out a word to see if it "looks right." They can be deeply affected by visual arts. They express feelings through facial expressions.

Visual learners need to see something to learn it.

We can help them learn by using visual aids! We want to provide pictures, maps, charts, demonstrations, in a variety of media—poster board, overhead transparency, video, chalkboard, paper, flannel board, or bulletin board. We want to put instructions on paper or poster and add clip art to words. We can provide opportunities for them to read as well as hear us talk. We can encourage them to make flash cards, diagrams, charts of their own. We can invite them to "picture" a situation.

Observe the Impact of Their Culture

In 1981, David Elkind wrote *The Hurried Child* because he wanted to warn Americans that children were being treated differently than in the past. He was concerned because this treatment was making life harder for them. By 1988, he wrote a revision of that book with a goal to get the readers to acknowledge the pressures on children so that we can help them deal with those pressures as effectively as possible.

Others have taken up the banner. Children's leaders have many sources to study to help them understand how culture is affecting children. It would be helpful for every children's ministry leadership team to consider such material once a year. The challenge then becomes one of determining how the developments in culture are affecting local children so that adjustments can be made in the department's programs.

Design Effective Learning Experiences for Children

Set Goals

The leadership team must write a mission statement for the children's ministry. It should demonstrate how this department will carry out the church's mission in the lives of children. In their book, *Building a Children's Ministry* (44-45), Evelyn Johnson and Bobbie Bower explain it this way.

> A mission statement for children's ministry will iden-tify the local church's unique role within the larger Christian community. The mission statement will guide the processes of evaluating current activities, making appropriate choices for future programming, and determining needed resources. . . . Basic questions must be asked and answered. For example, What are the needs? What are the opportunities? What are the current strengths? What do we value? What do we believe is important? What do we see happening?

All programming decisions are then based on what will enable the children's ministry to carry out its mission.

Within each program, leaders need to set goals so that they can plan how they will help carry out the department's mission. Teachers and leaders in each teaching session and event then also will establish goals for the year, quarter, and session.

Training programs for volunteers need to include instruc-tion in selecting appropriate goals/objectives from curriculum materials. Teachers should ask themselves, "What do I want the children to do as a result of this lesson? How will they be differ-ent because they were in my class?"

Understand the Role of the Teacher

It is obvious from all that we know about how elementary children learn that teaching is more than talking by the teacher. In the book, *Introduction to Christian Education*, Eleanor Daniel explains the teacher's role well. She says that the teacher is a teller, a doer, a planner, a model (83-94). A teacher of elementary children must be all those to enable the children to develop the sense of belonging and participation needed for faith development. A teacher of elementary children must plan completely with the teaching team/partner every detail of the teaching session and be ready to be actively involved with the children. As those interactions take place, the children will see a model of what they are to become in the Christian community.

Follow the Outline of a Good Learning Experience

Arrival Time/Presession. When elementary children arrive for any learning session or event, teachers need to be ready to begin one or more activities. The session begins with the arrival of the first child! The activity(ies) should help carry out the goals for the session in some way. They may be activities that help students understand the background of the Bible story, new vocabulary words, or the life application content of the lesson. They could prepare a presentation for the rest of the class during the Bible study, or they may work on memorizing a Bible passage.

Attention/Life Need. When the class members come together for the Bible story, one of the teachers leads some brief learning activity to get them involved and directed toward the goals. This activity should be centered in the students' life experiences.

Bible Study. Select a method that will get the students involved in finding out what the Bible says. This means that your students are using their Bibles or hearing Bible information (like storytelling).

Life Application. Select learning activities that get the students involved in exploring how to apply the Bible truths. This time finds your students deciding how the Bible information applies today to the lives of people their age.

Select learning activities that get the students involved in exploring how to apply the Bible truths.

Life Response. Select an activity that allows the students to decide what they will do to put the Bible material into practice.

This is a brief, individual activity unless the class has decided on a group project to apply the Bible truth.

Select Effective Methods

Good curriculum materials provide a good foundation for teachers to develop class sessions. However, it is not uncommon for teachers to have to add large muscle learning activities for the kinesthetic learners or more visual stimulation. They can be selected from the following methods/learning activities.

Art. Most children enjoy art activities. Visual learners enjoy creating the pictures in their imaginations. Remember to let kinesthetic learners have big spaces in which to work. Even if the finished product is not perfect, students have learned from the process of putting the Bible information or the life application into concrete form.

Elementary children can:

- Paint (finger, sponge, soap, spatter, vegetable, string, blow)
- Use crayons (drawing, etching, melting, paint resisting, rubbing)
- Use overhead markers on overhead transparencies
- Make stained glass windows
- Sculpt with play dough, paper, or modeling clay
- Draw a frieze or mural
- Create a rebus (pictures replacing words)
- Design a badge, bumper sticker, cartoon, poster, T-shirt
- Illustrate a book
- Make a diorama, mobile, or peep scene
- Use magazine pictures to make a montage or add three-dimensional supplies to make it a collage
- Tear paper to make a silhouette
- Design a chart, time line, or graph
- Make a map (floor, paper, salt) model, or table top scene.
- Older children can try photography with one of the new one-time use cameras to illustrate a Bible passage, song, or life application.

Drama. Both visual and kinesthetic learners can enjoy reenacting the Bible story, portraying a life problem, or trying out a solution to a problem. The teacher can provide the script or help the students develop it. Pantomime works well for nonreaders. A large piece of fabric, some PVC pipe, and a map tripod or microphone stand can create a puppet stage for even a small classroom. Simple costumes can be made available in the church's resource room. Appropriate paper hats or name tags can also identify roles. Students can make and operate puppets while a prerecorded script is played or other students read the parts; children can act as reporters interviewing a Bible person. They can pose pictures; pantomime or act out the Bible story; older children can read a script with expression for Readers Theater or read the Bible story as Readers Theater. Children with confidence can role play life situations to apply the Bible truth.

Both visual and kinesthetic learners can enjoy reenacting the Bible story.

Games. Many Bible games have been produced through the years and may be found in a closet in the church building. They help children work with the Bible information while having fun. They can also help children memorize Bible verses or the books of the Bible. Some publishers provide basic games that can be personalized for a specific lesson, and curriculum materials will often include a game for a unit of study.

Music. Children have enjoyed praising God in worship with their voices and rhythm instruments for many years. But music can be used as a teaching method also. Children can:

✎ Sing a song that reinforces what they learned in Bible content or life application
✎ Write new verses to a song
✎ Draw pictures to illustrate a song
✎ Select slides that illustrate a song
✎ Listen to a song that relates to the Bible story or life application and discuss it.

Research. Some children enjoy working individually to discover facts. They can:

✎ Find information in Bible dictionaries, encyclopedias, atlases, or maps
✎ Go on field trips
✎ View a video
✎ Listen to an audio cassette
✎ Work on a computer
✎ Take a survey.

Children then report their discoveries to the class.

Verbal communication. Every Bible lesson includes verbal communication teacher to student, student to teacher, or student to student. Teachers can:

✎ Guide conversation while students work on projects; students will read the Bible
✎ Tell a story or present an object lesson

Students may:

✎ Make oral reports of their research or small group work
✎ Discuss an open-ended situation, picture, or agree/disagree statement
✎ Respond to an assignment or question in turn (circle response).

Writing. Many older elementary children enjoy writing. Younger children enjoy dictating their thoughts to a teacher or tape recorder. The writing can be related to a Bible person or an application situation. They can:

✎ Write a letter, a story, a simple script, a simple book that other students illustrate, or a journal entry
✎ Create an acrostic or a caption for a cartoon or picture
✎ Create entries on a graffiti poster
✎ Write stories or headlines for a newspaper
✎ Paraphrase a Bible verse
✎ Make a word search or crossword puzzle.

Try these tips in carrying out a new learning activity.

✎ Try it first yourself.
✎ Write out complete instructions on paper, poster, or chalkboard for readers. For nonreaders, use pictures on the poster or give step-by-step instructions. The latter approach is also effective with students who have learning difficulties.

✎ Have all materials on hand before students arrive.

✎ Walk around as children work, giving help to individuals.

✎ Encourage students with positive teacher-student interaction.

✎ Be flexible in changing assignments or expectations as students work.

✎ Be willing to try the activity again.

Develop Programs that Minister to Children

The choice of programs to minister to children is limited only by the needs of the community and a congregation's resources to meet those needs. Typical programs include Sunday school, extended session, children's church, Sunday or Wednesday evening youth groups, after-school clubs, and vacation Bible school.

Special ministries may exist across regular programming as teachers reach out to gifted children or exceptional children and provide missions education. The children's department ministers to families through family events, intergenerational events, support groups for special needs children, and parenting classes. Some churches offer child care, weekday preschool, mother's day out, day camp, or a formal Christian school. The department may develop its own camping program or cooperate in an area camping program.

p r o j e c t s

★ Observe a group of elementary children. What likenesses and differences did you observe, especially in faith development and learning styles? ★

★ Plan a teaching session for children, using 1 Kings 18:16-46 as the text. ★

For Further Reading

Perry Downs
Teaching for Spiritual Growth: An Introduction to Christian Education. Grand Rapids: Zondervan, 1994.

Findley B. Edge
Teaching for Results. Rev. ed. Nashville: Broadman, 1995.

Effective Christian Education: A National Study of Protestant Congregations: A Summary Report.
A four-part video series with discussion guide is also available. Search Institute, 122 West Franklin Avenue, Suite 525, Minneapolis, MN 55404.

Eddie and Billye Joyce Fine
Teachers Are Made, Not Born. Cincinnati: Standard Publishing, 1990.

James Fowler
Stages of Faith Development: The Psychology of Human Development and the Quest for Meaning. San Francisco: Harper and Row, 1981.

Wes and Sheryl Haystead, ed.
Sunday School Smart Pages. Ventura, CA: Gospel Light, 1992.

Wes Haystead
The 21st Century Sunday School: Strategies for Today and Tomorrow. Cincinnati: Standard Publishing, 1995.

Kids' Workers Clip Art, Computer Clip Art
Ventura: Gospel Light, 1994.

Marlene LeFever
Creative Teaching Method. Rev. ed. Colorado Springs: David C. Cook, 1996.
Learning Styles. Colorado Springs: David C. Cook, 1995.

Margie Morris
Volunteer Ministries. Cincinnati: Standard Publishing, 1994.

Doris Sanford
Helping Kids through Tough Times. Cincinnati: Standard Publishing, 1995.

John Westerhoff III
   Will Our Children Have Faith? San Francisco: Harper, 1976.

Dennis Williams and Kenneth Gangel
   Volunteers for Today's Church: How to Recruit and Retain Workers.
   Grand Rapids: Baker, 1993.

CHAPTER 9
THE CHURCH'S MINISTRY TO
TEENAGERS

Chapter Nine Summary
- ☑ Cultural keys to today's teens
- ☑ Multifaceted development of teens
- ☑ Joys of teaching teens
- ☑ Steps to successful teaching of teens
- ☑ Advantages of established cirricula
- ☑ Proactive discipline

"I can't wait to come to your class!"

The confession from the teenager startled me. So I just nodded.

"You never know what's going to happen. And I always leave wishing we had more time. I learn so much from you. I just wanted to say thanks."

I inconspicuously pinched myself. Nope, I wasn't dreaming. Despite my numerous miscues and classroom flubs, I must be connecting and ultimately making a difference. Teaching adolescents can be a tremendous joy!

Adolescents in the 21st century are a distinct American generation. Sometimes known as "millennial" kids (born after 1982), these kids think and act differently, largely the result of a societal shift in how children were viewed at the end of the 20th century. They arrived in minivans sporting "Baby on Board" signs and grew up in an age of technology (cell phones, digital television, e-mail) and information (Internet, infomercials). For these kids, it was cool to be intelligent and smart.

On the home front, this generation witnessed a drop in the divorce rate and a new emphasis placed upon "family values." A 1997 Franklin Covey Company survey discovered nearly eight in ten Americans would forgo a job promotion to spend more time at home. "Home Improvement" television shows, family hotel rates, Promise Keepers, children's menus, home schooling, and family newspapers became the rage.

Values, volunteerism, and God also mark today's teenagers. Religion in the 1990s was energized, and many churches witnessed growth, especially those who emphasized children's, youth, and family ministries. From WWJD (What Would Jesus Do) bracelets to contemporary Christian music to the megachurch phenomenon, Christianity was embraced and celebrated. Millennials also participated in a revival of volunteerism as youth ministries switched from water park trips to mission excursions. Honesty, integrity, and marital fidelity are cherished values to this generation.

Religion in the 1990s was energized.

Despite these positive images of the millennial generation, a few disturbing portraits also emerge. While values are important, objective truth has given way to relativism, even among the most committed, churched teens. While the schoolroom and home were emphasized, crime and violence in both institutions are common. And despite the blessing of technological advancement, there is still no cure for the common hopelessness. Euthanasia, abortion, and AIDS remain problem issues.

Why is it so important to reveal this millennial montage?

One reason is because the first step in adolescent ministry is to understand their culture—not to condone it, but to confront it, not to accept it, but to apply scriptural teaching to it. Ironically, teenagers have many teachers who seek to influence their values: Madison Avenue, Hollywood, MTV. These corporate institutions have researched well today's young people to understand (and reach) them. Effective Christian educators must also understand the teenager's world.

But culture isn't the only matter teachers need to learn about teenagers. Adolescence is the second revolution in development: physically, emotionally, socially, morally, and intellectually. Between the ages of 10 and 20, a new person will emerge, shaped by influences of family, friends, church, and society.

This difficult process is commonly known as puberty.

Physical Development

Growing up isn't easy. It is a period of traumas, whether it be pimples or voice changes or menstruation. Hormonal changes abound as testosterone and estrogen flow forcefully. Body hair emerges, first in the genital and underarm regions, and later, on the male's face. In the female, breasts develop as early as age seven. However, the average age for the arrival of puberty is age twelve for girls, about two years later for boys.

These diverse physical changes produce many consequences. Adolescents can strangely bounce between emotional highs and lows, from exhilaration to depression. Societal influences about the "perfect body" can push young people, especially girls, into eating disorders such as anorexia nervosa or bulimia. Others simply get fat. Some teenagers explore physical pleasures, including alcohol and drugs. And many become sexually active as they attempt to appease social norms, emotional desires, and physical needs. Pregnancy and sexually transmitted diseases are often a tragic consequence.

As teachers of adolescents, we must understand that kids change constantly. And we must be sensitive to their self-beliefs and careful to help them accept and love their bodies, as designed by God. We must also avoid teaching methods which might produce embarrassment or encourage peer put-downs.

Cognitive Development

The Swiss psychologist Jean Piaget proposed that adolescents are able to think more abstractly, as opposed to children who view things in a more concrete manner. Essentially, where children see the world as it is, teenagers can now project a world as it could be. They can see different sides of the same coin—new perspectives, unique ideas, novel concepts.

Teenagers can hypothesize, analyze, synthesize, and evaluate information. They can create solutions and list arguments. Essentially, they learn how to think, not just what to think.

As youth workers, we must continually open their minds to new ideas. Christian teenagers crave a real faith that is based on objective facts. They welcome a reasonable faith that sharpens logical skills. Reasoned disagreement in the classroom should be encouraged (even disagreement with the teacher or Scripture) as it produces thinking skills. The teenage classroom should be less teacher-centered lecture and more student-based discussion. The teacher's role is to guide the class toward truth. Ideally, a lesson should produce questions in adolescent minds to fuel further thirst to study God's Word.

Moral/Spiritual Development

Teenagers experience a moral and spiritual revolution in puberty. They begin to question values, beliefs, and faith systems. It isn't surprising when today's teen rejects objective truth. Think about it. Television and movies preach, "Do your own thing." Role models live double lives. Mom will say, "Stay off drugs" and then swallow a sleeping pill every night. Teens detect and reject such hypocrisy.

The home is the center for moral and spiritual development, while peers help influence values and beliefs. Even so, many adolescents reject both family and friend influence, sometimes for the good, sometimes for the bad.

Adolescents behave morally for many reasons. Some fear punishment or rejection or a violation of personal principle. Regardless of the reason, Christian teachers must help teenagers make right choices and discover objective truth. Effective teachers also realize the influence of the home on an adolescent and seek to minister to the whole family. Ideally, an effective teenage class will be a safe place of faith with positive peer influence.

Adolescents behave morally for many reasons.

Personality and Emotional Development

Teenagers ask two central questions during their adolescent journey: *"Who am I?"* (identity) and *"Do I belong?"* (inclusion). And answering these two will help a teenager understand a third life question: *"Where am I going?"* (destiny).

Psychologist Erik Erikson proposed that teenagers experience an "identity crisis" between the ages of twelve and nineteen. During this "crisis," they discover who they are and their place in the world. Usually this identiy is forged through previously discovered strengths, abilities, hobbies, or interests—the high school football team, the cheerleading squad, the debate club. Sometimes this identity is forged in unhealthy pursuits like Friday night parties, gangbanging, or some forms of music expression. The dating process is largely a quest for personal identity: *"Will someone love me for me?"*

Another developmental psychologist, David Elkind, suggested teenagers as they discover personal identity are always performing to "imaginary audiences" (1984, 33-36). This assumption that the world is watching them explains how adolescents can be easily embarrassed and yet, at the same time, wear fashions, haircuts, and jewelry to create notice. Depending on the audience—parent, peer, or society—teenagers often act a part to either draw or deter attention.

Teenagers as they discover personal identity are always performing to "imaginary audiences."

As teachers of adolescents, we must recognize the need for identity and belonging, and foster the process through community building, affirmation, and teamwork. We must provide opportunities for teens to use their gifts, abilities, and interests for ministry. Finally, an effective adolescent classroom will be an emotionally safe sanctuary where teenagers sense belonging, power, and a freedom to be themselves, whether it is with a nose ring, cowboy hat, or necktie.

Why Work with Teenagers?

So why would anyone want to teach teenagers?

First, adolescents are impressionable and open. For many, even in the church, basic Christianity can be a radical concept, a faith not built on laws and rules, but rather upon a loving relationship with Jesus Christ. As everyone knows, teenagers do rebel. But who says that rebellion must be bad?

Secondly, teens are honest in some matters and will gradually open up and be authentic with a teacher as the teacher provides authentic, nonjudgmental acceptance and gains the trust of teens, but they'll let you know when your teaching is boring. They will sometimes vote with their feet and not show up. They'll act up in class—a clue that you're not connecting. But they will also affirm you. They will share their affection for you. And they will sacrifice to follow.

Adolescents are wonderful students but they don't become energized and revived overnight.

Finally, adolescents can be world changers. They are old enough to make adult decisions and able enough to get the job done. And yet they aren't limited. They can travel for several days without losing their job; they can willingly quit employment to participate in a program or activity. They tend to be less prejudiced and biased than adults. And they welcome new experiences more than adults who come to enjoy routine. Therefore, the classroom is the world. It is summer mission trips or Saturday morning service projects. Or it is simply holding class outside on the lawn, in a tree, or in the van.

Adolescents are wonderful students. But they don't become energized and revived overnight. To teach a group of teenagers requires work, patience, and prayer. And there is no age limit on who can teach. One of the best high school teachers I know was a great-grandmother who taught well into her 60s. You also don't need a hot car, an impressive stereo unit, or the latest fashion to teach kids. But you do need heart. You need to like teenagers. And you need to learn, love, and live the principles for "success."

Teaching Teenagers with S.U.C.C.E.S.S.

Shape (Prepare Thoroughly)

My college homiletics professor quipped that the secret to a great sermon was preparation. And the process was simple: First, read yourself full. Second, think yourself clear. Third, pray yourself hot. And, finally, let yourself go. This simple process parallels the commitment necessary to teach teenagers. After all, master teachers are prepared teachers.

And teenagers, especially, can recognize an unprepared teacher (it's one of the primary reasons they act up). Therefore, ninety percent of the success in the classroom is due to what is done prior to class in three primary areas.

Ninety percent of the success in the classroom is due to what is done prior to class.

First is proper preparation of the lesson. The key is an early start. Saturday night specials exhaust not only the teacher but wear thin on young people too. Essentially, the next lesson begins the moment the former one ends. It involves studying the curriculum plan for the coming week and memorizing it if possible so as to avoid reading from the manual. It involves outside study in the Scripture, discovering new insights and interpretations, including memorizing the Scriptures yourself. Finally, it means open eyes and ears to illustrations from life or the teen's world that can give the lesson a personal touch. Many a lesson is helped by incorporating a Top 40 hit song, a favorite movie or television show, or a front page news article.

A second area of preparation includes the learners. How well do you know your students? What is happening in their lives right now? A simple phone call each week to every student is a good start. Many times teenagers say their Sunday school lessons are irrelevant. What they are really saying is my teacher hasn't taken the time to know me and my world.

A final way to prepare for a lesson is in your own life. Each lesson must be taught to yourself first. After all, you cannot expect to lead young people where you have not gone yourself. Take some time to refresh, revive, and restore your own walk with God before challenging the teens to do the same.

Unconditional
(Abundant Grace)

Being a teenager isn't easy.

There are a lot of mistakes, a lot of regrets, and far too many misunderstandings. It is difficult to dance through adolescence when every step seems like a landmine. And it doesn't help when adults around, whether parents, youth leaders, or school teachers, view such missteps as bad or unacceptable or even evil.

Every teenager needs to hear three basic messages from an adult.

Every teenager needs to hear three basic messages from an adult. First of all: *"The past is the past and, in Christ, it is forgiven."* Many adolescents are crippled by past sin. Sometimes it is by their own choice. Often it is because someone else abused them in various forms. Regardless, they desperately desire a clean slate. As Christian teachers, we can help this understanding by letting bygones be bygones. I have witnessed many "bad" kids, as defined by other adults, blossom into wonderful Christian people because they finally met someone who didn't remind them constantly about their past.

Teenagers also need to hear a second message: *"You are okay in my eyes and in God's."* Adolescence is a weird time. Their bodies are doing strange things and it is confusing and often embarrassing. Furthermore, modern science has basically convinced many kids they are worth only a few bucks in chemicals.

This message not only depresses but can cause kids to view any and all imperfections as bad. Therefore, as adults, we must constantly encourage teenagers (every week): affirm their abilities, take note of their uniqueness, value their person, fortify their positive beliefs about themselves. Essentially, help them see themselves as God sees them.

A final message is: *"You can be somebody and God has a plan for your life!"* Too many teenagers, even churched kids, live in a hopeless vacuum. Riddled by criticism from parents, peers, and even self, and crippled by past regrets and mistakes, many kids view the future as rather dark. Nevertheless, we have the wonderful honor to help young people dream about their futures. And dare them to go where no dream has gone before.

Creativity (Awesome Variety)

The first step to boredom is predictability.

And creating learning situations that change from week to week is crucial when teaching teens. In fact, it is a wonderful compliment when students come to class because they never know what is going to happen. Naturally, the use of a good teen curriculum should help resolve creativity issues. But many teen teachers like to write their own lessons and, tragically, rely upon the same learning methods week after week after week. Nevertheless, there are dozens of great learning methods to use when teaching adolescents:

* Art: murals, collages, paper tears, cartoons, montages, mosaics, advertisments, banners, bumper stickers, charts, doodles
* Drama: role-play, pantomime, monologue, dramatic reading, videos
* Discussion: agree/disagree, circle response, debate, pair share, Q&A, word association, brainstorming, panel discussion
* Writing: letter writing, scripts, poetry, newspaper articles, diaries, acrostics, graffiti, parables
* Music: singing, music videos, songwriting

The two most overused methods with teenagers are lecture and discussion, followed closely by role-plays or skits. Teens tire of these rather quickly. If you must lecture, dress it up with visual aids (overheads, props, models). Discussions can also be varied (pairs, trios, quads). The best rule: use no method two weeks in succession.

Concentrate (Purposeful Focus)

The number one mistake many Christian teachers make with teens is the "content dump." This happens when a teacher simply unloads information without providing opportunity to digest (understand) or apply it—lists, pages of outline, or, worse, an hour of "teacher talk." *"All we do is sit"* is a common complaint of teenagers about their teachers.

The number one mistake many Christian teachers make with teens is the "content dump."

Effective teachers of adolescents understand that a single focus—one point learning—is far better. It is a simple process. Reduce the lesson to a one-sentence point, such as "Jesus is coming; get ready" or "Love everyone as yourself." And then hammer the point repeatedly by using various angles, applications, and assumptions. Use different methods to make the point. And, by all means, connect the point to the lives of the teen. This can be effectively done through pair shares and discussion groups.

Explore (Amazing Adventures)

Many have mused that it is a sin to bore a kid and that is true. But it is probably more wicked to bury a bored kid with seemingly endless information. Too much of a good thing only makes a person sick, exhausted, or resentful.

The world is a classroom. And the world is a mighty big place. Far too many Christian teachers think the church, especially the church classroom, is the only place where learning can take place. Not true.

The senses are important to learning. Educational research has concluded that the more senses that are involved at the same time, the more vivid the memory experience. And so where Teacher Amy may tell her teens about missions and challenge them to consider such work, Teacher Bob takes them to a soup kitchen or a week-long Mexico mission trip. Or where Teacher Charlie does a Scripture search on death, Teacher Donna takes her class to a cemetery for a grave rubbing and Bible discussion. Do you see the difference?

Teenagers like to learn on the move.

Teenagers like to learn on the move. Are you dealing with comparative religions? Then attend a Catholic mass or visit a New Age bookshop. Do you want to talk about evangelism? Then go fishing and brainstorm techniques that "fish for men." Do you want to discover how Peter felt when he walked on water or learn about his faith? Then go boating or sit around a fire and discuss the consequences in denying Jesus for Peter and for a teenager.

Even if the curriculum doesn't encourage such experiences, either incorporate the lesson into an experience or create an additional time outside of class for such activities. Personal, positive, and powerful experiences are what make a teenager's faith come alive. And they are what make for memorable teachers and lessons.

Study (Seasoned Expert)

To teach teenagers is to learn.

Young people are full of questions and if they believe you can answer their doubts, they will unload: *"Why is Christianity the only true religion?" "What happens when I die?" "Are there dinosaurs in the Bible?" "Does God really exist?" "What about the Shroud of Turin?" "Can a person go to Heaven and not be baptized?"*

"What is a Jehovah's Witness?" "Is the Bible the only Word of God?" "What about extraterrestrials?" "Why do good people suffer?"

The bottom line: you need to keep learning yourself.

Effective teachers will be schooled in the basics of the faith. They will understand who God is, what Jesus did, and how the Holy Spirit operates. They will know how the church works in Scripture and what comprises salvation.

Effective teachers of adolescents will also be educated in teaching skills. They will know how to create a good lesson, how to lead a discussion, or apply a point. They will understand how learners learn, why they act up in class, or how to create a positive learning environment.

Finally, effective teachers of teenagers can defend the faith. They can provide evidences for God, the resurrection, and the Bible. They can explain the differences in various religions and cults or give a framework for the biblical doctrine of creation.

How do teachers stay current? They do it by teaching new studies (new book or topic) or by using spare time to become further educated in apologetics, theology, or teaching practices. They read a new book every month or subscribe to periodicals that help answer such questions.

Skill (Model Equipper)

A primary goal of teaching is to produce equipped leaders. In fact, Jesus said a student will "be like his teacher" (Matthew 10:25). Therefore, every adolescent Bible class should be focused towards moving teenagers into areas of ministry. Teenagers must be unleashed within the church to do acts of service: lead worship, run the soundboard, prepare communion, create a newsletter, teach a younger age class, give a devotional thought, lead a church activity, or develop a ministry (puppet, drama, music, nursing home, homeless, etc.).

Teenagers must be unleashed within the church.

Naturally, the critics will say kids will mess up (they will). And they will also fail (more than once). They will not always do their best (tragic, but true). And they will probably make a few people angry in the process (guaranteed). Equip them anyway. One of the reasons adolescents leave the church is because they sense they do not belong. They don't see a place to fit or work. They don't feel at home. And if the church doesn't meet that need, teens will find a place that will!

Teenagers are the church of today, not tomorrow. They have a legitimate right to contribute. They can make decisions. And express themselves through art, drama, music, or writing. They can help design, deliver, distribute, deliberate, or discuss whatever adults are doing. And they should.

A few other thoughts are crucial. Teach every lesson as if it is the last. Never assume a teenage visitor will return. Conclude every lesson with a "life action" challenge. Don't just talk about how the Scriptures apply; do something. Finally, hold learners accountable for personal life commitments. Make sure they are doing what they promised to do.

What about Writing My Own Lessons?

Many teen teachers write their own material. Unfortunately, many of those lessons can be boring, or over the student's head, or biblically shallow.

Building a lesson is like making a camera. It takes some time, a lot of work, and in the end, it will probably develop something. However, it is easier and usually better to leave the job to those who make cameras for a living.

Curriculum is no different. Purchased curriculum from a reputable company is far superior to most homemade jobs. They have more creative learning methods. They list established objectives. They write better questions and transition statements. And they require less personal preparation. Today's youth curriculum is more cutting edge, innovative, and creative than ever and is quite adaptable to any size group.

Skillful teachers tend to use (and enjoy) established curricula.

It is interesting that those who are skillful teachers tend to use (and enjoy) established curricula. Why? They can then spend their time in classroom preparation rather than lesson development, calling students, doing research, developing a creative twist, or pursuing personal spiritual growth. In the end, these activities make teaching much more enjoyable.

What about Discipline Problems?

It sounds strange but true: *it may be good for a kid to act up in class*. Why? The young person is sending a message to you, an important message that communicates something is wrong. Either your teaching subject is too hard or too shallow or your activities are a bit goofy. Perhaps you haven't paid them any attention for awhile. Or maybe they just feel a bit out of place.

Remember that "belonging" is a basic adolescent need. And, according to psychologist Rudolf Dreikurs, when the goal of belonging is not met, the teenager will pursue other "mistaken" goals. The first is simple "attention-getting." Ninety percent of classroom problems are just flags for attention, but most are easily resolved.

If appropriate attention isn't gained, the student will move to power plays. The purpose is to assume a winner (who tends to be the teacher). Consequently, ill-fated power plays lead to "revenge" where the student vows to hurt the learning environment, including the teacher, in any way possible. Finally, if things don't change or the student is punished into submission, a student simply withdraws altogether—silent, seething submission—all because the primary need to belong wasn't met.

Proactive discipline prevents many classroom problems. Remove objects ("let me see that hat, please") or eliminate distractions ("let's shut that curtain now") or control the classroom environment (heat/cold, lighting) before the lesson begins. It is also important to pay every student some attention prior to and during class. Learn about their week or a personal hobby. Talk about Friday's ball game or ask about a prayer need. Address them by name while teaching. Make eye contact. And smile.

**A student must be plugged in, turned on, and tuned in
for maximum attention.**

Finally, use creative methods to bring distracted students back on track. Insert their name into a sentence. Use a visual (toss an apple) or audio (noisemaker) cue. Stand on a chair. Or simply lip-synch (mouth the words) what you should be saying aloud. You will get their attention and a few smiles. And then make a quick assessment of the situation to figure out why they disengaged. A student is like a radio. It must be plugged in (participating), turned on (listening), and tuned in (applying) for maximum attention.

Conclusion

Adolescent ministry, including teaching, is wonderful, exciting, and rewarding. Young people are quite impressionable by those whom they have come to admire and respect. Furthermore, the quest to help all teenagers mature in positive ways—whether physically, emotionally, mentally, morally, or spiritually—is a privileged honor.

---

p r o j e c t s

★ Go to a teenage hangout (mall, amusement park, ballgame) and observe teenage behavior. How are they alike? Different? ★

★ Research how the media portrays teenagers. View television shows or movies with adolescents. Read a teenage magazine (*16*, *Young Miss*, *Rolling Stone*). Or watch MTV. How would you think a teenager would view these materials? Why? Are there any illustrations the church (or a teacher) could use to reach her adolescents? Which ones? ★

★ Think back to your own teenage Bible class. What do you remember? Which lessons do you recall? What impressions do you have of your teacher? Why? Any memorable learning experiences? Explain. ★

For Further Reading

Bo Boshers
Student Ministry for the 21st Century. Grand Rapids: Zondervan, 1997.

Les Christie
How to Work with Rude, Obnoxious and Apathetic Kids. Wheaton, IL: Victor, 1994.

David Elkind
All Grown Up and No Place to Go. Reading, MA: Addison-Wesley, 1984.

Doug Fields
Purpose-Driven Youth Ministry. Grand Rapids: Youth Specialties/Zondervan, 1998.

Howard Hendricks
Teaching to Change Lives. Sisters, OR: Multnomah Press, 1987.

David Lynn
Talksheets. Grand Rapids: Youth Specialties/Zondervan, 1987.

Bill McNabb and Steven Mabry
Teaching the Bible Creatively: How to Awaken Your Kids to Scripture. Grand Rapids: Youth Specialties/Zondervan, 1987.

Thom and Joani Schultz
Do It! Active Learning in Youth Ministry. Loveland, CO: Group, 1989.
Why Nobody Learns Much of Anything at Church (And How to Fix It). Loveland, CO: Group, 1993.

Bruce Wilkinson
The Seven Laws of the Learner. Sisters, OR: Multnomah Press, 1992.

CHAPTER 10
THE CHURCH'S MINISTRY TO
ADULTS

Chapter Ten Summary
- ☑ Adult S.S. member profiles/scenarios
- ☑ Characteristics of each level of adulthood
- ☑ Ministry to singles
- ☑ Adult learner assumptions
- ☑ Adult programming possibilities

Adults come in all sizes and shapes—young, old, well-to-do, needy, well educated, minimally educated, large, small, outgoing, shy. But they, of all people in the church, need to grow to maturity in Jesus Christ. After all, they lead families and churches and communities who look to them to model a growing faith in Christ.

Every church must invest in its adults. Though children and youth are important—and often called "the church of tomorrow"—adults are the church of today, and they shape the lives of children and adults far more than church leadership alone can. The church that intends to develop a strong program of Christian education must know who the adults are in the congregation, unique features of adult learning, and how to shape adult programs and lessons to stimulate growth.

Who Are These Adults

Join me for a visit to a real class in a real church—Any Church, we will call it. This class has been in existence for a couple of years. It was begun with the intent that anyone of any age or marital status would feel welcome. Meet:

✎ Dale and Jane, a couple in their 50s. Owners of their own business, they work long hours, but they are quite involved in the church, he as an elder and children's teacher, she in women's ministries and adult Bible studies. They have two children—both adults living in other states. They helped launch this class, providing strong leadership. She is on the leadership team for the class.

✎ Gail, a married woman in her 50s. Though her husband attends worship fairly regularly, he does not attend Bible classes. They have two children, both married and living some distance away. They frequently visit one of their children, the one who is the parent of their only grandchild. She is a nurse at a local hospital.

✎ Bill and Donna, a couple in their late 40s. Both Bill's mother and stepfather have died within the past year. Both work in human resource areas in their respective companies. They have two children, one an adult living in their city, the other away at college. He has been an elder in the church in the past. She grew up in the congregation.

✎ Eric and Barbara, a couple in their mid-40s. They are the parents of two daughters—one married with a preschool child, the other to be married in a few months. He supervises and opens facilities for a major store chain; she is a receptionist for a dentist. Both are involved in the church, she more consistently than he. She sings in the choir, works in the nursery once a month, and leads in women's work.

✎ Leah, a married woman in her 50s. Her husband attends worship services regularly, but does not participate in a Bible class. She is an early childhood teacher. At church she works with children. She has two children, one married, the other in college.

✎ Jim and Connie, a couple in their 40s. They recently moved to the community. On the way, they experienced a serious automobile accident that they miraculously escaped without permanent physical damage. He has children from a previous marriage. They are working hard to begin a new business and are overwhelmed with all that has happened to them in the past six months.

- Joe and Susan, a couple in their 50s. Both have been married before: her first husband died of cancer; he was divorced. She has two children, he one. He is an engineer, she a teacher. He is a shy man who finds it difficult to participate in groups.
- Roger and Carol, a couple in their 30s. His father died less than a year ago. They have two preschool daughters.
- Sergio and Alzira, a couple from South America. In their early 30s, he is a student at a local seminary. They have one preschool daughter. He preached in his native country. They have a struggle making ends meet because of the devalued currency from their home country and the limitation on how many hours he can work while he is in school.
- Carol, a single woman in her early 40s. She has a PhD and is a professor at a nearby Christian college. She spends her summers in her home state helping in the family business.
- Thelma, a single woman in her 60s. A retired nurse, she moved to this community from a southern state. She is involved in many community events.
- Frances, a married woman in her 70s. Her husband teaches a Bible class away from the church building on Sunday morning. They spent many years in ministry. She is a retired teacher.
- Jean, a divorced woman in her early 40s. She is a bank teller and quite involved in a variety of community activities. She also serves on the leadership team for the class.
- Ann, a divorced woman in her late 60s. She is retired. Since retirement, she has contended with cancer. As a result, she is erratic in attendance.
- Tom, a divorced man in his 40s. A physician, he is a quiet man who has experienced a spiritual reawakening since his divorce. He has one small daughter to whom he is devoted. He serves on the leadership team for the class.
- Joy, a married woman in her 60s. A longtime member of the church, she attends the class, though her husband does not, because she is seeking a deepening faith.
- Tim and Grace, a couple in their early 50s. He is a development officer for a local institution, she a real estate agent. They have two adult children, both living in the city from which they moved a few years ago.

✎ Russ and Pam, a couple in their 50s. Both have professional positions. They have two children, both adults and both living away from their city.

✎ George, a married man in his 40s. His wife teaches children in the Sunday school so attends only social events with him. They have two children, one in college, the other a senior in high school. He is an engineer. He is a Roman Catholic who has attended this congregation for several years. He is on the leadership team for the class.

✎ Rebecca, a divorced woman in her 60s. Though she retired as a librarian several years ago, she again works part-time as a librarian for a local Christian college. She has one son who lives in a neighboring state.

✎ Jill, a married woman in her early 40s. Her husband attends social events with her but rarely attends worship or a Bible class. She is an accountant. They have one preschool daughter.

✎ Joan, a divorced woman in her late 40s. She is a teacher, but this year she has taken a leave of absence and is completing her masters degree at the local university.

✎ Gil and Allison, a couple in their 40s. Both work at the local university, he in an administrative position. They have three children. She is working on a masters degree. He is on the leadership team for the class and is a deacon.

✎ Joel and Jeanne, a fortyish couple. They both work, he a lot of overtime. His mother died a few weeks ago. They have one son, an early teenager.

✎ Graham and Margaret, a thirtyish couple. Both are physical therapists. They recently had their first child, a little boy, who was born several weeks prematurely. They are still waiting to bring him home from the hospital.

✎ Julie, a single woman in her 40s. She lives with chronic and severe pain. A newcomer to the class, she is as faithful to the class as her pain allows her to be.

✎ Jack and Karen, a couple in their 40s. He is an insurance adjuster, she a teacher. They are new to the congregation within the past year. She serves on the leadership team for the class.

Add to that list another eight or ten folks who attend now and then. And when you scan the list, you find a montage demonstrating the immense diversity of almost any adult group. This class is unlikely to be vastly different from an adult class in many different churches.

We could categorize these adults in many different ways. One helpful way is to describe the developmental changes that occur through the adult life span.

Young Adults

Young adulthood extends from age 18 or 19 to approximately age 40. At least four distinct subperiods can be identified.

The years from 18-22, or perhaps 23, can be described as a time of "pulling up roots." These young adults are leaving home, if not physically, certainly emotionally. Many of them leave their homes, at least for most of the year, as they enroll in colleges and live in housing on or near their campus. If they enroll in a college near home, they still undergo major changes.

Young adults must finish off psychological identification, i.e., they must decide who they are as a person apart from their parents. This is usually marked by reconsideration of values and faith. They must decide if they will adopt for their own the values they have been taught by their families and church. It is also a time of decision-making—whether or not to go to college, what vocation to pursue, entering more serious dating relationships. Unless the church makes an intentional, sustained effort to minister to young adults, they all too easily can put the church at the periphery of their lives. Sensitive leaders who understand the changes of this age can make a significant contribution to the lives of these young adults.

Young adults must decide who they are as persons apart from their parents.

After college, or a few years in the work force, young adults make a transition to the responsibilities of adulthood. They get started in their vocations—or pursue graduate work, often while working; they get married; they may have their first child; they often buy a house and take on added financial obligations. They must learn to live intimately with others, usually worked out in marriage. They are often transient on Sunday—the weekend, after all, is their free time, they reason. A positive young adult study group meets the need for learning to live in accountability with others. The effective leader understands the on-again, off-again nature of their attendance—but ministers anyway.

Young adults move into a 30s transition from 28-32 (or thereabouts). This is often a time of vague unrest and reevaluation, especially in regard to vocation. Couples who have delayed having children often revisit that decision. Many young adults at this age are taking on civic and church responsibilities. Leaders and teachers of these young adults must minister to the needs that may be easily hidden from view.

The 30s take on a definite orderliness that was nonexistent in the 20s. That is often the result of taking on additional family, civic, and church responsibilities. For many, children are reaching middle school age, with all of the demands that makes on parents and children. Some, those who were the younger children in their families, watch their parents grow older, perhaps die. This reality often shakes their security—and elicits a time of reevaluation not unlike that of a decade earlier. For some, the demands become overwhelming. This is too often a time when marriages fail and family relationships are disrupted. Some who have been away from the church for years revisit their faith and find there solace and strength for their challenges and failures.

Middle Adulthood

Middle adulthood extends from about age 40 to 65, again a wide span with many changes to confront. The decade of the 40s seems to be an especially vulnerable time. Some describe those in this age range as the sandwich generation: their children are moving away from the family while parents are growing older, sometimes dying. All of this occurs when professionals are taking on added responsibility in their jobs. In recent years, the job climate has been uncertain and workers feel pressured to perform in their work. If the 30s seemed overwhelming, the 40s are more so.

Middle adults not only experience the pressures of family and work; they are also changing physically themselves, a reminder that aging is a reality of life. It isn't that they are old, but they do receive frequent reminders that aging is real: bifocal glasses, an assortment of physical maladies, sometimes the beginning of menopause for women, graying hair. Any of these signs can become a symbol to the person experiencing it and raise certain insecurities.

Some who study adult development suggest that the decade of the 40s is critical in determining how we will grow old. They suggest that we may take one of three routes—and that we probably have made the decision by about age 50. Some become middle-aged kids. They abdicate responsibility and revert to adolescent behavior. Others, however, settle into defenders of the status quo. They expect not to change themselves—and they want no one else to either. They settle down and grow old prematurely. Others consider the issues and develop an understanding of what is occurring. They reconsider their values and perhaps make significant adjustments. But in the end, they are renewed and grow older gracefully.

**Some suggest that the decade of the 40s
is critical in determining how we will grow old.**

The decade of the 50s and early 60s brings additional changes, often a refinement of the changes begun in the 40s. It is a time of the empty nest in a marriage, an opportunity to renew the marriage. It is a time of planning for retirement—even sometimes actually retiring. For those who have renewed themselves as they enter the latter years of middle age, wisdom becomes valued above physical skills. It is frequently a time for spiritual reevaluation. An awareness that they are the older generation often pushes them into deciding how they will leave their legacy. That, of course, may be realized by investing in children and grandchildren. But it may also be experienced through mentoring and service to others.

Older Adulthood

Not a "period of decline," as some have described older adulthood in the past, older adulthood nonetheless brings significant changes. But these changes often are a satisfying conclusion to life.

Younger older adults are usually still quite active and can use their early retirement years traveling, working part-time, becoming involved in ministry activities, and doing volunteer work in the community. Though most experience some physical ailments, they are by no means "old." They are especially effective in carrying out ministry to their peers and those just older themselves. Many adults fit this description until well into their 70s—or even early 80s. Sooner or later, however, the aging process begins to take its toll, slowing seniors down, though by no means totally debilitating most of them.

Aging is experienced differently by different adults.

Aging is experienced differently by different adults. Aging is an interaction of genetic endowment, lifestyle, and attitudinal outlook. Some do grow old early because of physical problems such as Alzheimer's or heart trouble or disabling arthritis. The aging process in others is slowed significantly because of good physical and medical care, good nutrition, and a positive attitude.

Older adults are defined by far more than physical features. The major task of older adulthood is to bring their lives to a close with integrity. They are making sense out of their stories. And they need to sense satisfaction with their stories. This becomes increasingly an issue as people move into their waning years. They often tell stories reflecting on their childhood and young adulthood. They may have issues to settle with their families. But in the end, they need to come to a sense of satisfaction with their lives, to say with the apostle Paul, "I have fought the good fight; I have kept the faith."

The Case of Singles

Our description of adulthood provides a sweep of the general changes that occur. But some experience adulthood somewhat differently because they are single.

Singles comprise an increasingly larger proportion of American adults. In 1996, 47 percent of adults were single (compared to 5 percent in 1900): never married, divorced, widowed, or separated. The total adult population includes 27 percent never married, 7 percent widowed, 9 percent divorced, and 3 percent separated.

Most churches have many singles at the various stages of adulthood. I was asked several years ago to develop an adult class for women 35 to 65 years of age. When we surveyed the congregation to determine our potential audience, we found about 15 per cent of the adult attendance composed of single women in this category. Add to that the younger singles, older singles, and men, and you have the picture. It was a real surprise to a congregation that liked to think of itself as a "family church."

The adult population includes 27% never married, 7% widowed, 9% divorced, and 3% separated.

Divorced singles are represented especially in the middle adult ages. Divorce at any age and for either gender brings with it guilt and anger and the need to resolve the issues that contributed to the divorce in the first place. Many divorced people return to the church, realizing for the first time in a long time their spiritual needs. They need a place of warmth and caring so they do not have to seek that in unproductive places. They may need practical caring: help with children, financial advice, dating skills, to name a few.

The church has often had difficulty understanding the realities of divorce and dealing with the divorced. By definition, the church is committed to monogamous, lifelong marriage. But regardless of the commitment, many experience failure and need the healing the church can give. Church leaders must decide how to minister to the divorced without condoning the action.

Widowed adults are those who have lost a spouse. Although those at any age may experience the grief of losing a loved one, most widowed adults are in their 60s and beyond. These singles experience most of the same needs as divorced adults.

Never married singles have never been married. Most of these are in their 20s and early 30s. It would be more accurate to say they are temporarily single. Perhaps the major issue for them is the need to meet other singles of faith. Older never marrieds must find productive ways to determine that they have left a legacy to the next generation. Since they do not have children and grandchildren, they may need extra care and teaching to resolve this challenge positively.

What May We Assume about Adult Learners?

Malcolm Knowles, often called the "Father of Adult Education," has developed what he calls the science of *andragogy*, i.e., the science of teaching adults. In his books *The Adult Learner: A Neglected Species* (1973) and *The Modern Practice of Adult Education* (1980), he gives careful attention to the unique characteristics of adult learners. The following list is adapted from his work:

✎ Adults can learn. The old adage, "You can't teach an old dog new tricks," is absolutely false. The New Testament makes it clear that adult believers are expected to grow in their Christian walk. Research demonstrates that the average adult engages in eight learning projects each year (Tough, 1967, 1979).

✎ Adults are experienced. They have a range of experiences—both good and bad—that they bring with them to classes. Those experiences are educational, vocational, family, and spiritual.

✎ Adults attend learning groups for a variety of reasons. Cyril Houle (1979) found that adults he studied attend because they are goal-oriented (they have clear objectives), activity-oriented (they are there to enjoy the people and the process), and learner-oriented (they learn for the sake of learning).

✎ Adult learners want to be respected. They do not tolerate ridicule, condescension, embarrassment, and irrelevancy.

✎ They expect comfort in the classroom. This ranges from physical to psychological comfort.

✎ Adults may not always attend. Sometimes they do not attend for good reason—family responsibilities or work, for example. But they make the choice to attend.

✎ Adults sometimes resist change. They have accumulated enough experience to know that not every change is positive. Sometimes they experience overwhelming change over which they have no control, making them more resistant to the change they can control. But adults can change and most will change if they are respected and given enough time and reason to change.

✎ Adults learn best when they are involved. Involvement need not mean physical activity or even talking. But it does mean that the learner must discover the relevancy of what is being learned and has been engaged in the mental process.

Adults learn best when they are involved.

Adult teachers are well advised to understand these principles, wrestle with the implications for their teaching, and weave them into their teaching style.

Designing Adult Education Programs

The Importance of Adult Education

In 1990, the Search Institute released its seminal study reported in *Effective Christian Education: A National Study of Protestant Congregations* (Benson and Eklin). The study reported that only 28 percent of adults in the average congregation participated in any kind of adult study group. The report further outlined the sad status of adult faith development among adults. The study also identified factors in congregations engaging in effective Christian education for adults. Though the study can be criticized for some of the operational definitions used, it, as a whole, still gives helpful insight into what is involved in effective Christian education for adults.

Five key factors were identified as contributing to the development of faith among adults.

❶ A warm climate. Though the worship service contributes to this sense, it alone cannot achieve the sense of a warm climate. It is done best through a small group, such as an adult Sunday school class.

❷ A thinking climate. Our faith has both cognitive and emotional components. The adult study group contributes significantly to both.

❸ Uplifting worship. Worship should be dynamic and inspirational. Preaching needs to make sense of the struggle of life. The liturgy itself should be built carefully and feature the reading of God's Word.

❹ Receiving care. Adult classes and groups can play a crucial role in providing the pastoral care that everyone needs at one time or another.

❺ Service to others. Churches and adult small groups must plan and implement meaningful service opportunities both inside and outside the congregation.

If these are the key factors, churches must decide how they will implement them through the various worship, teaching, and service opportunities offered to the congregation.

Sara Little in a chapter entitled "Rethinking Christian Education," in *Rethinking Christian Education* (Schuller, 106-110) suggests that adult Christian education needs to be guided by the following principles in the future:

✎ Adults may learn as much from knowing-in-action as from formal study. This isn't to denigrate formal study, but it is to insist that we plan a balanced program of adult education.

✎ Proactive plans need to be developed by leaders for what adults need to know and be able to do if they are to fulfill their responsibilities to grow and to contribute to the common good.

✎ Consideration of a variety of settings is essential to comprehensive planning for adult education.

✎ The metaphor of "spiderweb" may be more appropriate than "stairsteps" for planning adult education. Borrowing from Elliott Eisners' *The Educational Imagination*, she suggests that congregations think of a variety of resources, settings, and topics for Christian education.

✎ Self-directed learning or distance education or computer programs may present further possibilities. These will be especially valuable for self-directed learning projects.

✎ Adult education cannot further faith maturity unless it is undertaken in the context of some unifying purpose, cause, or mission.

Programming Possibilities

Sunday School Classes are perhaps the core of adult education in most congregations. The Sunday school allows adult learners to gather in groups smaller than the corporate worship service. Classes can provide warmth and caring. Service opportunities can be planned and carried out through classes. All of these components should be present. But it is the thinking climate that adult classes can best provide. Systematic, thoughtful biblical study should be at the heart of the adult class designed to promote the development of faith.

Small Groups. An increasingly popular approach to adult education over the past decade or so is the concept of small groups. These small groups are usually designed to provide some Bible study, though usually not as systematically developed as in the Sunday school. But groups are also small enough to provide a particularly warm and caring climate. This makes groups especially valuable for reaching out to those who would never attend a service at the church building. Small groups may meet at a restaurant during a meal, in homes, at places of business over the lunch hour, or at the church building. They can be formed as men only, women only, or mixed groups.

Small group studies are especially valuable for reaching out to those who would never attend a service at the church building.

Elective Classes. Many churches have meetings on Sunday evening and Wednesday evening. Education leaders are increasingly planning these to include studies in greater depth than can be pursued in either Sunday school or small groups. They often also include skills classes to encourage individuals to develop their own ministry competency.

Support Groups. Most churches include a number of people who have special needs, some ongoing, some shorter term. They may find a cluster of people in their congregation and community to form a support group. These groups have been formed using all kinds of themes: parents of prodigals, survivors of child abuse, women who are victims of spouse abuse, diet groups, alcoholism recovery, adult children of alcoholics, gamblers, and just about any other kind of topic you can imagine. Not every church can or should do all of these—but many churches could consider providing at least one support group. These groups contribute to warmth and caring, a bit to education.

A forgotten teaching source in many churches is the library.

Church Library. A forgotten teaching source in many churches is the library. Well developed with new and classical materials, a library can be a significant influence to those pursuing individual study projects. It can readily contribute to the development of a thinking climate. Though the library is by no means confined to meeting the needs of adults, it is an important adult education tool.

Retreats. Retreats contribute to the development and education of adults. These may be family retreats or couples' retreats or marriage enrichment or a women's or men's retreat. But if they are planned carefully, they serve a valuable educational purpose.

Alvin Kuest's chapter "Developing a Balanced Christian Education Program" explores these—and more—opportunities for adult education in the church. Read it with this survey of possibilities in mind.

Structuring Adult Lessons

Adult teachers should understand the particular purposes for the class they are teaching. Though the proportion of time will vary from one purpose to another and from one teaching session to another, adult classes should have built into each session a time of fellowship, interaction and prayer, Bible teaching, Bible application, and call for response. Each session must be developed carefully and thoroughly in order to provide a thinking environment. Class interaction, both inside and outside of class, must also become a priority—and be just as carefully planned as the lesson itself.

Consult the chapter "Curriculum for Christian Education" for a detailed description of how to develop a teaching session. This is especially useful in preparing adult class sessions. In short, however, we may picture a class session in this way.

Title: The Visited Planet (1)

Scripture: Matthew 1:18-25

Central Truth: God chose to visit planet Earth in wholly unexpected ways to reach the humble and outcast.

Objectives:

1. Contrast the reality of the first Christmas with how we often observe it.
2. Thank God that He came to redeem the humble, outcast, and downtrodden as well as the "accepted" or "elite" of society.

Fellowship (9:40-9:50)	
	Rebecca—have coffee ready when class members come.
	Eleanor—greet and talk with people as they come.
	Rebecca—preside over opening—prayer requests, announcements, and opening prayer.

Hook (9:50-10:00)	Put a variety of Christmas cards on each table before class begins.
Last week we took our first look at Jesus and how He is described inside and outside the church. Let's move now to a natural starting place—His birth.	
Look at the Christmas cards on your table. Share the messages with each other.	
After class members have had time to look at the cards, ask:	
1. What kinds of scenes did you find?	
2. What kinds of statements were in the cards?	
3. What do these statements say to Christians?	
4. What do the statements say to non-Christians?	
Book (10:00-10:20)	
✦ Matthew 1:18-25	Read
✦ Now let's look at a dramatic portrayal of Joseph's concerns.	Video clip
Jewish marriage customs:	
1. Engagement—arranged by parents	
2. Betrothal—ratification of the engagement; binding; for one year; terminated only by divorce.	
3. Marriage	
✦ How did the Bible account compare/contrast with the video portrayal?	Discussion
✦ How did the video portrayal help you understand the biblical text?	
✦ What aspect of this account seems most incredible?	
Look (10:20-10:27)	
✦ What do we learn about God from this account?	Discussion
Comes to the humble	
Approachable	
Underdog	
Courageous	

Took (10:27-10:30)	Read p. 42 in Yancey, *The Jesus I Never Knew*
Prayer	

Adult teachers have a variety of methods from which to choose. The primary methods of teaching are discussion, lecture, learning activities, or a combination of the three. Even a dominantly discussion or activity-based lesson will include some lecture, though the lecture sections should be short. Many of the methods used for children—some kinds of art, music, and drama—are effective in teaching adults if it is used to achieve a specific purpose. Adults, however, do not enjoy activities that have no purpose or meaning other than to provide variety. Any method may be an effective method if it is chosen carefully to achieve a specific purpose. An important principle is to plan for variety in presentation: never let the learners be able to predict exactly what will happen in a teaching session.

Conclusion

Adults are a precious resource for the church. They have particular needs that should be met in the teaching program of the church. They can and do learn. But they learn best when teachers understand their unique needs and learning characteristics and design lessons and experiences to stimulate thinking and involve them in the learning process. Adult education is crucial—both for now and the future—as these capable learners are motivated to grow more and more into the image of Christ.

p r o j e c t s

★ Interview a dozen adults. Be sure that they represent the various divisions of adulthood. Find out what they see as their biggest concerns. Find out what appeals to them in an adult Bible class. Compare your interview results with the textbook descriptions. ★

★ Observe an adult Bible class. How was it taught? Compare the class with the guidelines described in this chapter. Did the teacher understand adult learners? ·How was this demonstrated? What could the teacher have done better? ★

★ Plan a Bible lesson for adults using Ephesians 4:17–5:7 as your text. Use the lesson plan in this chapter as your pattern. ★

For Further Reading

Kenneth Gangel and James Wilhoit
The Christian Educator's Handbook of Adult Education. Glen Ellyn, IL: Victor Books, 1993.

Cyril Houle
The Inquiring Mind. Madison, WI: University of Wisconsin Press, 1961.

Albert Y. Hsu
Singles at the Crossroads. Downers Grove, IL: NavPress, 1997.

Malcolm Knowles
The Adult Learner: A Neglected Species. Houston: Gulf Publishing Company, 1973.
The Modern Practice of Adult Education. Rev. ed. Chicago: Follett, 1980.

Neil McBride
How to Build a Small Groups Ministry. Colorado Springs: NavPress, 1996.

Eugene Roehlkepartain
The Teaching Church. Nashville: Abingdon Press, 1993.

David S. Schuller, ed.

Rethinking Christian Education. St. Louis: Chalice Press, 1993.

Charles Sell

Transitions. Grand Rapids: Zondervan, 1991.

Alan Tough

Learning without a Teacher. Toronto: Ontario Institute for Studies in Education, 1967.

The Adult's Learning Projects. 2nd ed. Toronto: Ontario Institute for Studies in Education, 1979.

CHAPTER 11
PROVIDING CHRISTIAN EDUCATION FOR
PERSONS WITH DISABILITIES

Chapter Eleven Summary

- ☑ 6 concepts for developing a disabilities program ministry
- ☑ Common disability categories
- ☑ What to avoid in a disability ministry
- ☑ Ministry to the families of the disabled

A teacher in the Sunday school reports that a six-year-old with cerebral palsy is attending her class regularly and she needs some help.

A new family, with a ten-year-old daughter with autism, wants to join the congregation. They ask the Thursday night caller what programs the church has for their daughter.

A teenager in your youth group has just been involved in a head-on collision, sustaining a severe spinal cord injury. A therapist recommends that he should stay involved in the youth group.

A young couple in your church has just had their first child, a little boy with Down's syndrome.

If you, as a prospective Christian educator, were faced with providing service to these students and their families, what would you do? If you don't know, the material in this chapter is meant to give you the basic information to develop plans for ministry.

The likelihood of dealing with such situations is real. In America, 54 million people have some type of disability. This census fact means one in five people. It also means some of them are living in the area served by your present or future church. Further, it means you have a challenge to teach the eternal truth of God's Word to some people who really need it.

Church leaders often report, "We don't have any of those people in our church. So, we don't need to start a program." If no one with a disability is attending your church, the reason could be that there is not a program or an accepting environment. Work to change the report to, "Let's search for people with disabilities in our community and invite them to learn about Jesus in the loving, accepting environment of our congregation."

To accomplish this worthy goal, you should know six concepts:
- ❶ Build on Jesus' principles
- ❷ Know some facts about the disability community
- ❸ Develop congregational awareness
- ❹ Make the Christian education program inclusive
- ❺ Minister with the family
- ❻ Realize the result of sharing the gospel makes an eternal difference.

Concept #1: Build on Jesus' Principles

The motivation for including persons with disabilities in the education program of the church should be based on Jesus' mission statement to His disciples before He returned to His Father, "Go into all the world, and preach the gospel to *every* creature" (Mark 16:15, KJV; my emphasis). There is no footnote about exclusions, no suggestion that too much or too little ability makes a difference, no disclaimer. Everyone needs the gospel.

Jesus expects us to follow His example in interacting with people who have disabilities and including them in His church. If we follow Jesus' example, we need to examine some of the principles He used in relation to people with disabilities.

✎ Jesus looked for people with disabilities. If we actively seek them, our Christian education program can provide them with a wonderful banquet featuring the Bread of Life (Luke 14:21-23).

✎ He worked with them one-on-one. Jesus was *seated* when "the lame, the blind, the crippled, the mute, and many others were brought to Him. This fact suggests Jesus interacted with each person individually, not the whole group at the same time (Matthew 15:29-30).

✎ Helping people is more important to Jesus than keeping rules. Critics criticized His healing the man at the pool of Bethesda on the Sabbath (John 5:1-14)!

✎ Our Lord modeled a quick, personal and thorough response to the person's need. He touched a leper. He stopped in mid-step when He heard a plea for help (Luke 5:12-14; 18:40).

Jesus looked for people with disabilities.

✎ Follow-through was a hallmark of His ministry. Jesus first met the person's immediate needs, and then discussed deeper spiritual needs. In the case of healing the blind man, Jesus found him in the temple and encouraged him to stop sinning (John 5:14).

✎ Jesus involved the person with the disability in the ministry process. Jesus didn't discuss the case with a committee or even launch a plan of His own. He asked a man who was blind and a man with a physical disability what they wanted. His approach suggests the focus of the ministry should be *with* the person, not *to* (Mark 10:51 and John 5:6).

✎ He ministered to the family with sensitivity. Jesus radiated a warm concern for the family of the person with a disability by showing interest in them. He asked the father of a young boy how long his son had been disabled (Mark 9:20-24).

✎ He helped the family find meaning in disability. When parents are made to feel blame for the disability of their child, such an approach did not originate with Jesus. In the story in John 9:1-3, He provided a clear answer to the reason for the man's blindness. It was not due to either his sin or that of his parents. It happened "so that the work of God might be displayed in his life." There is no reason to blame, but every reason to support the family, and to extend mercy, kindness, love and hope to each family member.

✎ Friendship is a good ministry method. It gets Jesus' attention. Jesus will respond to the friendship we show to people with disabilities. The faith of the four friends brought healing to the man with a physical disability. Christians should be eager to ignite faith on behalf of persons with disabilities so they and we can grow spiritually (Mark 2:1-5).

Concept #2: Know Some Facts about the Disability Community

A few facts about the disability will help in initiating a Christian education program. It is necessary to know the categories of people with disability. Before we name them, it is urgent to stress that disability, whatever it is named, happens to real people who have God-given souls. See the person, not the disability.

Common Categories of Disability

The school system's categories provide a good place to start.

› **Learning disabilities**. Children with learning disabilities are the largest group receiving special education services in the school system. Students with learning disabilities make up the largest disability group enrolling in college. Three of the most common diagnoses likely to require special attention are dyslexia, Attention Deficit Disorder (ADD) and Attention Deficit with Hyperactivity Disorder (ADHD).

People with learning disabilities have normal and above IQs. Academically, mathematics and reading are difficult. Directions to sit still and to listen create social problems for them. The person will have to learn to cope or use medicine to control the feelings resulting from it.

› **Mental retardation**. These individuals learn more slowly and retain less information than their age-mates. They need help and supervision to be independent. Down's syndrome and Fragile X syndrome are two well-known diagnoses in this category.

› **Gifted**. These students learn quickly, are creative, artistic, have high IQs, excel at academics, are talented, and have broad interests. Christian education can enhance the possibilities of capturing the creative energy of this group for the benefit of the Lord's church.

› **Visual impairment**. This group is the smallest in the disability world. People with vision difficulties fall into two groups. *Visually impaired* means that they use large print to learn, and those who are blind use braille.

› **Hearing impairment**. People with auditory difficulties fall into three groups. Those born without hearing and who did not develop speech are *deaf*; those who had hearing and developed speech, but lost both have been *deafened*. Those whose acuity level has been weakened are *hard-of-hearing*.

It is urgent to stress that disability, whatever it is named, happens to real people, who have God-given souls.

› **Communication disorder**. This category includes students with delays in speech and language abilities. Students with speech disorders experience problems with articulation (not speaking plainly), voice (not appropriate to sex and age), and fluency (stuttering). There may be receptive problems (reading and listening), in which case children with language disorders have difficulty understanding, or problems expressing themselves (speaking and writing), which create difficulties in being understood.

› **Orthopedic impairment**. Learners with cerebral palsy, spina bifida, muscular dystrophy, or missing limbs are representatives of this group.

› **Other health impairment**. People with heart problems, diabetes, asthma, and sickle cell anemia are in this category.

› **Serious emotional disturbance**. Severe problems in relating, coping, and responding are characteristic of these students. Such behaviors interfere with their education and social pursuits.

› **Traumatic brain and spinal cord injury.** Since 1990 the school system has treated this as a separate category. Students with neurological injuries caused by motor vehicle and bicycle accidents, abuse, and sports accidents are assisted with speech production, language comprehension, social skills, learning, psychological problems, and orthopedic needs.

› **Autism (pervasive developmental disorder).** When traumatic brain injury (TBI) became a separate category, so did autism. Learners with a diagnosis of autism receive more focused attention on serious communication and relational deficiencies.

Some other information will further define the disability community and give insights in how to offer meaningful ministry.

✎ Not all people with disabilities are the same. The *degree* or *severity* of the disability can range from mild to severe. Each person has a distinctive personality. Just remember, however, no one functions at a level too low to respond to love and warmth of caring.

Not all people with disabilities are the same.

✎ It is important to know that the age of the person with the disability will determine the services available through public agencies.

✎ From birth to 3 years of age, early intervention developmental programs are standard. They include physical, occupational, and speech therapies, and support for the family and informational programs.

✎ From 3 to 21 years of age, the local school system is responsible for education. Governed by IDEA (Individuals with Disabilities Education Act, Public Law 105-17), the child's educational needs are met if deemed appropriate by a child study committee, commonly called a multi-disciplinary team.

✎ After age 21 or 22, depending on when the person's birthday occurs, community programs in residential, vocational, recreational, and educational areas are available.

✎ The disability world is a world of special transportation limited by the boundaries of the person's ability. After the person is out of school, getting to work, to the mall, or to a sporting event generally does not happen without the help of a family member or friend.

✎ The world of disability is often more medical than the typical world. Persons with disabilities require more medical specialists, more assistive devices, more medications, and more therapy than people without disabilities.

✎ Income in the world of disability varies. It can range from a lot of money to income from sheltered workshops to Social Security. Money can come from a trust fund provided by the family.

✎ Living arrangements may be in a group home, independent, or supported living in the community, at home with the family, or in a house of their own.

✎ The language of the world of disability is more than politically correct; it is kinder and more gentle. "Disability" is the in-word. "Handicapped" is the correct word to use when talking about a person being hampered by architectural barriers or attitudes. For example, "He is handicapped by the low expectations of his parents."

Use people-first language. Don't say, "the retarded" or "the cerebral palsied." Say rather, "Sue has mental retardation" or "people with cerebral palsy.

Avoid the words, "cripple," "deaf and dumb," "slow," "crazy," "invalid," "acts funny." In the same vein, expressions like "afflicted with," "a victim of," and "suffers from" lead to pity and sympathy rather than respect and acceptance. When conveying that the person does not have a disability, avoid the word "normal." The terms "typical" or a "person without a disability" are nicer.

Don't describe people with disabilities as special, overly courageous, exceptionally brave, or superhuman.

Don't describe people with disabilities as special, overly courageous, exceptionally brave, or superhuman.

The language of assistive devices, mobility, and adaptive equipment should be kind and gentle. Choose "Fred uses a wheelchair" rather than "Fred is confined to a wheelchair," "Joyce uses sign language" instead of "Joyce talks with her hands."

Concept #3: Make the Christian Education Program Inclusive

The concept of inclusion has developed steadily in the American community in the last few years. The growth started in 1975 when a mandatory education act (then Public Law 94-142, now IDEA) was passed. The law mandates that students with a disability be educated in their neighborhood school with their age-mates. "Mainstreaming" became "inclusion" and now we deal with "full inclusion." Inclusion is the process of offering more independence and more complete participation in the community. The process creates a good arena for people to develop their potential.

The concept of inclusion has developed steadily in the American community in the last few years.

The legal community has provided impetus for inclusion. Coupled with the 1990 Americans with Disabilities Act, the concept of equality under the law continues to expand. While the laws that have made the community more accessible to persons with disabilities do not address their spiritual needs, the church has a higher law and a stronger example to govern its actions.

How are churches across America doing with inclusion? The evidence is mixed. Some families say that their congregations have nothing to offer their children with a disability. Other families report that their congregations are doing a great job meeting their spiritual needs and those of their children.

The church has a higher law and a stronger example to govern its actions.

A recent Louis Harris poll [National Organization on Disability, *Closing the Gap: The N.O.D./Harris Survey of Americans with Disabilities—A Summary*, Washington, DC, 1994] reported that 36 percent of Americans with disabilities attend religious services at least once a week, and 49 percent attend at least once a month. These attendance levels are just a little lower than among adults without disabilities, 58 percent of whom attend religious services at least once a month. From some unknown source, I have quoted the statistic that only 5 percent of persons with disabilities have a relationship with the church. If the percentage is correct, the Harris poll seems to suggest that this situation is improving. Reports of churches opening their doors to persons with disabilities are increasing. It is a trend that will continue when Christian educators include all learners in their efforts.

The answer to achieving full inclusion is to provide the church community with the information that will assist in including the disability community. Follow these steps.

STEP ONE: Educate church leaders about the disability community, reminding them that the soul is the most important part of the person. The church staff should realize that while people with disabilities may have specific limitations, they can learn about Jesus' love and God's word.

Sharing the following statistics with the church leadership will underscore the reason for the church's involvement.

- Nine out of ten women who find through amniocentesis that their unborn child has Down's syndrome choose to abort.
- Four out of five marriages that either produce a child with a disability or include a spouse who becomes disabled through accident or disease will end in divorce.
- The incidence of abuse in families with a disabled child is twice that of typical families.
- Children with cognitive problems are subject to abuse ten times more than typical children.

✎ Siblings of a child with a disability are four times more likely to be maladjusted than their peers who have typical siblings.

✎ 85 percent of persons with mental retardation can learn on an adult level. The important factor in learning and functioning is mental age, not chronological age.

STEP TWO: Recommend that the church host a disability awareness Sunday or weekend. Such an event will enable members to know more about people with disabilities, be more sensitive to their needs, know that their spiritual needs are as important as those of typical people, be motivated to include them, and know that the most important part of the person is the soul.

Suggest that the event have the following components:

✎ A theme. "The Variety in Ability" and "Christ's Love Is Inclusive and Accessible" are good suggestions. Stress the theme on an attractive bulletin cover.

✎ A sermon. Using a Scripture event describing Jesus' encounter with disability is always good. It gives a biblical foundation for the ministry.

✎ Music. Using any of the many hymns written by Fanny Crosby will speak to the value of people with disabilities using their talents in the church. (Fanny Crosby was blind from the age of six weeks.)

The most important part of the person is the soul.

✎ Special music. There are many possibilities; a good one is "Sometimes Miracles Hide" (Word, 1991).

✎ A testimony. Having a family tell of the importance of developing faith in their child helps the congregation see that all Christian parents treasure faith and want their children to have it.

✎ Personnel with disabilities. Use people with disabilities to serve as ushers, sing, play an instrument, or read Scripture.

✎ Sunday school. Have every teacher in the Sunday school department teach the same lesson, using a story from Jesus' ministry which can be applied to all age groups.

✎ Ideas. Have a member of the congregation spend the day in a wheelchair, another blindfolded, another with both hands bandaged, and another wearing earplugs. At some point, having them report their experiences will help everyone to have some indication of how disability feels.

STEP THREE: Suggest that a simple survey be put in a church publication to locate people with disabilities and families already associated with your congregation who need ministry. Define clearly what is meant by disability and what your church will do. Convey your interest in people with disabilities and your desire to minister to them. Use a follow-up survey to identify needs in the church family and members who are willing to be involved in meeting those needs.

STEP FOUR: Organize a disability ministry team task force to analyze the results of the two surveys. Put into place the services or programs that will accommodate the spiritual needs of the people already associated in some way. The Sunday school is an ideal place to begin.

Concept # 4: Make the Christian Education Program Inclusive

Teaching the broad range of people with disabilities in the Christian education programs is not as difficult as it might seem. It takes a plan. Study the following eight steps.

❶ Assemble an inclusion team made up of the minister or his representative, Christian education staff member, parents of a child with disabilities, parents of children without disabilities, and the teachers. This group discusses what the students, parents, and the church will do to meet the spiritual needs of the student. Having representatives of parents without a child with a disability will provide assurances that every child's needs will be met and the program understood.

❷ Record the Individual Christian Education Plan. Put the plan in writing. Set goals. Provide time limits. Assign responsibilities.

❸ Prepare the learners with disabilities and those without disabilities for the process. Explaining to the children without disabilities the nature of the disability will make the first meeting easier.

❹ Provide assistance for the teacher. Be sure there is enough help in the classroom. Train volunteers.

❺ Train the students without disabilities to help. Having peer tutors and "buddies" in place will enhance learning for everyone and encourage relationships.

❻ Evaluate the progress the learner is making. Record the results of the strides the student is making in his learning of Sunday school materials.

❼ Plan activities that will open the community for the child. Making it easy for the child to go on picnics, and other church outings will carry over the purpose of the inclusion process.

❽ Offer some practical tips to the Sunday school teacher to aid the inclusion of students with specific diagnoses.

Having peer tutors and "buddies" in place will enhance learning for everyone and encourage relationships.

Students with Mental Retardation

1. Routine is important. It provides stability and continuity.

2. Use concrete language. Teach concepts that can be illustrated by the five senses.

3. Remember that these students need more time for learning. Repetition is the key to retention. Be patient and unhurried in teaching.

4. Use concise one- or two-step directions. Avoid confusion by giving no more than two directions at a time.

5. Be sure the lesson is presented sequentially in small, easy-to-follow steps.

6. Make each lesson meaningful and applicable. Apply your lesson to everyday life and encourage all students to put what they have learned into practice.

Students with Hearing Impairments

1. Do not shout!
2. If the child lipreads, be sure he or she has a clear view of your mouth and face.
3. If the child wears hearing aids, be sure you have extra batteries on hand. Ask the parents to teach you how to adjust the aids and how to replace the batteries.
4. Provide a sign language interpreter, as necessary.

Students with Visual Impairments

1. Use clear, uncluttered visual aids.
2. Address the student by name. Give explanations each time an activity changes or when movement is necessary in the classroom.
3. Familiarize yourself with appropriate sighted-guide techniques. Ask the parents for guidance in training nondisabled students to be guides.
4. Explain guidedog etiquette to your class if a dog will be attending class with their new classmate.
5. Provide braille or large-print materials. If you have purchased a student book for each student in your class, you do not need special permission to enlarge the pages of one book for your visually impaired student. Whenever you need more than one copy of a page, contact the publisher for special permission, unless the book is marked "reproducible."

Students with Physical Disabilities

1. Familiarize yourself with any special equipment, such as wheelchairs and/or braces. Help your students understand the use of this equipment and the need to respect and care for it.
2. Train student peers to assist with physical tasks beyond this student's capabilities.
3. Be sure your classroom is wheelchair accessible.
4. Obtain special supplies, such as double-handed scissors. These scissors, which allow a helper to hold the scissors

along with the child, can be purchased through any office supply store.

Students with Speech Disorders

1. Develop a successful means of communicating with the child.
2. Never pretend to understand. Ask the child to repeat a statement or tell you in a different way. If you still cannot understand, ask the child to show you or perhaps to draw a picture to illustrate what is meant.
3. Give the child time to finish her statement. Don't do it for her.

Students with Emotional Disorders

1. Be loving, but firm.
2. Plan for success. Students may come to you with a negative self-image after repeated failures in other areas of life. Encourage them with praise for even the smallest success, and provide opportunities to demonstrate areas of competence.
3. Ask the student's parents to explain the behavioral interventions and discipline plan used at home and school. Implement the same interventions and plan in your classroom.
4. Being consistent applies not only to your management of behavior, but also to your response to the child. For instance, be consistent with recognition, encouragement, and praise.
5. Don't make promises you cannot keep. If you say you are going to give the person a call during the week, do it! Don't disappoint.

Students with Learning Disabilities

1. Provide for needed breaks in concentration. Don't talk for extended periods. Break your schedule into segments so that the student is not expected to sit still and listen for long periods of time.

2. Continually refocus the student's attention. Use his or her name or touch the shoulder to draw attention to the task at hand.

3. Reduce distracting noises and limit the visual environment behind you.

4. Use active learning strategies. Engaging in pencil and paper tasks only will be especially difficult for these students. Vary the approach by using clay, interest centers, games, music, drama, and other activities to heighten interest and involvement.

5. Be visually direct. Looking the students in the eye as you teach affirms the value you have placed on them as individuals.

6. Use motivational techniques. Watch all of your students and "catch them being good." Reward attentiveness and cooperation.

There are two situations that might require a self-contained classroom.

Is inclusion always the best approach? There are two situations that might require a self-contained classroom. First, older students with mental retardation and other cognitive delays will probably learn better in a separate classroom. The social differences are more noticeable. While a twenty-five-year-old man without disabilities is dealing with finishing a master's degree and rearing a family, his age-mate with a disability is dealing with training for a job at a fast food restaurant and adjusting to living in a sheltered apartment. Second, a student with severe mobility and communication functions will not be best served sitting in a classroom just to satisfy a philosophy. Age and functional level are real issues.

If a noninclusive approach is best, use some inclusion principles. Let the person know that the members of his or her age-appropriate class care about him or her as a person. The regular class for young adults could be assigned to members of the special class. Calling them during the week, sending a birthday card, or inviting them to the class party will build positive relationships. The student with a severe disability could be a part of the opening, singing, and other group activities of the class. The teaching session could be done by an assistant who presents the lesson on a level the student will comprehend.

Concept #5: Minister with Families

A part of a meaningful Christian education program is an outreach to the parents. The toll is heavy on marriages experiencing disability. Parents of children with disabilities report the insensitive, unkind statements people make to them. They range from, "What do you think God is punishing you for?" to "God knew what He was doing when He selected a strong person like you to have a child like this."

As a Christian educator, learn and teach words that will encourage. These examples will help you phrase positive sentences:

✎ I have learned so much from you as I've watched you handle your child.

✎ You are the expert on the needs of your child.

✎ I see a lot of love in you.

✎ It is not your fault.

People also often pull away from families with members who have disabilities because they believe "We don't know what to say or do." Perhaps, too, they think they don't know how to help with the feelings the families are experiencing. Four suggestions will help to know what to do.

First, knowing that there are four times of universal concern for the family will enable the church family to know when to be available. First, when the diagnosis is made; second, when the child starts to school; third, when the child is finished with school; fourth, when the parents realize they can no longer provide care for their child.

Second, your congregation can be a great source of encouragement and assistance to the family. Find out what they need by being close enough to notice. The family's number one need will likely be respite care. Simply stated, they need some time away, some extra hands occasionally, and someone to do the chores when time gets tight. Putting yourself in the family's place will allow you to add chores to the following list that will make their days easier: provide transportation, shop for groceries, care for the lawn, do the laundry, write letters, baby-sit, etc.

Third, providing Sunday school and worship experiences for the child will serve the family. Christian parents want their child to develop faith, become a Christian, have church friends, and grow spiritually. The parents also need to be nurtured spiritually and relieved of caregiving responsibilities during that weekly time.

Siblings of the child with a disability also need attention.

Fourth, siblings of the child with a disability also need attention. Some siblings will overachieve to make up for the child with the disability, some will resent the time the parents spend with the child with a disability; some will be fine and choose a special education or helping profession; and some will be embarrassed. Whatever the case, a little extra attention from the Christian education staff and program will be a great benefit to the siblings.

Concept #6: Realize the Results of Sharing the Gospel Makes an Eternal Difference

The result of participation in the inclusive Christian education programs of the church should be the same as the regular programs. The goal is to teach who Jesus is, how to embrace Him in faith, how to live the Christian life, and how to have the hope of Heaven.

Over the years, I have observed many professionals whose work has made a difference in the lives of people with disabilities. The changes have been amazing. An occupational therapist designs a switch which allows a young wheelchair user to control his chair with his breath. He has freedom. The family had been told that the child might not walk. A physical therapist saw the possibilities. After months of therapy, the child walked.

Acquiring speech, learning to walk, and developing social skills are important. It is more important to develop the soul. Doing so brings hope. The promise of Isaiah 35:4-6 is available to students with disabilities: "Your God will come . . . he will come to save you. Then will the eyes of the blind be opened and ears of the deaf unstopped. Then will the lame leap like a deer, and the mute tongue shout for joy."

Baptism raises questions. Do persons with cognitive problems know enough to understand the elements of faith? The question of how much comprehension takes place is easy to answer. The people who will have the most trouble understanding faith matters are those with mental retardation, but of this group, 85 percent can be taught the facts of faith. Do not worry about how much they understand. Your role is to get them into a Christian education program where learning can take place.

Will God understand? In cases where the person's level of function is so low that he simply cannot comprehend basic facts, the answer is "yes." In those situations the person is surrounded by God's love and mercy. But in situations where the mental age is sufficient to learn, the person should be taught. The results will produce eternal consequences.

Acquiring speech, learning to walk, and developing social skills are important. It is more important to develop the soul.

Rachel and I have been friends from the first time we met. When we are in restaurants, we sit together. She likes lettuce, and enjoys Special Olympics and her pets. Rachel has Down's syndrome. During a visit with her family, I learned her awareness of Bible truths. On the way to church, Rachel said, "Dr. Jim, I am going to miss you."

I'll miss you too, Rachel," I replied. She repeated her statement.

"See those clouds, Rachel? Someday, Jesus will walk out on them, get us, and take us to Heaven. Then we won't be sad when I have to go back home to my family and my work and you stay here with your family and go to school," I comforted.

"Dr. Jim, I know. But how will He do it?"

She answered her question with some questions, "Are there steps behind the clouds? Will Jesus walk down them and say, 'Let's go, Rachel?' Then we will we walk back up together?"

My reply, "That is exactly the way it will be, Rachel."

Where did she learn the fact that Jesus will come get her? She has been taught by her family, her Sunday school teachers, and her vacation Bible school teachers. Because of their efforts, she is a Christian. Her Christian educators have made an eternal difference. Some day Rachel will stand in God's presence without Down's syndrome.

Conclusion

After studying the material in this chapter, how would you, as a director of Christian education, provide ministry for the examples in the introduction?

✎ Because the six-year-old with cerebral palsy is included in a regular Sunday school class, provide an assistant to be available to her. The child should not be made to feel that she is the only one who needs help. Let the assistant work with other children. Provide the help that will lead to more independence for her.

✎ Assemble the Christian education team and meet with the family of the child with autism. Develop an Individual Christian Education Plan.

✎ Explain to the members of the youth group the nature of their friend's needs and encourage them to be supportive. Stress that he is the same person he was. He has just lost some functional ability. One of his major needs is to continue to feel that he belongs and has something to offer. Stress his abilities. Include him in group activities. Assign him jobs to do.

✎ Support the family with the new baby with Down's syndrome. Do some training sessions for the nursery staff.

Train church members to provide respite care. Keep the family involved in church life.

In all four cases, know that your ministry will make an eternal difference.

An Acronym

This acronym provides a good summary of the contents and the intended results of this chapter. Written by Jennifer Heck, a student of mine in disability ministry and a lady with cerebral palsy, it was the response to an examination question: How can the church minister to a person with a disability and his family? She answered: UNDERSTANDING.

United in vision to welcome all people.
Not afraid to ask questions and learn about disabilities.
Develop new attitudes about people with disabilities.
Earnestly believe and obey the Bible.
Restore spiritual strength, joy, and hope to people.
Serve their immediate needs (financial, emotional, household chores, etc.)
Train church staff, lay leaders, volunteers, youth buddies.
Arrange for respite care, prayer chains, visitations, etc.
Never restrict them from using their spiritual gifts.
Devoted to pray for guidance and compassion.
Invest time and energy into creative ways of ministering.
Never underestimate God's power to transform lives.
Grow together and function as one body in God's family!

---

p r o j e c t

☆ Interview a person with a disability or the parents of a child with a disability. Let them tell you about the nature of the disability and what they need in Christian education. Discuss how well the church meets these needs. ☆

For Further Reading

Jim Pierson
No Disabled Souls. Cincinnati: Standard Publishing Company, 1998.

CHAPTER 12
MEDIA AND TECHNOLOGY
IN TEACHING

Chapter Twelve Summary
- ☑ Biblical examples of audiovisuals
- ☑ The role of media in Christian Education
- ☑ Multiple intelligences
- ☑ Types of and uses for media in the classroom
- ☑ The Internet as teaching tool

Sesame Street, Blue's Clues, Teletubbies . . . and the list continues, the list of television programs targeted to young children. The children and students we teach in church today are products of a media-pervasive world. To the media producers they are proof that implementation of the ancient Chinese proverb "a picture is worth a thousand words" draws an audience, sells products, and makes money. It is important to remember that while society has changed, in that we live in a postmodern world with radically enhanced forms of communication, the essential child or adult has not changed. To teach, we need to make effective use of the tools that are a part of our students' subculture. Wise teachers choose to use the most effective tools to communicate the message of God's Truth.

Wise teachers choose to use the most effective tools to communicate the message of God's Truth.

Biblical Perspectives of the Use of Media in Education

We find no examples of computers, DVD players, and multimedia productions in the Scriptures, but we do find people using culturally appropriate visuals to communicate their message.

Old Testament Examples

The Old Testament is full of the use of audio and visual tools as a part of the teaching process. Let's look at a few.

Imagine Noah standing on dry land building a huge boat and telling people that it was going to rain, something they had never seen, and imagine him continuing to build for 80 years (Genesis 6:9–7:5). This is an example of an early use of objects as visuals. Just a little further in the story God put a rainbow in the sky and told Noah that whenever he saw the rainbow, this would be a reminder of God's promise, another visual aid (Genesis 9:12-17).

When God wanted to attract Moses' attention, He used a burning bush.

When God wanted to attract Moses' attention and call him to a leadership role, He used a burning bush, yet a bush that did not burn. The Scriptures tell us that Moses thought, "I will go over and see this strange sight, why the bush does not burn up" (Exodus 3:3). Here is an example of the use of a visual to attract someone's attention so that one can share a message with him or her.

We read the story of the ten plagues that occurred after Moses' return to Egypt. Here we see the dramatic arrival of Moses, his interaction with Pharaoh, and God's action when Pharaoh refused to listen. Snakes, blood, frogs, gnats, flies, cattle disease, boils, hail, locusts, darkness and finally the death of the oldest son—these are graphic visuals that demonstrated God's power. Real objects played an important role in this learning experience (Exodus 7–11).

As Moses traveled through that hot, dreary desert with a crowd of complaining and tired people, God used a variety of visuals to communicate His message. Think about the nightly pillar of fire and the daily pillar of cloud that was always before them throughout the time they wandered in the desert. In a very graphic way, God reminded them continually of His presence (Exodus 13:21-22).

In a very graphic way, God reminded them continually of His presence.

Imagine the scene on Mt. Sinai when the people saw Moses and Aaron disappear up a mountain where there was thunder, lightning, and a loud trumpet blast, certainly an audio/visual demonstration. And then, many days later, Moses reappeared with two tablets of stone in his hands, which the Bible tells us, "were the work of God, the writing was the writing of God engraved on the tablet." How graphic was Moses' reaction when he took those tablets of stone and "threw them out of his hands, breaking them to pieces at the foot of the mountain." In modern terms, we have drama, visuals, and the effective use of sound and light to communicate the holiness of God (Exodus 20–32).

A little later in the Israelites' journey, God provided the directions for a phenomenal visual to daily remind His people of His presence and the response that should be theirs—the directions for the building and appearance of the tabernacle. In great detail we read how the tabernacle was to be built, the type of decorations, the color of the materials, the furniture to be placed in it, and even the exact requirements for the dress of the priests (Exodus 35–40). Every one of these directions had meaning and could be used as a tool to teach the children of Israel more about the God they worshipped. Exodus chapter 39 describes the clothes that the priest wore when he ministered in the sanctuary. To a people who had no written Scriptures (apart from the two tablets of stone) and a limited knowledge about God, these visual aids were an essential part of their religious education.

But the use of visuals did not end with the Pentateuch. In 1 Kings 11:29-33, the prophet Ahijah met Jeroboam as he left Jerusalem. Ahijah was wearing a new cloak, which he grasped and tore into 12 pieces. Ten of these pieces he gave to Jeroboam as he explained that this was a demonstration of what God was about to do when He tore the kingdom from one dynasty, divided it, and began a new dynasty in the person of Jeroboam and his family.

The book of Daniel gives many examples of the effective use of visuals to communicate God's message. Probably the most stunning is the appearance of a dismembered hand writing on a wall in front of the king and a thousand drunken noblemen. It is not surprising that the Scriptures tell us the king's face, "turned pale and he was so frightened that his knees knocked together and his legs gave way" (Daniel 5).

No one who saw him would forget the aids that Ezekiel used to communicate God's message to the exiles by the Kebar River. In chapter 4 we see him drawing a picture of the city of Jerusalem on a clay tablet, erecting seigeworks around it, and then dramatizing the situation by lying on his side and symbolically bearing the sin of the house of Israel on himself for 390 days—more than a year. We find Ezekiel using many symbolic visuals to help his learners understand and remember his prophecies. God helped him to dramatize the message.

No one who saw him would forget the aids that Ezekiel used.

New Testament Examples

We often talk about Jesus as the perfect teacher. The life and teaching ministry of Jesus show many examples of the use of objects in the teaching process. Jesus used a child whom He placed in the middle of the group as an object lesson (Matthew 18:3-6); He used parables that featured daily life and objects, for example a farmer, seed time and harvest, sheep, coins, a lost son, and fishing. Jesus directed people's attention to scenes around them as He taught them various truths. He said, "Consider the ravens: They do not sow or reap . . . yet God feeds them" (Luke 12:24). You are more valuable than these birds but with all your worrying you can't make your life any longer. Since you can't do this, why do you worry about the rest? Each time they saw birds in the sky, his audience would be prompted to remember His teaching. Jesus also used visuals as part of miracles. He made mud and used it in the healing of one blind man (John 9:1-12). He told the man with the deformed hand to stretch it out, and those around saw and surely remembered the changes that took place (Matthew 12:13). Probably the three most memorable visuals that Jesus introduced are baptism, the Lord's Supper, and his own crucifixion together with common criminals.

The Role of Media in Christian Education

Your Brain and Media

Recently a great deal of effort has gone into research about how our brains work. PET scans allow us to see at any instant the parts of the brain that are active in the learning process. As a result of both research and the growth of technology, we now know more about how children learn. From these understandings has come the theory of hemisphericity. This is the study of where in the brain, in the left or right hemisphere, different types of learning occur. We have discovered that the right cerebral hemisphere is involved with visual, spatial, nonverbal, intuitive, and divergent learning, whereas the objective functions are processed through the left hemisphere. This would be the cognitive, analytical, and convergent aspects of learning. Specifically, this means that the right side of your brain processes the visual elements that let you recognize a person, while the left side stores information about that person. When you meet the person again, the left and right sides of your brain work together to identify the person and remember his or her name, address, and other information that you stored in the left side of your brain. This understanding of brain function helps us to understand why media plays such an important role in the learning process. Too often formal education has tended to emphasize only left hemispheric activities. It is important that lessons are planned to involve both hemispheres for maximum learning to take place. Therefore, effective use of media and technology become imperative.

It is important that lessons are planned to involve both hemispheres for maximum learning to take place.

Your Learning Style and Media

The Bible tells us that humankind was created in the image of God. Just as God's creation of this world reflects tremendous diversity, so does His creation of men and women. It is safe to say that no two people learn in exactly the same way. Not only does our cultural background and our personal experience affect the way we learn, but also our own personal learning style is a significant factor. Serious research into student learning styles probably began with the work of Kenneth and Rita Dunn who analyzed the importance of learning environment, emotional support, peer interaction, and personal and physical preferences on a student's learning. The research of Gregorc followed their work. A summary of Gregorc's analysis can be seen in the following chart.

Cluster	Thinking Patterns	Preferred Learning Environment
Concrete Sequential	Linear, sequential processing of concrete world	Ordered, linear, and stable
Abstract Sequential	Abstract, analytical thinking	Mentally stimulating, but ordered
Abstract Random	Emotional, imaginative	Active, colorful, and free
Concrete Random	Concrete world of activity; non-linear and intuitive	Stimulus-rich, with emphasis on problem solving

Gregorc's identification of the concrete random thinker explains why visuals and real-life experiences are so important for many students. While the theories are new, we can see from biblical examples that good teachers have always employed different types of visuals to reinforce the concepts being taught. Biblical stories have their roots in an agrarian culture. Most of our students live in an urban or suburban late 20th century technological society. Visuals and media are essential components if real understanding and learning is to take place.

Your Multiple Intelligences and Media

Closely related to an understanding of learning styles are three key findings about human intelligence. First, intelligence is a dynamic quality that is not fixed at birth. Second, through appropriate learning experiences intelligence can be enhanced. Third, intelligence has many different facets (Gardner, 1993). This third concept is a key element in lesson planning. From it, Gardner has developed his work on multiple intelligences. He suggests that we all possess eight intelligences, but traditional education develops only the first two, verbal/linguistic and logical/mathematical.

Gardner's Multiple Intelligences

* Verbal/linguistic   * Logical/mathematical   * Visual/spatial
* Body/kinesthetic   * Musical/rhythmic   * Interpersonal
* Intrapersonal   * Naturalistic

Figure 12.2

From these eight intelligences, Lazear has developed a toolbox to help teachers make sure they are addressing each intelligence as they teach. Media are strongly referenced in the visual/spatial, body/kinesthetic, musical/rhythmic, interpersonal, and naturalistic sections of his toolbox (Lazear, 1991). As we consider the use of media in Christian education, it is important for us to apply it as appropriate in our lesson planning.

Exploring Different Types of Media

There are many ways to classify media and technology. All are artificial, but most are helpful to different types of learners. Media here will be divided into two main sections with several branches, that is, traditional media and contemporary technology. Consideration of contemporary technology will be deferred to a later section.

Traditional Media

Some of these types of media have been used for many generations. One of the earliest aids to become an integral part of the educational process was the chalkboard, which found its place in the early nineteenth century classroom. As the one-room school disappeared, total class teaching became popular and a chalkboard was an inexpensive useful tool (Ryan, 1998, 199).

Some of these types of media have increased in popularity as technology has made them more obtainable. But with the development of newer technologies, once popular forms of media are less frequently seen and have become obsolete. One example would be the filmstrip and filmstrip projector.

Taxonomy of Traditional Media

1. Flat Media
   a. Boards
      1) Bulletin   2) Felt   3) Chalk
      4) Flannelgraph   5) White   6) Hook & Loop
   b. Visuals
      1) Maps   2) Pictures   3) Murals
      4) Photographs
   c. Charts
      1) Pull-off charts 2) Cartoons   3) Sketches
      4) Diagrams   5) Flip   6) Poster
      7) Graphs
         a) Pie   b) Bar   c) Line   d) Scatter
2. Projected Media—analog and digital
   a. Film—16 mm, video tape, CD-ROM, DVD

    b. Slides—35 mm slides, digital pictures, "PowerPoint" type presentations

    c. Overhead transparencies—computer generated and printed by color laser or inkjet printers, copy machine produced in black and white or color, professionally produced

3. Recorded Media

    a. Cassettes   b. CD's—audio and data

    c. CD-R   d. CD-RW

    e. DVD   f. DVD-ROM

4. 3-Dimensional Models

    a. Globes   b. Exhibits   c. Objects

    d. Puppets   e. Games   f. Artifacts

    g. Models

Evaluating Media

Today there is a wealth of audio/visual resources available to Christian educators. These vary in quality from professional level productions to very amateur, poorly made materials. It is important to establish selection criteria before beginning a church collection or when evaluating an already existing collection.

Daniel (1980, 183) suggests the following criteria:

1. Does the visual give a true picture of the idea it represents?
2. Does it contribute meaningful content to the topic?
3. Is it appropriate for the age, intelligence, and experience of the learners?
4. Is the physical condition of the visual satisfactory?
5. Will the visual stimulate thinking?
6. Is it worth the time, expense, and effort involved?

One might add to this list what is the value of the visual to a contemporary audience?

Organizing Media

A well-designed audio/visual center should be equipped with appropriate storage facilities. Catalogs from audio/visual equipment storage and furniture companies give many ideas regarding the appropriate organization and storage of visual aids and equipment. If there is no local dealer, pictures and details of these resources are readily available on the Internet where you can "shop" for the most appropriate system at the best price. Arrange resources so that supplies and teaching resources can easily be found. Establish a database that keys materials to both the type and the biblical stories for which they are applicable. Easy retrieval and easy access are vital if materials are to be used effectively. Within the Christian education ministry team there is the opportunity for a small group to assume responsibility for this area and be involved in the evaluation, classification, and promotion of the resources. Helping teachers have what they need when they need it is an essential part of organizing audio/visual materials. Frequently, it is more effective to have age-appropriate materials stored where they are most frequently used and are readily available for the teacher, rather than in some distant, centralized location. Expensive equipment needs to be checked out in accordance with church policies.

Exploring Contemporary Technology

Most of the contemporary technology with which our children are extremely familiar uses digital technology. The miniaturization of the integrated circuit and the development of more and more complex computer chips have fueled a burgeoning digital educational and entertainment industry. Most children interact with computers early in life; many of their toys contain computer components, which perform actions undreamed of in previous generations. The digital revolution and the information age are already with us.

The digital revolution and the information age are already with us.

The Internet, which only a few years ago was an unknown entity to most people, has now become a part of their everyday lives. People communicate, book airline tickets, find travel directions, perform sophisticated research, video conference with friends around the world, and even shop for everything from cars to groceries on the Internet. Search engines regularly access hundreds of thousands of sites worldwide and index the information in ways that make it easily available to everybody.

Technology offers us in Christian education an exciting tool or a scary nightmare.

As we approach the beginning of the 21st century, technology is fueling many changes in lifestyle. Today's Christians expect multiple choices and variety, both in delivery systems and in the topics to be studied. The rapid growth of effective accredited distance learning programs on the Internet are already changing the face of many college campuses, a change that will accelerate in the new century. Rapid and frequent changes of jobs are forcing people to become lifelong learners. The ability to communicate and work effectively in teams, the members of which are separated by miles, time zones, or even continents, is changing the way we interact.

Technology offers us in Christian education an exciting tool or a scary nightmare. Jesus called us to make disciples and to communicate the gospel to people throughout the world. Technological advances give us new and exciting ways of fulfilling this commission to make disciples and teach them the things that we have been taught. It is not the message that has changed, but the means of fulfilling Christ's command. Using technology, the Christian educator can effectively teach, train, and communicate with people whose lifestyles are busy, and who do not have or make the time for the traditional meetings where such communication took place in previous generations.

Using your church website in conjunction with a discussion area, a list server for Sunday school teachers, a chat room to answer questions, and multimedia presentations are some ways to communicate in a contemporary manner. These resources that deal with key issues can be accessed day and night at the learners' convenience. Another possibility is a virtual classroom with courses taught by church educators that are available to all church members at times that are convenient to them. All of this and more is possible using current and emerging technology.

So, what do we need in order to use current technology in our teaching? The answers to this question have to be general because specific types of hardware and software are out of date almost before they are generally available. This next section considers three main areas: equipment, software, and the use of the Internet in teaching.

Necessary Equipment

At the present time, some form of computer is an essential component in this teaching paradigm. Decisions regarding laptop, desktop, size, and power should be governed by the following criteria:

For teaching using multimedia and off-site communication, you need to buy a computer with:

1. Components that can be upgraded
2. As much memory as possible
3. As large a hard drive as possible
4. The possibility to add a second or third hard drive
5. As fast a processor as you can afford
6. A good audio card and excellent speakers
7. A video card with a lot of VRAM installed and space to add more
8. A current and upgradable operating system

What is needed varies from one situation to another.

An important consideration as we consider equipment is the addition of peripherals. What is needed varies from one situation to another. In some situations a youth ministry can be significantly enhanced with a multimedia station available where youth group members can develop presentations and digital video. In other churches enough members of the congregation already have their own personal equipment which will allow for the development of many of these materials using existing congregational resources. For effective development of technology in teaching, easy access to the following peripherals is important:

9. Color scanner
10. Digital camera
11. Video camera
12. Digital video camera
13. Laser and color printers
14. MIDI interface and keyboard
15. DVD drive
16. CD-R or CD-RW drive to allow for digital CD production

An important factor that must be considered when making a commitment to using technology appropriately in Christian education is how you will distribute your educational materials. The resources available in your community will in part influence this decision. In areas where the web is transmitted using high-speed cable modems, the distribution of multimedia presentations on the web is effective. Where most people are still accessing using a lower speed modem, it is probably more appropriate to develop some form of distribution system. Developing and making CDs has become a very inexpensive and easy process. The same will soon be true using DVD technology.

Software

Computer hardware and networked buildings are becoming very common in our nation's schools. Effective use of this technology often lags far behind the equipment that is available. However, in most areas one can find schools or teachers who are effectively using the computer as a tool in the educational process. When a church seeks to make software decisions for Christian education, two factors need to be born in mind: first, what type of software are children and youth accustomed to using at school and second, what software is available on home computers in the church community. Any discussion of software has to start with an understanding of software licenses and the U.S. copyright law. Unless site licenses or multiple machine licenses are purchased, the normal rule is that each piece of software can be loaded on only one computer. Software use policies that emphasize high ethical standards are essential in any Christian education ministry.

Software use policies that emphasize high ethical standards are essential in any Christian education ministry.

To use technology effectively in education, the following types of software should be available for church programs.

1. Tool Software—for example: office suites that include integrated word processors, databases, and spreadsheets such as Microsoft Office and child appropriate graphic word processors such as Kid Pix and Kid Pix Studio.
2. Technology Support Tools
   a. Materials generators such as desktop publishing software, worksheet generators, and puzzle generators.
   b. Graphics tools such as Print Shop, Print Shop Deluxe, and Corel Draw; presentation software such as PowerPoint; charting/graphing software features usually found in general tool packages and clipart and sound collections. Royalty free collections are available on many CDs, including collections of biblical and religious images. Video development systems such as Avid Cinema are also helpful.
   c. Planning and organizing tools—brainstorming tools such as Inspiration; lesson planning tools such as Parsons Lesson Maker; and schedule and calendar makers, usually found in larger graphics packages.
   d. Research and Reference Tools—encyclopedias on CD ROM, both biblical and general encyclopedias, and atlases such as The Visual Atlas.
   e. Hypermedia/Multimedia Tools such as HyperStudio. This type of software can also be used by students to express an outcome of the learning that has taken place.

f. Biblical Resources—An expanding collection of quality biblical resources are now available for the Christian educator. Current examples of these would be: teaching CDs such as Focus on the Family's *Jesus, The Man, The Message, The Messiah*; Parsons Technology's *A Walk in the Footsteps of Jesus*; Compton's *Multimedia Biblical Encyclopedia*; electronically indexed versions of the Bible such as: *The Online Bible* or *PCBible*.

When considering software, it is important to explore what is currently available because technology is changing so rapidly.

Using the Internet in Teaching

The "Information Superhighway," more properly the Internet, is a global interconnected collection of computers, servers, and networks linked using a TCP/IP protocol. Using the Internet actually involves using a variety of Internet resources and services such as email, chat rooms, FTP, discussion groups, and the World Wide Web (www). There are many resources on the Internet that will significantly enrich a Christian education program.

There are many resources on the Internet that will significantly enrich a Christian education program.

Let's consider missions education first. Your church missionary can establish a keypad link between children on the mission field and children in the sponsoring church. In many areas, live online communication is possible using software such as NetMeeting or CUSeeMe. Inexpensive digital video cameras allow for "live" video communication between the mission field and the home church. The addition of a hookup in the sanctuary and a video projector allows the missionary to communicate current news during a local worship service. E-mail has revolutionized contact between churches and individuals around the world. Events that happen in the middle of India can be communicated to everyone using a distribution list within minutes or hours of their occurrence. Praying for the immediate needs of Christian workers around the world is now a reality. Groups such as Mission Services and Brigada send out daily or weekly e-mail mission information updates.

Teenagers who have traditionally spent hours on the telephone, frequently spend that time visiting in chat rooms. Christian educators and youth ministers need to establish area chat rooms where they can interact with their young people.

Many Christian discussion groups are available on the Internet on topics such as practical Christian living, apologetics, theology, Bible study, home schooling, and Christian education. While many of these are unmoderated, and therefore subject to abuse or off-topic posting, much useful information and communication occurs.

Probably the area of the Internet with which most people are familiar is the World Wide Web. Christian sites on the web and sites, which provide background to biblical sites and resources are numerous. Jason Baker, in his latest edition of *Christian Cyberspace Companion* (1997) includes a 70-page, two-column directory of Internet sites. The Christian presence on the Web is expanding weekly. To find links to Christian resources, it is often helpful to go to a central site such as http://www.goshen.net, which indexes a large number of Christian sites.

It is true that much on the Web is unhelpful and unacceptable to Christians. It must be remembered that the Web is a mirror of our society. Christians are called to be lights in the darkness, so we need to find effective ways to use this exciting tool in Christian education and evangelism.

Looking to the Future

Because of the way people learn, visuals and technology will always be an important component in the teaching/learning process. The principles are timeless. It is the responsibility of the Christian educator to ensure that these principles are implemented in a culturally appropriate, contemporary manner so that Christ is glorified in every aspect of our teaching.

p r o j e c t s

★ Find out what equipment and resources are available within your church. ★

★ Plan your own dream media center. ★

★ Plan a teaching session for an age level of your choice. Plan media and materials that will appeal to each learning style. ★

For Further Reading

James Baker
Christian Cyberspace Companion. 2nd ed. Grand Rapids: Baker, 1997.

Howard Gardner
Multiple Intelligences: The Theory in Practice. New York: Basic Books, 1993.

Anthony Gregorc
Gregorc Style Delineator. Maynard, MA: Gabriel Systems, 1985.

D.G. Lazear
Teaching for Multiple Intelligences. Bloomington, IN: Phi Delta Kappa Educational Foundation, 1992.

K. Ryan
Those Who Can, Teach. Boston: Houghton Mifflin, 1998.

CHAPTER 13
THE CHURCH'S MINISTRY TO
FAMILIES

Chapter Thirteen Summary
- ☑ Changing family demographics
- ☑ The need for family ministry
- ☑ Strategy for family ministry
- ☑ 7 exercises for evaluating family ministry needs
- ☑ 9 areas which affect the family
- ☑ Family ministry goals

During the past twelve years, I have ministered in blue collar and white collar churches. I have been involved with rural, inner city, and suburban ministries. The people, settings, specific needs, and approaches to ministry have varied. However, one characteristic has been the same: confusion, even utter chaos, in what was once considered "traditional" or "normal" family values.

I have attempted to teach elementary Sunday school lessons about a Heavenly Father by making comparisons to earthly fathers. On more than one occasion, I have listened to young children tell me they do not know where their father is, or that it has been so long since they have seen him that they don't remember his face. I have attempted to teach high school classes about ethics, only to be told that decisions are purely situational and depend on how others treat you. This situational approach to ethics covers everything from sex, family, and marriage to integrity. I have seen churchgoing adults neglect and abuse their children, sometimes intentionally, other times because they did not know better or because that was how they were reared. I have had adults and children share about how hard it is to trust and love others or God because they have always been hurt and let down by the people they care about most. I have watched marriages begin and end almost simultaneously and seen children left to pick up the pieces as they are juggled to any interested party.

These illustrations are heartbreaking and real. These stories happen in the biggest churches and in the smallest churches. They penetrate the rich and the poor. These situations and these broken people are all around us. The church needs to respond. We must develop an approach to a society and a family that has become situational and calloused. These negative cycles must be broken; otherwise, they will be repeated by each successive generation.

Stories of dysfunctional and broken families happen in the biggest churches and in the smallest churches and penetrate the rich and the poor.

It is crucial that the church recognize how family life is changing in our society. The church must develop programs to support, educate and train the various members of the family throughout their life cycle.

The task of family ministry can easily become overwhelming. The term "family" has become almost indefinable in today's society because family can refer to many different groups of people. The label "family" has been expanded to include any group wishing to claim the name. This labeling grants almost any group access to privileges and programs that were intended to support the "traditional" family (Craig, 1994). For many children, the realization is that a home with one mom and one dad forever exists only in 1950s reruns.

Controversy arose in New York City when parents realized that books on the homosexual lifestyle were included in the curriculum for their children's first grade class. *Heather Has Two*

Mommies describes a lesbian couple creating a family through artificial insemination. *Daddy's Roommate* supposedly offers a child the opportunity to understand a different kind of love as portrayed through male parents (McDonald & McDonald, 1994). Such episodes from news headlines show that family ministry may require the broadening and questioning of the definitions in a number of areas.

The Changing Face of Family

The U.S. Census Bureau perceives the family as continuously changing. This truth is demonstrated in the transformation of family units from the year 1980 to projected changes by the year 2000.

Family Composition 1980 and 2000

Family Type	Married Couples with Children	Other Families with Children	Other Non-Families
1980	30.9%	7.5%	3.6%
2000	23.9%	8.2%	5.2%

(U.S. Census Bureau, 1995).

If these statistics are true, even if a church is family oriented, it may be reaching only a minority of the families. We must recognize that the households in our communities are made up of single individuals, single-parent families, blended families, newly married couples, couples without children, cohabitating couples with or without children, middle-aged couples dealing with adult children, middle-aged couples rearing their grandchildren, and senior citizens. There are countless needs to be met.

The Call for Family Ministry

Family ministry is composed of more than intergenerational activities or a few summer events. Families need day-to-day and year-round support that will enable them to care for ever-changing needs. Family ministry is not a trendy area for the church to work into after the essentials of worship are in place. Family ministry needs to be a philosophy of ministry, not necessarily a program within a church.

Family ministry will vary in form from one church to another. It may be preventive or therapeutic in style depending upon the needs of the congregation and community. A ministry that can assist and support the family unit will have the opportunity to instill God's values and principles.

Family ministry may be preventive or therapeutic in style depending upon the needs of the congregation and community.

The differing needs are overwhelming. However, the church is one of the few organizations that has the opportunity to touch, educate, and heal people and their families at every developing stage of the life cycle. Education, employment, and hobby associations and relationships are more temporary. The church can become a family of households ministering to each other's needs. The church could reach the various needs of the family more effectively than any other organization if it would realize its opportunity and accept its responsibility to be the family of God (Wynn, 1991).

Scripture does not offer us a distinct definition of family. In the Old Testament, no Hebrew word describes the family as we know it. The New Testament word *oikia* (household), often translated as family, is not an exact translation. This Greek word refers to every person living in a residence, which could include servants, friends, and relatives. Indeed, maybe this Greek reference is perfect for today's situations.

One definition of family is "a married couple or other group of adult kinfolk who cooperate economically in the upbringing of children, and all or most of whom share a common dwelling" (Gough, 1971, 760). Whether or not we agree on a definition, we can all certainly acknowledge that today's family is different than it was 40 years ago.

Regardless of the lack of specifics, the importance of a solid family life is described in the Old and New Testament references given to the family in the Pentateuch. Families are instructed to teach godly values in such a way as to "impress them on your children" (Deut 6:6-8). Specifically, honoring parents (Exod 20:12) is mentioned to insure a recognition of authority and godly values. Sexual sins are forbidden (Exod 20:14), and coveting a neighbor's wife (Exod 20:17) is equally unacceptable. The goal of these prohibitions was to strengthen, protect, and purify the family (McDonald & McDonald, 1994).

God's ideal for marriage is presented in Genesis 1:27-28. We read of the creation of humankind and of God's desire for men and women to "be fruitful and increase in number [to] fill the earth." A household with children was viewed as being a manifestation of God's love (Psalm 127:3-5). Parents had the responsibility to model and nurture as mentioned in Deuteronomy 6:4-7. In addition, Proverbs 23:13 emphasizes parental responsibility for discipline. The Apostle Paul in Ephesians 6:4 describes the parent's task of educating children, "Fathers, do not exasperate your children; instead, bring them up in the training and instruction of the Lord."

At times less than ideal circumstances have to be accepted.

Of course, society is far from the ideal pictured in Scripture. At times less than ideal circumstances have to be accepted, for example, when a parent dies or abandons the family, leaving a single adult alone struggling to keep the family together and functioning. Other situations may demand that a child be reared by a grandparent or other relative. Consequently, the church must be prepared to respond to every form of family and family situation. Some families are healthy, but others battered, torn, and scarred. But we are called to meet their needs. In some cases, the church's intervention could offer the necessary assistance to insure healthy physical lives. In other cases, it could ensure spiritual and eternal well-being. By God's direct intervention, it can offer both.

Scripture promises, "I will not leave you as orphans; I will come to you" (John 14:18). Could God use the church as the vehicle that offers a struggling family the values, education, and resources necessary to become functional again? Perhaps a better question is: If the Church does not, then who will? Secular ideas and philosophies are floundering.

The picture of family life may appear bleak. However, the church has the opportunity to offer hope and is beginning to take action. The response required from each individual church will vary. We cannot set up specific programs without first giving families the opportunity to provide input and take control of the care and support that they perceive as necessary. This requires listening to families' priorities, hopes, and dreams. It also requires believing in the power of God working through the church and other Christians to respond to family needs. It requires developing specific approaches, times and places that offer support and ministry to families in crisis.

The church has the opportunity to offer hope and is beginning to take action.

Divorce is perhaps the most prevalent and common dilemma to be faced. Statistics reveal perhaps 60% of marriages will end in divorce. Three-quarters of divorced individuals remarry within two years (18 months for men, 24 months for women) and 60% of these marriages fail. The average first marriage lasts 7-8 years and the typical second marriage lasts 4-5 years. This ongoing problem causes difficult adjustments for adults and especially children who may have several sets of step- and half-siblings.

Other families hurt in a number of different ways: financially, through abuse and neglect, dependency, etc. Every family faces crises at one time or another, some of them devastating. Our sophisticated society has perpetuated the fallacy that every problem has a solution. But family difficulties are becoming so complex that at times there are no easy answers. Some families need coping mechanisms to survive.

From November 1996 until March 1997, the National Board of Christian Education of the Church of God, Anderson, Indiana, conducted six forums on family ministry in an attempt to identify how to develop a "family friendly, family sensitive" congregation. One hundred forty-one participants from 81 congregations cited the following seven priorities as crucial for families:

❶ Balancing family time
❷ Fathering
❸ Money
❹ Developing meaningful family times
❺ Communicating in the family
❻ Nurturing faith in children
❼ Mothering

(Kelly & Cookston, 1998).

The Roman Catholic Church of the United States conducted their "Liberty and Justice for All" program with over 800,000 responses. The relationship of the family to church was listed as the greatest concern. Consequently, the church responded with "The Plan of Pastoral Action for Family Ministry: A Vision and Strategy." The plan does not offer a specific plan, but a structure in which to respond to the family:

> The anguish and fragmentation of so many married couples and family members call for both a preventive and remedial ministry for families. This includes specialized counseling, and a ministry of reconciliation that touches the psychological, economic and spiritual realities of family life. Clergy and couples engaged in family ministry should be encouraged and helped to acquire specialized skills for dealing with such complex issues as poverty, aging alcoholism, drug abuse and homosexuality. There is great need for family ministry to separated and divorced persons as well as to children of divorced parents. The needs of families with handicapped members and those with members living in institutions should not be overlooked in this area of pastoral ministry (Thomas, 1980).

Developing a Strategy
for Family Ministry

A number of questions must be asked to ascertain the specific needs of individual congregations. A systematic process is the way to begin change in the local church and its community. The assessment process for family ministry begins by discovering the makeup of your congregation: financial resources, ethnicity, educational level, perceptions, assets, and deficits.

In *Church and Family Together: A Congregational Manual for Black Ministry*, seven exercises, to be done in group settings, are suggested to evaluate family ministry needs.

Exercise 1: Inventory existing family ministry programs. List activities, support groups, clubs, and programs that meet the needs of the various members of the family.

Exercise 2: Perceive the difficulties facing the family. Group members should be asked to respond with the assurance that their responses will not be critiqued or judged. Then reflections should occur comparing the list from Exercise 1 with Exercise 2.

Exercise 3: Investigating the community allows groups to collect data related to various areas of the community (schools, family resources, businesses, recreational outlets, religious centers, problem areas, etc.) Then have reports given of findings.

Exercise 4: Identify major concerns. Compare Exercise 2 and 3. Pray for guidance and the realization of limitations. Prioritize and brainstorm ministry approaches.

Exercise 5: Develop goals. Goals are general statements of desired outcomes. Goals offer direction that leads to plans of action.

Exercise 6: Develop objectives. Objectives offer the specifics needed to reach goals. They describe what will be done, when it will be done, where it will be done, and how it will be accomplished.

Exercise 7. Prepare a budget. This requires research into expenses related to staffing, programing and ministry-related events to be offered (Bernstine, 1996).

Studies on the developmental factors of the life cycle offer additional information. This includes a description of the typical needs of family members in the average environment through the developmental phases of life. Such information provides sensitivity for the typically vulnerable areas of life that may require support and assistance. In turn, education and insight can be offered to develop ministries to meet the needs of the local church and its community.

The National Council of Family Relations has developed a framework to assist in developing family life education programs that reach the various developmental needs of the family throughout the lifespan. It details nine areas which affect the family:

❶ Families in Society
❷ Internal Dynamics of Families
❸ Human Growth and Development
❹ Human Sexuality
❺ Interpersonal Relationships
❻ Family Resource Management
❼ Parent Education and Guidance
❽ Family Law and Public Policy
❾ Ethics

More specifically, the structure targets each of these areas and how it affects the family at each level of the life cycle: childhood, adolescence, adulthood, and later adulthood (NCFR, 1991).

The task of family ministry requires good organization and direction.

The task of family ministry requires good organization and direction. Information must be accumulated and acted upon. Therefore, it is important to consider who will serve as the director of family ministries and how the group's research will be implemented in the local church. Hiring a full-time family life minister may be a goal, but it may not be feasible, especially for small church budgets. A full-time staff member is only one option. Perhaps a qualified individual would be willing to fill this need on a part-time basis. Team leadership with two or three volunteers dividing the responsibilities while using their talents to implement family ministry is another option. Some churches have begun to write family life ministry into the portfolio of job expectations for their age-level specialists.

Some churches have begun to write family life ministry into the portfolio of job expectations for their age-level specialists.

Decisions regarding the specific form and style must also be determined. Questions regarding whether a preventive education system or a corrective education system is needed must be answered. Preventive education is the pathway the majority of churches choose. Under this umbrella, activities could include marriage enrichment seminars, parenting classes, financial planning, etc. Corrective education such as counseling centers or clinics increase legal liabilities and require investigation into state guidelines and principles before implementation.

The specific form of preventive, corrective, or a blending of the two approaches depends on the specific needs of each individual congregation. However, family ministry awareness should be driven by the following:

- Individuals are recognized by name, accepting diversity.
- Family-led worship is encouraged.
- Everyone becomes a part of the family of believers.
- Leaders and teachers are aware of family needs throughout the life cycle.
- Ministries provide family activities (mental, physical, educational, and spiritual).
- Community concern and outreach to families is promoted on the same level as concern and outreach to church families.
- Staff members demonstrate awareness and support to the various developmental needs of the family.
- Assistance is offered or sought through the religious organization or community resources to assist the dysfunctional family.

✎ Family ministry is not an isolated activity, but a philosophy for ministry that touches every individual regardless of developmental stage.

✎ Communication skills are taught and modeled with non-judgmental attitudes.

(Kelly & Cookston, 1998).

Families often come to churches with agendas in mind. They are looking for assistance with specific problems. The church must develop relationships and gain respect from its members. Once this acceptance is established, the church can "scratch" the family's "itch." The church, in so doing, has applied the salve of Christianity and established what will hopefully be a lifelong relationship. The church can be a necessary asset that promotes security.

Research shows that a network of support is crucial. Assets such as quality schools, quality peers, and religious affiliation are a part of the lives of young people who are functioning well in today's society. Young people who succeed despite dysfunctional families are twice as likely to have these active support systems (Olson & Leonard, 1996).

Young people who succeed despite dysfunctional families are twice as likely to have active support systems outside the family.

With the problems, difficulties, and lack of traditional values of today, a variety of needs have to be approached. These could likely be needs that the church has never before regarded as their responsibility or as a part of its educational programs. Such areas might include:

✎ Financial management. Families are working hard not to improve life, but to stay afloat. Families feel the need for two wage earners to meet the desired standard of living. The average number of hours worked has increased, leaving less time for family.

✎ Assistance for those living in poverty. This could include job training, parental training, or basic educational assistance (reading, writing) to offer the possibility for better employment in the future.

✎ Health care. In 1995-96, over 15% of our country lacked health care with between 9.8 and 10.6 million children lacking care. What is the church doing?

✎ Care for the elderly. In 1987, seven million families offered unpaid care for adults over the age of 50. In 1996, 22.4 million families were caring for seniors. These families need assistance as well as training.

✎ Counseling/shelter for victims of domestic abuse and violence. Child protection agencies suggest that 15 out of every 1000 children suffer from abuse or neglect. Six times as many women are victimized by those they have relationships with as compared to those victimized by strangers.

✎ Dependency relationships. Dependency occurs when one family member believes that he or she needs someone to assure self-value or to enable success. This defective relationship falsely allows the dependent person to be excused from his actions.

A dependency relationship falsely allows the dependent person to be excused from his actions.

This is by no means an exhaustive list, but a list for thought as congregations consider family ministry.

In regard to specific planning, churches have often verbally expressed pro-family ideals, but in practical terms have done little to promote family bonds. Most church programs separate the family into age-related groupings. As strange as it sounds, perhaps a cut in programming would encourage family bonding. One church proclaims the last Sunday night of each month as Family Night and cancels evening services. A sign on the church door states:

> Sorry We Missed You! We believe in the importance of family. Families that do things together build strength, therefore, we have dismissed formal services tonight (as well as the last Sunday night of each month) so

that our families can be together. Please return next week. Meanwhile if we can be of any assistance just call our preaching minster. . . . (Thornton, 1992).

Some churches formulate their Family Ministry by implementing counseling and small support group ministries. This has taken form in many churches as dynamic lay ministries.

The Stephen Ministry Program began with the idea of developing support ministry. Its success has become an international, interdenominational approach that offers 50 class-hours of training in such areas as depression, loss of a child, ministering to families of homosexuals and lesbians, suicidal individuals and their families, grief, dying, mental and physical illness, and divorce. These areas present just the tip of the iceberg, depending on the need of a specific congregation.

Professional counseling services for the family can also be developed by the churches. Unfortunately, few churches have the resources to sustain a counseling program on their own. However, churches can unite quite successfully to offer services to their community.

Churches can unite quite successfully to offer professional counseling services to their community.

A group of San Francisco area churches formed the Christian Ministry of Counseling and Help. This pool of resources includes professionals such as medical doctors, licensed counselors, ministers, and family educators. The group had three goals:

❶ To win individuals to Christ.
❷ To assist families with various problems.
❸ To be a catalyst for spiritual growth.

(Deal, 1996, 26).

Every community has Christian professionals who could work together across the country to provide similar community resources or even national networks for specialized needs.

Conclusion

The local church must take several steps to develop healthy family ministry ministers.

✎ Define family ministry for the specific church. (This may include defining stances on divorce, remarriage, unwed pregnancies, etc.)

✎ Develop leadership to meet family needs.

✎ Create a vision for family needs that will continuously grow and adapt to the changing needs of the family.

✎ Identify resources for the families in the local church. This includes education programs and professionals.

✎ Evaluate current family programs.

(Vogelsang & Norton, 1998).

It is time to be a part of the solution to family problems in society instead of being idle bystanders.

It is easy to point out the problems in our families and the failures of our churches to meet their needs. However, it is time to be a part of the solution instead of being idle bystanders. The family was instituted by God. The church has the resources and abilities to support the family. Now is the time to seize this incredible opportunity.

Satan has ambushed the family in many ways and confused the traditional values that form the foundation of the family. He has offered the possibility of a better life for the adult who abandons a difficult marriage because someone better might be out there. He has promised family programs through the government to meet health, social, economic, and educational needs that have taken a values-free approach to life and the family.

No quick fix or easy solution exists. Every congregation must make a conscientious effort to strengthen the family. The salvation of our country's families is a calling. It is not a task, but a God-sent privilege and responsibility.

I have stood over both my daughters at night saying the same prayer:

Help me have the strength, commitment and patience to be a good role model. Help me nurture them physically, socially, and most importantly, spiritually. Allow the church to provide capable teachers, leaders, and experiences that will lead these little girls to Christ. Allow their paths to cross with Christian friends who may offer positive peer pressure. Develop these girls into dynamic Christian women. Provide Christian spouses, if marriage is in your will. Help them to be godly mothers, like their own, if they are blessed with children.

I am sure this is not an original prayer, but one that is uttered by many parents. However, praying alone will not ensure these things. It is time that we as the church do more than pray over our children and families. It is time that we access needs and take action to assist our congregation's families and offer them assistance where they are.

What does Jesus think of family ministry? During his ministry, He offered assistance to an immoral woman. He provided healing for those who were sick. He counseled the rich. He comforted the grieving. He loved the orphaned, dysfunctional, and traditional family. Isn't it time we follow the Master and do the same?

projects

★ Discuss with five or six families in your congregation about how they find the congregation ministering to and meeting their needs. Ask what else the church could do. ★

★ Design two methods and two programs, not currently available in your church, for reaching families. ★

For Further Reading

K.J. Bernstine, ed.
Church and Family Together: A Congregational Manual for Black Family Ministry. Valley Forge, PA: Judson Press, 1996.

Patrick Carnes
Out of the Shadows: Understanding Sexual Addiction. Center City, MN: Hazelden, 1992.

Gary R. Collins
Family Shock: Keeping Families Strong in the Midst of Earth-Shaking Change. Wheaton, IL: Tyndale House, 1995.

J.D. Craig
"New Family Structures: A Christian Counselor's View." *Christian Standard.* October 11, 1994, 15.

R.L. Deal
"The Church as Lifesaving Station: A Model Program Training Lay Counselors for the Ministry of Healing." *Journal of Family Ministry.* 10:1, 24-32.

James Dobson and Gary Bauer
Children at Risk. Dallas: Word, 1990.

Julie Gorman
Community That Is Christian. Wheaton: Victor Books, 1993.

M. Joseph and S. Preister
"A Model for Family Ministry at the Parish Level." J. Hiesberger. *Paths of Life.* New York: Paulist Press, 1980, 25-32.

A.M. Kelly and J.L. Cookston
"The National Family Ministry Forums—One Denominational Design for Discovery." *Journal of Family Ministry.* 12:1, 41-51.

W.C. McCready
"Family Healing: A Sociological Perspective." J. Hiesberger. *Paths of Life.* New York: Paulist Press, 1980, 6-11.

Cleveland McDonald and Philip McDonald
Creating a Successful Marriage. Grand Rapids: Baker, 1994.

Dean Merrill and Marshall Shelley, eds.
Fresh Ideas for Discipleship and Nurture. Carol Stream, IL: Victor Books, 1994.

National Council on Family Relations
"Family Education Life Span" Poster, 1998.

R.P. Olson and J.H. Leonard
A New Day for Family Ministry. New York: The Alban Institute.

James Osterhaus
Family Ties Don't Have to Bind. Nashville: Nelson, 1994.

Les Parrott III
Helping the Struggling Adolescent. Grand Rapids: Zondervan, 1993.

K. Pasley
Remarried Families. Presented at the National Council on Family Relations Conference "Moral Discourse on Families." November 14, 1993.

S.L. Rodman
"Stephen Ministry Program: Second Presbyterian Church, Louisville, Kentucky." *Journal of Family Ministry.* 11:4, 70-71.

C.M. Sell
Family Ministry. 2nd ed. Grand Rapids: Zondervan, 1995.

G.W. Sheek
The Word on Families. Nashville: Abingdon Press, 1995.

Michael J. Sporakowski, ed.
Family Life Education Teacher's Kit. Minneapolis: National Council on Family Relations, 1993.

D.M. Thomas
"Church as a Community of Compassion." J.M. Hiesberger. *Paths of Life.* New York: Paulist Press, 1980, 12-15.

S. Thomas
Your Church Can Be. . .Family Friendly. Joplin, MO: College Press, 1996.

S. Thornton
"Family Sunday." *Christian Standard.* 1992, 14.

J.D. Vogelsang and M.P. Norton
"What is Happening to Families at the End of the 20th Century?" *Journal of Family Ministry*. 12:1, 10-29.

K.L. Woodward
"The New Holy War." *Newsweek*. June 1, 1998, 26.

J.C. Wynn
Family Therapy in Pastoral Ministry: Counseling for the Nineties. New York: Harper Collins, 1991.

PART THREE

PLANNING

CHAPTER 14
PLANNING
FOR CHRISTIAN EDUCATION

Chapter Fourteen Summary
- ☑ The importance of planning in Christian Education
- ☑ Trends impacting the local church
- ☑ The necessity of change in remaining relevant
- ☑ 9 skills for effective Christian Education
- ☑ The planning process
- ☑ Structuring a Christian Education Planning Team
- ☑ Major tasks of the Christian Education Planning Team
- ☑ 4 principles for effective, efficient facility usage

Effective Christian education stimulates a person's growth in faith. So concluded Search Institute, a research organization based in Minneapolis, in their report entitled, "Effective Christian Education: A National Study of Protestant Congregations" (Benson & Eklin, 1990, 2, 4). Of the eighteen major conclusions documented, two identified the "amount of exposure to Christian education" as one of the "two experiences most associated with higher faith maturity" in both youth and adults. But it was not just exposure to Christian education that impacted one's faith in God. Rather, "the congregational factor most associated with helping people grow in faith maturity is the *degree of effectiveness in Christian education programming*" (italics in original). Of all the areas they examined in congregational life, "nothing matters more than effective Christian education." Yet, effectiveness in Christian education tends to be an elusive aspect—it does not occur accidentally. Effectiveness results from intentional planning. Strategic planning provides the pillar upon which effective Christian education rests.

Effectiveness results from intentional planning.

The Changing Shape of Christian Education

Planning becomes all the more vital in light of the revolutionary changes leading up to the twenty-first century. Knowledge is exploding faster than it can be printed. Technological advances have shattered many skills formerly regarded as necessary to survive in American culture. New skills, previously unheard of, and continuously changing, are needed to function as a member of society. Nothing will escape being affected by all the changes of the future. Barna declares that "effective ministry in the years ahead will be quite different from meaningful ministry today. In fact, it is likely that ministry in the year 2000 will be as different from ministry in 1980, as ministry in 1980 was from ministry in 1900. Change is occurring that quickly" (Barna, 1990, 27).

Trends Facing the Local Church

Christian educators need to be like the men of Issachar in 1 Chronicles 12:32 who "understood the times and knew what Israel should do." Gangel warns, ". . . educators cannot *impact* the future through Christian education until they first *understand* the future" (Gangel, 1989, 320). Analysis of culture to determine the prevalent trends that shape people's lives helps educators to identify the needs in society that the church could address. Ruth Picker's chapter, "Sociological Foundations," identified many such trends facing the church today. As educators "understand the times," they will know what the church should do to reach this generation for Christ. Trends not only reveal needs in society. They translate into potential opportunities for

Christian education ministry. The issue facing the church is not the fact that the world is changing sociologically, culturally, and technologically. Rather, the focal point centers upon how well she responds to this onslaught of change.

Trends translate into potential opportunities for Christian education ministry.

Change: The Necessary Ingredient of Relevance

Effective Christian education ministry requires relevance. The timeless truths of the Bible need to be interwoven with the ever-changing, contemporary needs of people in a technologically-driven culture. Though the message remains constant, the methods for conveying that message must change. Traditionally, the church has been years behind in adapting to the changing culture. Russell Chandler, in his book *Racing Toward 2001*, suggests that effective education requires the integration of tomorrow's media systems in the educating of today's "video-sophisticated" students (1992, 104). Failure to make the necessary changes would lead the church to become one of the most impotent institutions in society. Educational programs will need to be redesigned. Adult and children's ministries will need to be repackaged. Consideration needs to be given to both cross-cultural and cross-generational contact and interaction. Christian education effectiveness will depend upon whether those in educational leadership can clearly understand the trends that impact the church and then respond creatively. But to design and innovate new programs and to implement these changes to become relevant, Christian educators will need to acquire certain skills.

The Skills Needed for Effective Christian Education Ministry

The research project, "Christian Education Ministry in the Twenty-First Century" (Oakes, 1993) sought to determine the most important knowledge, attitudes, and skills for effective ministry at the start of the twenty-first century. Based upon the collection of data through five rounds of surveys directed to Christian education professors and Christian education practitioners in the local church, the project identified the skills essential for effective Christian education ministry. They were rank-ordered on a Likert scale (6 = strongly agree; 1 = strongly disagree) to determine the ten most important skills as perceived by both professors and practitioners. These skills are listed in order of priority along with a descriptive phrase that further describes the skill:

❶ Interpersonal Relationship Skills—ability to relate and work in harmony with others

❷ Equipping Skills—ability to train, develop, and disciple people for ministry

❸ Christian Living Skills—ability to be a testimony of personal holiness

❹ Volunteer Staff Skills—ability to recruit, train, and model teaching

❺ Biblical Skills—ability to study, interpret, defend, and apply truths to contemporary life

❻ Decision-Making Skills—ability to decide after careful evaluation of alternatives

❼ Organization Skills—ability to structure facilities, programs, people, and tasks

❽ Coordination Skills—ability to combine people, programs, and tasks for a common purpose

❾ Motivational Skills—ability to initiate programs and influence assumption of responsibilities

❿ Planning Skills—ability to set long range, intermediate, and short-term goals

Out of the top five skill categories, two of them (Equipping Skills and Volunteer Staff Skills) will be addressed in chapter 17 of this book. Two others (Interpersonal Relationship Skills and Christian Living Skills) focus upon the character of Christian educators in their ability to cultivate a vertical relationship with God and a harmonious horizontal relationship with others. The fifth skill category (Biblical Skills) is developed through biblical and theological courses. The last five skill categories, however, specifically relate to this chapter on planning for Christian education. They all involve administrative management responsibilities.

Decision-Making Skills

Christian education ministers must be decisive. Many administrative decisions are made every week regarding curriculum, room scheduling, selection of workers, solving problems, and organizational issues. Leaders need to be able to decide after careful evaluation of alternatives. Sometimes bad decisions are made because of failure to consider the characteristics of bad decision making.

Characteristics of Bad
Decision-Making

- ✎ Failure to make a decision. Indecisiveness is, by default, a decision not to decide. Such decisions—whether prompted by the push to gather more information or the fear of possible consequences—hinder ministerial effectiveness.
- ✎ Failure to consider the mission and goals. Every decision needs to be made in light of the institution's mission and goals and the program's objectives.
- ✎ Failure to gather sufficient information. Making decisions with too little information or without consideration for other points of view hinders effectiveness.
- ✎ Failure to walk by faith. Sometimes decisions need to be made that involve risk. Such decisions need to be bathed in prayer and entrusted to God.

Characteristics of Good
Decision-Making.

- ✎ Consideration of the mission and goals. All programs and decisions must be directed toward the institution's mission and goals.
- ✎ Involvement of others in the process. Good decisions are not independently made—they involve the Christian education planning team. Proverbs 15:22 says, "Plans fail for lack of counsel, but with many advisers they succeed."
- ✎ Careful evaluation of all opinions and other points of view.

Effective leaders seek out all opinions and seriously consider each one. Sometimes opinions that initially sound good are discounted once considered in light of actual practice.

✎ Facilitation of group consensus. Group decision-making blends the wisdom, experience and gifts of the members into a collaborative process that yields positive results. Consensus results when members carefully evaluate the alternatives and substantially agree that one course is preferred over the others.

Organizational Skills

Effective organization is a necessary tool for ministry. When Jethro, Moses' father-in-law, saw how Moses was judging the people from morning till evening, he said, "What you are doing is not good" (Exod 18:17). He then gave some organizational advice. "Select capable men from all the people—men who fear God, trustworthy men who hate dishonest gain—and appoint them as officials over thousands, hundreds, fifties and tens. . . . have them bring every difficult case to you; the simple cases they can decide themselves. . . . and all these people will go home satisfied" (Exod 18:21-23). This ability to structure facilities, programs, and tasks facilitates effective ministry—the people went home satisfied. Organization helps share the load of responsibility and enables effective ministry to take place.

Every program requires not just a number of people but also a number of tasks to be completed—usually in a given sequence.

Coordination Skills

Another aspect of administrative management is this ability to combine people, programs, and tasks for a common purpose. Every program requires not just a number of people but also a number of tasks to be completed—usually in a given sequence. Christian education ministers need to be able to recruit the people, delegate the tasks, and oversee their completion within the proper time schedule. This coordination is all focused upon the common goal for the program.

Motivational Skills

Motivational skills provide the ability to initiate programs and influence assumption of responsibility. This ability to motivate self and others is a necessary skill for effective Christian education ministry. Self-discipline provides the diligence needed to design and set up programs directed toward the meeting of educational needs. Motivating people to participate and to assume clearly described responsibilities is one key to a broad-based, widely-supported Christian educational program.

Planning Skills

Every program should have a written purpose that explains its reason for existence. That purpose is met by the fulfillment of the program's stated goals. Whether it is a lesson to be taught, a program to be developed, or a ministry to be started, this ability to write goals—whether long-term (3-5 years), intermediate (1-2 years), or short-term (1-12 months)—is essential for effective Christian education ministry. These planning skills provide both purpose and direction. They guide the continuous growth and development of Christian education.

Every program should have a written purpose that explains its reason for existence.

The Planning Process in the Local Church

Planning is a shared process of seeing the future and determining the steps to bring it to reality. Several key truths stand out in this definition. First, planning is *shared*. It involves the participation and contribution of others. The Christian education planning team works together in the development of educational plans. People support the plans they develop. Goal ownership results when people participate. Second, planning is a *process*. There is a distinct, ongoing, cyclical sequence of steps to follow. Planning analyzes the present to determine needs, develops the goals to meet those needs, determines the strategies to apply, evaluates the results, and revises the plans as needed. Whether planning a ministry, a program, or even a lesson, the same process exists. Third, planning *sees the future*. It projects a vision of what the future ministry will look like. That vision translates into goals that are specific, measurable, and reachable. Directed by the church's mission or purpose, the Christian education leadership establishes these "mile markers" along the road to an exciting ministry filled with possibilities. Fourth, planning *determines the specific steps needed to bring these goals to completion*. Whether these steps are called strategies or tasks, they represent the specific actions needed to accomplish each goal. These four truths define and describe planning. The planning process in the church, however, is broader than the definition of planning. It contains the following key steps.

Clarify the Mission and Vision

The first step in the church's planning process is to clarify the purpose for her existence. A clear mission statement describes why the church exists. For example, the mission of one congregation states "We exist to introduce people to Jesus Christ and encourage their responsible worship, fellowship, witness, and service." Each church must first of all clarify its purpose. From this purpose flows a vision of what God wants the church to do or become. This vision is defined as "a clear and challenging picture of the future of a ministry as its leadership believes it can and must be" (Malphurs, 1992, 31). The Christian education planning team starts with these two pictures of why the church exists, and what the church will do. Together they provide the direction and motivation for effective leadership ministry in the 21st century.

Whether planning a ministry, a program, or even a lesson, the same process exists.

Analyze the Situation

The second step in the planning process is to analyze the current situation. This involves looking in two directions: out the window and in the mirror. Looking out the window means exploring the environment outside the church. The church cannot control these external factors: political, economic, social forces, and trends. But the church is greatly affected by changes within them. For example, a church whose membership consists largely of workers in a cookie factory would be economically and socially affected if the factory closed. Consideration of the external environment helps to identify not only the possible threats like the closing of a factory, but also the potential ministries. What are the demographic breakdowns of the community? What age group is predominant? Are the families "white-collar" or "blue-collar?" What religious affiliation is dominant? These questions help formulate the possibilities for growth and the opportunities for ministry. Looking in the mirror means looking within the church to those factors that the church can control. The leadership should carefully evaluate all programs, ministries, services, facilities, teachers, and classes to determine present strengths and weaknesses.

Identify the Needs

After analyzing the external and internal environments of the church, the leadership should next identify the needs. The threats and opportunities (external) and strengths and weaknesses (internal) help raise awareness of both needs and issues to be resolved. These needs are then stated in the form of questions: How can the church attract more young adults to attend Bible school? What can be done to improve the effectiveness of the nursery program? How can visitors feel acceptance and a sense of belonging? Once these needs are stated, the Christian education leadership must then determine the consequences for failure to respond. If no consequences result, then the need is not an important strategic issue. If, however, negative consequences would result from failure to respond, then the need should be considered a high priority.

Construct the Goals

Once needs are determined, the planning team constructs goals to address those needs. Written goals clearly state "the precise kinds of things God expects of *your* congregation in *your* location at this time in history" (Gangel, 1989, 86). They project what the educational program or structure would be like in the future. Goals are measurable—the leadership can know when they are achieved. They provide direction for intentional planning. For example, "The young adult ministry plans to contact thirty new young adults for Bible school by developing an eight-week sand volleyball outreach program during the summer of 1999." This goal grows out of the need stated above, "How can the church attract more young adults to attend Bible school?" It focuses the planning efforts and provides a specific, measurable evaluation for determining accomplishment and effectiveness.

Simply writing a goal does not ensure its completion.

Determine and Apply the Strategies

Simply writing a goal does not ensure its completion. Goals need to be broken down into the specific strategies or tasks that need to be accomplished to bring them about. Strategies involve a category, a sequence, a time frame, and a person responsible. One of the best ways to determine all that needs to be done to reach a goal is to have the planning team brainstorm. Write down every idea or task suggested. Next, group all the items into categories like "facilities," "publicity and promotion," "staffing," and "equipment and supplies." Seeing the items under specific categories often leads to additional tasks being suggested. Then arrange all of the items under each category into the proper sequence. Obviously, writing a letter of invitation would need to occur prior to sending the invitation to the targeted age group. Assign a specific date for each task to be completed within each category as well as a specific person to be responsible for each task. Then arrange all tasks from all categories by the date assigned. Place all of these items on the calendar and each week the required task will be remembered and completed at the proper time.

Evaluate and Revise

The Christian education minister evaluates constantly. Evaluation uncovers the needs initially as well as determines the progress toward the accomplishment of goals. Both strategies and goals need to be "written in clay and not in concrete." That is, they are open to revision. Ministry is like a sail in the blowing winds of change. Christian education ministers must monitor changes both outside and inside the congregation. Adjustments to goals and strategies in the face of unforeseen events or circumstances are sometimes necessary. Failure to evaluate the status of various programs or projects could well result in unintentionally allowing them to degenerate beyond the point of remediation. By following a regular process of evaluation Christian education ministers can detect potential problems and make revision as necessary.

The Structure of the Christian Education Planning Team

Planning for Christian education involves the group effort of the Christian Education Planning Team. Some churches call this administrative group a council, a committee, or a board. Regardless of its name, this Christian Education Planning Team administrates the church's educational program. In some churches its area of responsibility includes more than the Sunday morning Bible school program. The children's church ministry, the youth program, the vacation Bible school program, Wednesday night classes, and the educational resource center are often included in the oversight function of this team. Though having all the educational endeavors of the church under the responsibility of this team has administrative advantages, many churches have restricted their area of jurisdiction to the Sunday morning Bible school program. Youth and children's church programs are often the responsibility of the youth ministry team. Special task force groups may direct the vacation Bible school programs. Even the nursery programs are often placed into the responsibility of the nursery ministry team. So for purposes of this chapter, the Christian Education Planning Team focuses upon the Sunday morning Bible school programs. The team meets regularly, usually monthly, and provides the administrative management and oversight of the Bible school.

The Christian Education Planning Team includes at least seven key individuals.

As such, the organizational structure of this team includes at least seven key individuals. The first is the professional Christian Education minister. As a salaried position on the church staff, this person administrates and oversees the total educational program of the church. Eleanor Daniel's chapter 20, "The Professional Christian Educator," identifies the various positions and responsibilities. As a primary responsibility, she chairs the planning team and provides guidance to the educational ministry of the Bible school. The second key individual who serves on the planning team is the Bible school director or superintendent. Given the primary task of managing the Bible school, he recruits teachers, orders curriculum and supplies, assigns rooms, and provides the record keeping necessary for informed decision making.

These first two individuals are joined by four age-division coordinators as illustrated in Diagram 14.1. The preschool division coordinator oversees the staffing and programs for children from birth through kindergarten. The children's division coordinator supervises the teachers and classes for children, grades 1 through 6. Youth, grades 7 through 12, and their teachers fall under the oversight of the youth division coordinator. And the adult division coordinator is responsible for all adult classes. Each coordinator oversees her particular age division. She plans, leads, organizes, staffs, and evaluates her division to ensure that the educational objectives are being met.

The last person included in this planning team is the Outreach Ministry Leader. With a calling and a passion to reach people for Christ, he "is responsible to see that the goal of reaching new people remains a top priority in everything done through educational programs" (Haystead, 1995, p. 130).

Diagram 14.1: The Christian Education Planning Team

Christian Education Minister			
Bible School Director		Outreach Ministry Leader	
Preschool Division Coordinator	Children's Division Coordinator	Youth Division Coordinator	Adult Division Coordinator

The Major Tasks of the Christian Education Planning Team

As the administrative arm of the educational ministry, this team exerts the leadership muscle in the implementation of a number of major responsibilities. One of the most critical tasks is the *establishment of educational policies and procedures*. What is the procedure for selecting and recruiting teachers? What policies are needed to ensure their theological accuracy? What decisions would provide physical and sexual protection for children and legally protect the church from lawsuits? How is the curriculum chosen and by whom? What disciplinary policies guide teachers in the classroom? These and other issues are discussed in this planning body. The decisions reached and the policies and procedures formed guide the church's educational ministry.

A second key task is to *evaluate the context to determine educational needs*. Taking the time to carefully analyze both the external and internal environments of the church helps to determine ministry needs. Attendance records, program and personnel evaluation, new member integration studies and retention, and demographic comparisons between the community and the church all provide indicators of potential needs. Both the opportunities and threats in the external environment outside the church and the strengths and weaknesses of the internal environment inside the church need to be identified. As these areas are assessed, the leadership team will clearly see the needs to be addressed.

Third, *develop ministries and goals to meet the educational needs.* Churches should use their opportunities and strengths to overcome their threats and weaknesses. Ministries may need to be designed to meet these needs. Goals will need to be stated. Together they direct the efforts of the congregation toward those areas that are most needed. The key point to understand is that needs determine ministry and goals—not the other way around. To develop ministries and goals not based upon needs is both ineffective and irresponsible.

Develop ministries and goals to meet educational needs.

Fourth, *design and coordinate strategies to accomplish the ministries and goals.* Strategies are the specific tasks that bring about the various ministries and goals. Coordination ensures that the tasks and schedules of the educational ministry programs mesh with the other church activities. Wise leadership consolidates the various opportunities for ministry on meeting nights thereby avoiding the fragmentation of families every night of the week.

Fifth, *assign space and provide supplies and equipment.* The planning team decides where classes meet and after evaluation, recommends when additional space is required for the ongoing educational ministry. They oversee the acquisition of supplies and equipment to ensure that teachers have the tools necessary for effective instruction. Rooms may even need to be reassigned depending upon the size of the class to make efficient use of available space.

Sixth, *evaluate, select, and provide curriculum.* When teachers choose their own material to teach, serious gaps in biblical instruction result. Otherwise material is duplicated needlessly. Either way, a purposeful, well-balanced, biblical instruction does not occur. The leadership team looks at the total educational program and makes curricular decisions that meet the needs of the people.

Seventh, *select, recruit, and provide an ongoing training program for teachers and leaders*. An evaluation and approval process for prospective teachers and leaders needs to be determined by the leadership team. The quality of instruction is directly related to the quality of the individual providing the instruction. Therefore, careful selection and screening, and intentional recruiting must take place. Training should include both preservice (prior to becoming a teacher) and in-service (after and during the time of being a teacher) instruction. Daniel's chapter 16, "Recruiting, Training and Keeping Volunteer Leaders" provides specific instruction in this task.

Training should include both preservice and in-service instruction.

Eighth, *provide continuous evaluation and revision (as needed) of needs, goals, and strategies*. Monitoring the various educational ministries of the church provides effective management. By discovering weaknesses early, a process for remediation and correction can be determined and implemented. For example, carefully monitoring attendance patterns of the high school class with a new teacher revealed a steady attendance drop in four consecutive weeks. Upon consultation with the students, the team discovered a methods problem—the new teacher only used the lecture with no interaction among the students. Intervention and instruction corrected the situation and reversed the downward trend.

The Principles for Effective and Efficient Facility Usage

One task of the Christian education planning team mentioned above was assigning rooms in which learning experiences occur. This task cannot be handled haphazardly. There are definite principles to guide the allocation of space to maximize the building's efficiency. Failure to adhere to these principles could well result in reduced learning, stymied growth, and improper decision-making.

Purpose-Driven

Educational decisions need to be made in light of both the institutional mission and the program's purpose statement. Yet far too often, the facility becomes the icon of God's presence and protective decisions prevent adorning the walls with educational materials. Some churches even restrict rearranging furniture, using glitter or glue, and eating or drinking in the classrooms. Rather than elevating the building to a museum-like holy edifice, the rooms and facilities need to be used as tools for ministry. Unfortunately, rooms often become the private possession of classes and groups who resist relocation. Even though class attendance has dwindled to less than ten, they still covet staying in the room that seats fifty. To allow such to continue does not provide efficient facility usage. The purpose needs to drive the Christian education planning team's decision-making. Rooms need to be assigned—and reassigned—to maximize the potential for effective ministry. Facilities need to be used as tools to enhance the *educational experience*.

Rooms often become the private possession of classes and groups who resist relocation.

Philosophy-Governed

Educational space should be governed by a solid educational philosophy. Room sizes, furnishings, and arrangements are all determined by the age group meeting in the rooms and how they learn best. For example, preschool children need the largest amount of floor space per person but the smallest group size. Room furnishings should be age-appropriate. Room arrangements convey instructional methods. Rows of chairs facing a podium and chalkboard communicate a lecture format. A circle of chairs encourages interpersonal sharing. Individual tables with chairs around them give the impression of discussion groups. Adult learners come to class with life experiences that illustrate and apply biblical principles. Philosophically, they need to be involved in the learning process through methods that facilitate their participation. However, sometimes the size and structural layout of the classroom prevents their interaction with one another. To use each classroom effectively and efficiently, educational philosophy must be considered.

Effective facility use demands that the programs determine both room selection and usage.

Program-Considered

Another essential principle is to make room selection and usage program considered. Sometimes facilities contain and constrain the activities that take place there in the same way that water takes the shape of the container into which it is poured. To allow the facilities to determine the programs conducted within them is to limit the vision for what God can accomplish. Effective facility use demands that the programs determine both room selection and usage. Efficiency also demands that rooms be used by having multiple services each Sunday and by programs and ministries at other times. Flexibility makes it possible for leaders of two programs to share the same room and equipment at different times during the week. Rooms should be flexible enough to accommodate any age group, children through adult. Efficiency results when similar age groups use the same rooms. This limits the shifting of furnishings from room to room. Moveable walls increase flexibility and allow for a wide diversity of programs and activities. Some programs may need to take place in nearby facilities to accommodate the unique purposes of the program or even to provide additional space where none was available in the present facility.

People-Centered

Another key principle ensures that facility use is people-centered. The leadership team must never forget that all the administrative planning, scheduling, and organizing is directed

PLANNING

toward people. The effort expended and time sacrificed in planning for Christian education make it possible for effective ministry to occur. Sometimes leaders reject administration because they believe it takes them away from people. On the contrary, administration brings people together—and brings them together for a Kingdom purpose!

In light of this people-centered principle, consideration should be given to provide a personally appealing decor throughout the facility. Basic features such as proper lighting, heating, and air conditioning either detract from or enhance learning. Proper maintenance and cleaning ensure that rooms are well kept and provide a warm, comfortable setting. Even a simple coat of fresh paint can go a long way in appealing to people. Age-appropriate tables and chairs need to be furnished and arranged in a manner that facilitates learning—because people is what educational ministry is all about.

Conclusion

Christian education ministry in the 21st century will continue to change. New methods and ministries will probably be developed to reach people for Christ. Though the message of the Bible remains constant, the methods of teaching it will continue to be revised. Nevertheless, the skills needed for effective Christian education ministry and the planning process engaged in by the leadership team will probably remain. By performing the major tasks of the Christian education planning team and by following the principles for effective and efficient facility usage, Christian educators will become a catalyst for spiritual restoration both in the church and in the world.

p r o j e c t s

★ Using Oakes' guidelines, put together an effective Christian Education Planning Team for your church. ★

★ Design a layout for effective, efficient use of your current facility. Dream and design your *ideal* facility. ★

> ★ Interview a Christian education leader in your congregation. Find out how planning for Christian education is done and why it is done that way. ★

For Further Reading

Leith Anderson
A Church for the 21st Century: Bringing Change to Your Church to Meet the Challenges of a Changing Society. Minneapolis: Bethany House, 1992.

George Barna
The Frog in the Kettle: What Christians Need to Know about Life in the Year 2000. Ventura, CA: Regal, 1990.

Peter Benson and Carolyn Eklin
Effective Christian Education: A National Study of Protestant Congregations. Minneapolis: Search Institute, 1990.

Russell Chandler
Racing Toward 2001: The Forces Shaping America's Religious Future. Grand Rapids: Zondervan, 1992.

Robert Clark, Lin Johnson, and Allyn Sloat
Christian Education: Foundations for the Future. Chicago: Moody, 1991.

Kenneth Gangel
Feeding & Leading. Wheaton: Victor, 1989.

Team Leadership in Christian Ministry. Chicago: Moody, 1997.

"Ten Forces Shaping Christian Education." *Bibliotheca Sacra*. 146, 320.

Wes Haystead
The 21st Century Sunday School: Strategies for Today and Tomorrow. Cincinnati: Standard, 1995.

Michael Lawson and Robert Choun, Jr.
Directing Christian Education: The Changing Role of the Christian Education Specialist. Chicago: Moody, 1992.

A. Malphurs
Developing a Vision for Ministry in the 21st Century. Grand Rapids: Baker, 1992.

Ron Oakes
"Christian Education Ministry in the 21st Century." D. Min. Dissertation, Bethel Theological Seminary, 1993.

CHAPTER 15
DEVELOPING A **BALANCED**
CHRISTIAN EDUCATION PROGRAM

Chapter Fifteen Summary
- ☑ The needs-based ministry of the early church
- ☑ Sunday ministries
- ☑ Weekday Ministries
- ☑ Multiple Day Ministries
- ☑ Off-site Ministries

I have become all things to all men so that by all possible means I might save some. I do all this for the sake of the gospel, that I may share in its blessing (1 Cor 9:22b, 23).

The story is told about a teacher who, while teaching a unit on nutrition, asked her class to describe to her a balanced meal. One of her students immediately raised a hand and waved it wildly to get her attention. When called upon, the student quickly responded that the definition of a balanced meal was a piece of chocolate cake in each hand. To a child that may sound like a good example of a balanced diet, but to a nutritionist it falls drastically short. A balanced diet requires a variety of types of foods, with each providing a specific benefit to the body.

Financial investments require a balanced effort.

Financial investments require a balanced effort. Many consider checking and savings accounts with a life insurance policy an adequate way to prepare for the future. However, a financial advisor will recommend a more balanced approach, using stocks and bonds in a mixed ratio of high to low risk investments to create a portfolio that will best meet our needs as we look toward the future. As with nutrition, financial planning requires more than just two equal objects to present a balanced approach.

We have long worried about our physical health and financial health but have ignored the health of the church.

These two illustrations are applicable to the educational work of the church. Many churches look at a balanced education program as Sunday school on Sunday morning and a high school youth group on Sunday evening. Though this is a traditional view that has served many in the past, it does not present a balanced view of education. Many needs of the members, and nonmembers, are not being met. We have long worried about our physical health and financial health but have ignored the health of the church. As a result the spiritual growth and faith maturity of our congregations is lacking. Donald Griggs, in the foreword of *The Teaching Church*, writes:

> Will churches continue to identify Christian education primarily as a Sunday School program for children? Or will they explore ways to increase involvement of youth and adults in a through-the-week, lifelong process of learning about and growing in the faith? (Roehlkepartain, 1993, 9)

As with our health and financial investments, the church must present a balanced program to meet the needs of its members and the people it will try to evangelize. The early church had a needs-based ministry and its growth, both physically and spiritually, was phenomenal.

- The church met in small groups to better facilitate teaching (Acts 2:37-42).
- The needs of the widows were met (Acts 6:1-6).

✎ Believers prayed for each other and those outside of Christ (Acts 12:1-17).

✎ Churches saw opportunities to evangelize their communities and to those far off (Acts 6, 8, 13).

✎ The church held special conferences and studies to learn more about special needs and problems that arose (Acts 15).

✎ In Acts 6 the Apostles felt that they should be found in the study of Scripture and prayer. They could have made this the emphasis of the church, but they saw a need in the congregation and provided for it by selecting capable leaders to develop the ministry. The resulting leadership caused even more growth, as exemplified in the lives of Stephen and Philip. The example of the early church encourages us to look beyond traditional programs and provide a balanced ministry for the work of the church.

A balanced program looks beyond Sunday as the only day to offer services to the people of the church. Ministries need to be offered that go beyond the concept of the traditional Sunday school and youth groups as the only educational medium, allowing the church to envision the magnitude of its purpose. Christian education must look beyond the local congregation to the community and develop ways to present a caring Christ to them. Christian education must look both within and outside itself to present a balanced program for spiritual growth.

A balanced program looks beyond Sunday as the only day to offer services to the people of the church.

Sunday Ministries

The balanced program involves Sunday, weekday, multiple-day, off-site, and special needs programs. The different meeting days and ties offer a variety of special benefits to the church and the community. Each of these areas will be considered, and ideas given for effective implementation. First, consider the traditional day of worship—Sunday.

Sunday is the traditional day for worship and training. Though the day of worship was never commanded to be the first day, it was established as such because it was on the first day of the week that Jesus arose (Matt 28:1-8). Paul, as he wrote to the Romans (20:7), noted they accepted this day as their day of worship. In 1 Corinthians (16:2), Paul exhorts the church to collect an offering on the first day of the week. As a day of gathering it provided a focal point for worship.

As mentioned earlier, the day has been questioned, not as a day of worship and training, but as the only day for these opportunities to occur. Though maligned, the day does present great opportunities for teaching and outreach. Recognized as a day of worship in our society, it is also a common day of rest for most people. Members of the congregation and community are home and able to attend. They are more attuned to worship and study on this day, because it is the traditional day to attend church. This results in Sunday being a prime day for Christian education ministries to work.

Though originally developed outside the established church, Sunday school has been effectively assimilated.

Sunday School

The most recognizable and common Christian education ministry is that of the Sunday school or Bible school. Though originally a ministry developed outside the established church, it has been effectively assimilated into its educational programs. The advantages of Sunday school in a balanced educational program are many, but the most prevalent are as follows. First, it is a time of concentrated Bible study. Students are able to spend a larger amount of time, even weeks, focusing on a passage of Scripture. Secondly, Sunday school can offer studies designed more for the students' interest and needs, whereas, worship tends to emphasize generalized topics. Third, classes can be designed to reach specific groups. Age groupings can be made for children, youth, adults, and senior adults. In modern society the need to provide classes for singles, single parents, and those with special needs has become an imperative. Fourth, perhaps the greatest advantage lies in the neutrality of the Sunday school as an evangelistic outreach. Many will come to a Sunday school class who would never come to a worship service, finding it less threatening to attend a study group.

Opportunities for spiritual growth and outreach are lost when the SS program is limited to children only.

However, some drawbacks to Sunday school may hinder a balanced approach. Almost every church has a Sunday school, yet a large number offer few, if any, classes for adults. Perhaps an even greater tragedy is that some churches offer no classes for high school youth. Sunday school is regarded as a children's activity, and unimportant for youth and adults. In some mega-churches it has become fashionable to eliminate adult Bible school (generally because of logistics problem) in favor of small group studies at other times. Opportunities for spiritual growth and outreach are lost when the program is limited to children only. Perhaps the greatest detriment to a balanced approach is the lack of trained teachers. Classes can be created and special subjects offered, but if the educator has not been trained, the program is severely weakened and may even fail. Instructors must know the material, but most importantly they must understand the student and how to relate to them.

Children's Church or Extended Sessions

Another valuable ministry often seen only as babysitting is children's church, or extended sessions. Children's church uses materials developed for a church-time program of worship and learning, whereas extended sessions are extensions of the Sunday school with an element of worship added. These provide an opportunity for children to learn with their peers, rather than attending a worship service in which they would be restless and gain a minimal amount of understanding. Because children become fidgety in "big" church, parents send them to the "nursery" for care. Not only do parents see this as a nursery service, the children and their teachers also see it that way. With proper training, teachers can present an effective program that will allow their students to learn more about their relationship with God, and how to worship Him. Providing information about the children's church ministry and its mission to the parents will help them prepare their children for this valuable experience.

Youth Groups or Activity Clubs

In many churches, Sunday evening is for junior and senior high youth groups. The church often hires a youth minister to direct the youth program and places the program in the budget, demonstrating its importance. These groups provide an opportunity to teach students on their grade level, to present materials that meet their spiritual needs, and provide for social interaction. This is a needed and vital part of the educational program, but two other groups can also benefit from a special evening program: children and adults.

For the church to depend on the Sunday school to provide all of the education needs for children is like placing all of the weights on one pan of a balance scale and calling it balanced. Children need age-related studies and social experiences as much as older youth. This can be a time of growth and building of basics for future life in church and community. When adults are asked about their earliest faith commitments, few can point to a single moment of conversion, but many relate that faith development had grown gradually since early childhood.

To depend on the Sunday school to provide all of the education needs for children is like placing all of the weights on one pan of a balance scale and calling it balanced.

Children's programs can be developed by the church staff and volunteers. But many churches have added a minister to children to facilitate the development of these programs and to train personnel. Some excellent activity club curricula have been designed for students—Awana, Royal Rangers, Success with Youth, Pioneer Clubs. A well balanced youth program must include provisions for children.

Electives or Training Hour

The evening worship service is generally directed in most churches toward adults. The attendance in these services has waned in recent years. Some churches countered with a more contemporary service or with a general Bible study with varying degrees of success. One avenue of education that has been successful is the addition of adult electives with courses designed to meet adult needs. Bible studies allow students to do more research into the background and meanings of the Scriptures than the Sunday school hour will allow. Other courses are life related, family issues, finances, job training, etc. These electives allow adults to meet their specific life needs and interests.

The concept of the training hour is also successful. Churches have developed courses on what it means to be a member, church leadership, teacher development, and other topics that prepare members to become more effective in their work with the congregation.

One of the most successful evening educational programs for adults has been the development of small group studies. Often these occur on Sunday nights, although they may occur on any night of the week. These groups are developed on a geographical basis or through personal connections. They meet together to study the Bible, special interest subjects, or personal growth. At the same time group members spend time in prayer for each other and in fellowship. A well-designed program of small groups is an excellent way to involve adults, enhance spiritual growth, and expand the evangelistic outreach of the church.

Weekday Ministries

Often churches avoid weekday ministries because they feel they will be competing with school and family activities. However, research has shown that busyness may be less problematic than we sometimes think. We know, for example, that youth who tend to be involved in more outside activities also tend to be more (not less) active in church activities. Thus the problem may not be dealing with the busy people, but discovering ways to reach out and include those people who find time for what meets their needs (Roehlkepartain, 1993, 83).

The addition of quality Christian education programs may fill the void for many busy people. Many youth are involved in after school programs because most colleges and universities give preference to those applicants who can show commitment and leadership in extracurricular activities. Activities provided through the church can provide this experience with youth who also gain spiritually. The church gains by having program helpers and training future leaders.

Weekday ministries offer a time when attending church is less threatening.

Weekday ministries also offer a time when attending church is less threatening. Many find it less threatening to enter a church building for the first time on a day other than Sunday. Often when people are introduced to the church through weekday ministries, they find the church to be inviting and seek more information about joining the congregation.

Ministries during the week allow a more complete use of the church building. Buildings that cost hundreds of thousands, even millions of dollars may be only partially used during the week. Meeting rooms and teaching aids that would otherwise sit dormant can be put to good use.

The church can become more involved in its neighboring community because people who were gone on the weekends are now home and available for services the church can offer. Classes and programs that fill their needs will help draw them to the congregation. The demonstration of a church involved in its community will show that it cares for more than just its members.

Family Ministry

One of the biggest needs in most communities is help in caring for a family. The family is under attack from many fronts, and most families need help and support. Families are separated from their grandparents, aunts and uncles, and other family support systems. Both parents work, putting a strain in family and personal relationships. Children are active in school, sports, and community activities and are pulled away from family activities. Morals are being taught by many who deny the validity of wholesome standards. Many parents and children alike welcome informational help and training.

This opens the door for a family ministry. The church has long been a standard for family relations and morals. It now has the chance to minister to the community as well as its own membership. Classes and support groups can be of benefit in child rearing, husband and wife relationships, family relationships, finances, personal issues, and vocational guidance. Personnel from the church trained in these areas can be of great service to families.

**The church now has the chance to minister
to the community as well as its own membership.**

Many families do not spend an evening together, let alone a mealtime. If a family eats at least three meals a week together, relationships are smoothed and bonds are strengthened. The church cannot force families to sit down to three meals, but it can invite them to spend at least one evening together. The encouragement to develop a family night, by creating and providing materials to be used, providing training sessions on how to lead a family night, and counseling on relationships, can enhance these special nights.

Some churches conduct a family night at the church building. Many have found success in having a meal prepared for family members. The cost is kept at a minimum (possibly subsidized by the church). Though most churches use this as a time for Bible studies and youth groups, others have succeeded by keeping it as a true family night. Programs are planned which allow families to participate together in Bible studies, prayer, games, and open communication between family members. This type of family night allows those with busy schedules, who do not have time to prepare an effective get-together, to have this special time together. Family time together is never wasted time and is to be encouraged.

Day Care

In many families both parents work and one of their major concerns is who will care for the children. It is a real concern because the news media periodically reveals childcare centers that are understaffed and that abuse or ignore the children placed in their care.

Churches may already have the facilities to handle a day-care: fully equipped nurseries, rooms designed for small children, toilet facilities, a kitchen and fellowship hall, and quite often a play yard or an area that could easily be converted to play space. If day care facilities were opened, with trained personnel, a great service could be offered to the members of the community. Care offered by churches can readily advocate traditional family and moral standards. An announcement in the summer of 1998 indicated that government subsidy for child care now allows funds to go to churches without government intervention. This can help many churches establish their own program.

Churches may already have the facilities to handle a daycare.

Two words of warning. Know the standards for day care in your community and state. These standards are designed for the welfare of children; churches should observe—or even exceed them. The second is to select personnel carefully. Background checks are important—and required—but selection of pesonnel should be based on personal and spiritual criteria as well. This will provide strong assurance to parents.

Bible Clubs and Day Camps

Similar to youth groups, Bible clubs are designed for young children and generally meet in someone's backyard once a week. The advantage to this type of program is that it is held on a totally neutral site and most parents of neighborhood kids are not afraid to send their children. Bible study, activities, and refreshments are the core of these clubs. Child Evangelism Fellowship has been successful in this type of outreach. However, materials from other sources can be readily adapted or new material created for these studies.

The advantage to a Bible club program is that it is held on a totally neutral site.

One successful Bible club program met on Saturdays during the summer in a local movie theater. Wholesome movies were shown and promoted to attract children from the community. In between the movies, games were played and prizes given. Students were given tickets for special prizes to be given away on the final day—the more they attended the more chances they had to win. After the games, a teacher led them in a special Bible time, in which they were acquainted with the truths of the Bible. Clubs like this one offer a unique opportunity to teach children and evangelize the community. They are often short term, lasting only a summer, though some successful ones are run year round, but they are rewarding.

Day camps are like Bible clubs in that they are generally for younger children and meet away from the church on a weekly basis. They differ in the location and length of time the children meet together. Day camps are often found in parks and camping areas to give them a camping atmosphere. While Bible clubs last from one to two hours, day camps are generally half- to full-day activities. They also are an excellent way to evangelize the community because unchurched parents are often more comfortable sending their children to a neighbor's house than to a church building.

Bible clubs and day camps provide opportunities to educate children other than on Sundays. The most obvious advantage is the availability of more time. This allows the teacher to fully develop an idea without rushing. The relaxed atmosphere makes it easier to get the children involved physically and intellectually. The increased length of time permits the use of games and activities to enhance the lesson as well as to cure the wiggles. Bible clubs and day camps are an excellent way to enhance the educational program.

Bible Studies

As mentioned earlier, one of the growing ministries of the church is small groups. These groups can meet on Sunday or throughout the week. Women's study groups at the church, in a home, or at a restaurant provide the opportunity to study Scriptures and how they apply to daily life. Men's and teen's studies can meet at a restaurant early in the morning before work or school. Not all Bible studies have to take place at the church; weekly studies in homes have proven successful because they are at neutral sites. These studies allow members to speak more openly than when they are in a mixed Sunday class or small group.

Multiple-Day Ministries

Multiple-day ministries are a series of connected days on one subject. They offer some definite advantages. The ability to fully develop a concept is the most compelling benefit. Instead of students going home and returning a week later to continue the study and the teacher having to spend valuable time refreshing their minds, the class comes back the next day, or hour, and continues with the subject still fresh on their minds. A second advantage is the possibility of moving to a different location where the influences of work and family are lessened. Students are able to focus their full attention on the course. Sometimes the location will add to the material taught, such as meeting by a lake or seashore with lesson themes of becoming "fishers of men" or meeting at an inner-city location on the subject of "caring for the least of these." Multiple-day ministries offer many advantages and should be developed in the education program.

Vacation Bible School

Perhaps the most well-known multiple-day ministry is vacation Bible school. At one time VBS lasted for six weeks. It was then reduced to one month, then to ten days, and now most churches have five-day programs. Regardless of the length, a well-planned VBS offers a time when children, youth, and adults learn in an atmosphere that is both fun and practical. All elements of the two- to four-hour program are connected together by a theme to gain the most benefit. The VBS can be held during the day, though most adults cannot come at this time, or at night, which limits the amount of time for each session. Another possibility is a VBS that meets one day a week for a month or a summer, lasting all day. VBS is a traditional way to reach out to the community. Most parents are glad to have a quality program to which to send their children during the summer, and a good experience opens doors for further ministry.

Church Camps, Retreats, and Conferences

Other multiple-day ministries are actually extended-site ministries. They take place away from the church property, but are still influenced by the church atmosphere. These ministries are widely used in Christian education.

The first is church camp. Camps take place generally throughout the summer in a locality away from the church site. They usually last about a week. These weeks are designed for specific age groups (children through adult) or special interest groups, such as missions, singles, and families. Some churches conduct their own camps; others work together to develop a camping program.

A camping program is an effective way to build on what has been taught at the church. Camping is also an excellent way for the church staff to interact and bond with the children and youth of the congregation as they study the Bible and learn new Christian life skills together.

A camping program is an effective way to build on what has been taught at the church.

Camping programs do not have to be tied to the summer months or to a developed campsite. The camping experience can be enjoyed and used successfully year round. Many established camps have winter facilities and encourage their use. Wilderness, boating and canoeing, and stress camps are becoming more popular, especially for groups that want to create a bonding experience or to help their members find inner strength and confidence needed to build their faith.

Retreats and conferences are shorter term than camps and are more concentrated in their approach to learning. The subject matter will often concentrate on a single concept rather than the several generally found at camp. The time frame is either a two- or three-day weekend away at a camp, resort, or a hotel. The least effective location is on the church property because home and job are too close and may easily distract participants. Almost any subject can be covered during these times. Though fun and recreation may be a part of the time together, it should not be a major emphasis. The main reason to be at a retreat or conference is to benefit from concentrated study.

Libraries

The continual use of the church library is a special multiple-day ministry. Though most churches have a library, they are often not used much nor are they well promoted or funded. Church libraries can be of benefit to the members of the congregation, and especially those who teach. Many Bible study books are expensive and the general membership cannot justify buying them for their personal libraries, but these books would be a great asset in personal Bible study or preparation for teaching. Many people buy inspirational books, read them once, and then sell them at a garage sale. Those same books could be shared by many if they were in a church library. Children are trained to use school and public libraries for research. It would be of benefit to them to have materials that present worldviews, moral principles, and ethics from a Christian perspective. Properly promoted and funded, church libraries offer much to the education of the congregation.

A valuable resource in a library is to make tapes, videos, and computer resources available. Gaining permission in writing to use these materials is important. A simple way to gain the necessary authorizations is to contact organizations such as Christian Copyright Licensing, Inc. (music) and Motion Picture Licensing Corp. (video).

Off-site Ministries

Ministries that take place off the church site, or site extension, offer many possibilities to broaden the learning experience of participants. One public school developed a method to teach students how to swim. They went through all of the basic strokes and safety measures. It was only after several weeks that they were actually taken to a swimming pool to try out what they had learned. Needless to say many failures were recorded and the program was cancelled. The same thing happens within churches. Classes are arranged and students are trained, then they are allowed to flounder on their own. What if Jesus had never sent the disciples out on their own, asking them to later return and share their experiences? What if the only time they went out was after Jesus had left for heaven? The evangelistic efforts of the early church would have been severely changed. Off-site ministries are important if the church wants to effectively reach out to the community.

Christian education programs are often accused of existing in a "hothouse" environment.

Christian education programs are often accused of existing in a "hothouse" environment. Its members are said to be insulated from the world and unaware of what is really happening. When the church enters the world of the student, Bible teachings begin to make sense and to fit into modern life. When students begin to apply what they have learned by performing acts of service to the community, not only do the students grow in their faith, but the community sees the church as caring and concerned.

Service learning has made a big impact on public schools in recent years. This learning concept involves combining what students learn with service to the community. Basically, it is putting what is learned at school into practice, or bringing the lives of the student into the classroom. It is a format that churches have used to train ministers and missionaries by encouraging them to take weekend ministries or requiring them to serve internships. The idea of service learning should come naturally to the church. Christians have been commanded to love one another, and they are encouraged by Jesus' own example to care for each other. Caring and reaching out to those in need are at the heart of Christianity and are excellent ways to become involved with the community.

Caring for others can be shown by becoming involved in various organizations that already exist or by establishing the church's own. Helping those in need is among the easiest off-site ministries to find: soup kitchens, food pantries, rescue missions, and Habitat for Humanity are just a few of the possibilities. Caring for widows and orphans is another opportunity. Widows can be ministered to through neighborhood watch groups who contact them through phone calls and visits. The church can also develop its own ministries in which the physical needs of widows are met such as home repairs, transportation, etc. Orphans can be ministered to through involvement with children's homes, acting as big brothers and sisters, and becoming foster parents. Opportunities for these types of service in the community are many, and if the church responds to them, its members will grow spiritually and minister more effectively.

**Caring for others can be shown by becoming involved
in various organizations that already exist
or by establishing the church's own.**

One of the most popular off-site ministries is mission trips. Long seen as a way for youth to experience the worldwide ministry of the church and to gain cultural awareness, these trips are beginning to become an exciting ministry for adults too. These allow the student to experience firsthand the work of missions and opens greater understanding of the work being done. This awareness translates into a greater enthusiasm for missions and also helps awaken the possibility of students entering full-time ministry. Some discount such trips, saying that the costs could be more effectively used in other areas of ministry or the mission itself. However, the impact on the lives of the students and the feeling of connectedness by the missionary can never be expressed in dollars and cents. The educational experience pays off heavily in spiritual growth.

One off-site ministry that is overlooked by many churches is that of released school time.

One off-site ministry that is overlooked by many churches is that of released school time. Many states have laws that permit schools to allow time off during the school week for religious studies. This provides a golden opportunity to educate students further and to make the church known in the community. Students, with parental permission, must submit a request to attend an organized religious training session, and the school is required to work out a schedule to make that possible. Churches taking advantage of released time often establish classes in nearby homes, one church in California has converted a large travel trailer into a mobile classroom and travels to several different schools.

Balance in Perspective

The concept of a balanced Christian education program requires the consideration of a variety of questions and issues. In this chapter many ideas have been given to suggest ways in which a church can minister. It is not intended that a church adopt every one of the ministries suggested. Unless it is a mega-church, many of the ideas may not fit the congregation or the community in which the church is located. Purposeful time must be taken to establish educational programs that will meet the needs of the people.

In order to do this, leaders must find ways to evaluate the membership and the community in order to develop ministries that will be effective in strengthening the faith of its member-ship and evangelizing the community. Without some method of examination, programs will be hit and miss. Duffy Robbins in his book, *The Ministry of Nurture*, points out what has happened in churches because of the lack of investigation and focus on the needs of the membership.

> The goal of the church is to help its members grow spiritually. If we don't understand that at the outset, you can bet that we will eventually find our efforts upset. The church is littered with wasted programs, sermons, Bible studies, and projects which once seemed like wonderful ideas, but were never motivated and fueled from a sense of target. Over and over, people have walked away from the church, not nod-ding their heads and saying, "Bullseye," but shaking their heads and shouting, "Bull" (17).

All surveys should include members and nonmembers, those who actively attend and those who do not.

In order to minister to the congregation more effectively, and reach the community, surveys can be taken to see what the people want and need from the church. These surveys can be taken during church time, in church mailings, as door-to-door neighborhood polls, and possibly in local shopping malls. All surveys should include members and nonmembers, those who actively attend and those who do not. The purpose is to get a broad view of what people need in their Christian education.

Also interviews with church and community leaders will give invaluable insights into the needs of the people. Another avenue of input can be gained by evaluating the effectiveness of present activities. By taking the time to feel the pulse of the people, the church becomes more effective in nurturing spiritual maturity and drawing others to Christ.

Christian education must look beyond the Sunday school and youth groups in order to provide a healthy and balanced program. For too long the church has tried to live on chocolate cake alone; it is time to balance the diet. When it is balanced, Christian education looks at the whole life of a student, not just Sunday life, and makes efforts to develop programs to assist life development.

p r o j e c t s

★ List all of the Christian education programs in your congregation. Find out the purposes for each. How do these demonstrate a balanced Christian education program, or lack of one? ★

★ Plan a 2-day retreat for adults based on the book of Philippians. Incorporate principles found thus far in this book. ★

For Further Reading

J. Heck
"We ALL Can Serve the Lord." *The Lookout*. Mar. 1, 1998. 6,7.

Duffy Robbins
The Ministry of Nurture: How to Build Real-life Faith into Your Kids.
Grand Rapids: Zondervan, 1990.

Eugene Roehlkepartain
The Teaching Church: Moving Christian Education to Center Stage.
Nashville: Abingdon Press, 1990.

Copyright Information

Christian Copyright Licensing Inc.
17201 N.E. Sacramento, Portland, OR 97230.

Motion Picture Licensing Corp.
5455 Centinela, P.O. Box 66970, Los Angeles, CA 90066-6970.

CHAPTER 16
RECRUITING, TRAINING, AND KEEPING
VOLUNTEER LEADERS

Chapter Sixteen Summary
- ☑ Effective tools for volunteer recruitment
- ☑ The process of training Christian educators
- ☑ Ways to retain volunteers

Bill, a youth minister, is responsible for developing all of the programs designed to reach and teach youth from grades 6 through college in his congregation. Bill is responsible for 35 young people. But he is a frustrated youth minister because he has only two others helping him in this ministry, even though they have three Sunday school classes, two youth groups, and two Bible studies during the week. Every week, then, Bill is teaching three studies and trying to take care of the needs of all 35 of the young people. He has tried to get others to join the task of teaching, but no one seems interested. When he came to the church, eight volunteer leaders were doing what he and the two volunteers are doing now. What is wrong in Bill's church? Have they little or no commitment?

Debbie is a children's minister. She is responsible for 70 children from birth through fifth grade. She has 11 Sunday school classes, 3 children's church programs, 4 midweek groups, and 4 Sunday evening groups for which to plan. She needs a minimum of 45 workers if she is to give each only one job to complete. When she came to the church, she had only 25 workers, many of them teaching more than once each week. She has

311

now recruited 15 more workers, leaving only a few to carry out more than one job. Do people in Debbie's church have greater commitment than those people in Bill's?

Tom is an adult education minister. He is responsible for 7 adult Sunday school classes, 6 weekly small groups, and the two electives offered on Wednesday evening, creating a need for 15 teachers/leaders each week. When he came to the church, he taught a Sunday school class, led a small group, and taught a Wednesday evening elective class. But this year Tom has enough leaders so that he teaches only a Wednesday evening class and fills in occasionally for a Sunday school or small group. In fact, this year, he has two apprentice teachers in classes and groups. Next year he will be able to begin a new class, with one of the apprentices taking the leadership. Is Tom's church a church of super saints? How come they are more committed than those in Bill's church?

The task of recruiting leadership is one of the most important—and most difficult—of the leadership functions in Christian education.

No simple answers exist to the questions posed. Admittedly, the problem could be the commitment of the people, but it is far more likely to be the recruiting, training, and retention skills of Tom, Debbie, and Bill.

The work of Christian education depends on willing, competent, trained volunteer leaders who commit themselves to the awesome task of sharing God's Word with the learners entrusted to their care. But willing, competent, trained volunteers do not "just happen." They must be recruited, trained, and retained.

Recruiting Leadership for Christian Education

The task of recruiting leadership is one of the most important—and most difficult—of the leadership functions in Christian education. Yet, most churches—perhaps all—have human resources available who can be encouraged to join the leadership team. Though it takes *work*, it is a task that can even be enjoyable, if those responsible follow some basic principles.

Plan Carefully

Effective recruitment means that someone has taken the time to clearly identify the Christian education ministry tasks that are required: administrative leaders, media support staff, teachers and their assistants, musicians, storytellers, recreation leaders, social planners, visitation, youth coaches, worship leaders, and perhaps even others. Make a list of those needed to carry out this ministry. Dream a bit. What would be the ideal situation?

Few of us work in ideal situations, of course. But we will never be able to recruit enough leaders if we do not know whom we need. After the ideal list has been developed, some of the tasks can be combined in the event not enough people are identified to carry out each task separately.

It is also helpful to develop brief descriptions of the responsibilities involved in each task. This should be written up in a half page or less and given to prospective workers. The job analysis may take a form such as the one in chart 16.1 designed for a Sunday school teacher.

Chart 16.1

Ministry Description

Ministry: Teacher of Grades 3-4 Sunday School Class

Time: 9:30-10:20 a.m. Sunday

Duration: First Sunday in September through last Sunday in May

Responsibilities:
> Prepare each week to teach.
> Teach the children each Sunday, using the curriculum you are given and maintaining appropriate classroom decorum.
> Contact each absentee each week.
> Plan an occasional social activity with your class.
> Attend the quarterly meeting of teachers.
> Attend one training event each year.

Supervisor: Children's Division Coordinator

Resources: Curriculum packet, church library, resource room, Christian education leadership team

---

Think through every position and develop a similar description of the ministry. Presenting these to those you are trying to recruit helps the person have a clear idea of what is involved in the ministry.

Pray Fervently

Effective recruitment is established on a foundation of prayer. Scripture tells us that Jesus instructed the disciples, "The harvest is plentiful, but the workers are few. Ask the Lord of the harvest, therefore, to send out workers into his harvest field" (Luke 10:2). The Lord is concerned that enough laborers are available to carry out the tasks of evangelism and nurture. Though that Scripture is often applied to praying for evangelists and missionaries, and rightfully so, it is equally applicable to the work of the local congregation.

Effective recruitment is established on a foundation of prayer.

Proceed Prudently

Effective leaders never expect prayer to replace work, of course. But they do understand that the Spirit is at work in the world to convict the hearts of people to bring them to salvation and to empower them for ministry. They become partners with the Spirit in this engaging task of calling others to ministry.

Develop a recruitment strategy that informs the congregation of needs and approaches people to fill those identified needs. This involves several facets.

The congregation must be made aware of the need for teachers and leaders. This can be done by using bulletin boards, testimonies, videos, and printed communication to identify ministries within the Christian education program and how these meet the needs of those to whom the program ministers. This can be accomplished only with consistent communication and keeping needs before the congregation not to beg for workers, but to show the joys and rewards of ministry to those who participate.

A part of the adult education program should incorporate classes and seminars that challenge adults for ministry. This should include opportunities for people to assess their gifts and learn about ministries in which they could find satisfaction. This kind of program does not directly recruit for specific positions, but it helps individuals decide where they can best be used by God to minister.

A well designed strategy for approaching people should also be developed. Usually it is best for the person most directly related to a ministry position to recruit the person. But it is important that a procedure be developed by which names are approved before they are involved in the ministry. This is essential to assure that those on the staff have high spiritual standards. It also provides valuable protection from overly zealous litigants.

A frequently debated question is whether churches should do a background check on potential prospects for volunteer ministry. It may be uncomfortable to have to discuss this matter, but church leaders must. It is probably advisable to have the prospective teacher answer some basic questions: name, telephone number, previous church, experience, reason to want to teach, and names of a couple of references. Then follow up on the references. Some churches choose to follow the same procedure they are required to do for preschool, day care, or school employees. Many insurance carriers have begun to press churches to follow sound recruitment procedures.

Recruitment occurs most successfully when people are approached individually or in small groups.

Recruitment occurs most successfully when people are approached individually or in small groups. Invitations to join in educational ministry should indicate to prospects why they are being considered for the ministry, help them assess what the challenges and rewards would be, outline the tasks they are asked to perform (give them the ministry description developed in the planning stage), and assure them of the support they will receive as they carry out their ministry. It is best to plan recruitment visits to allow prospects a few days to pray about their decision. Then at the appointed time, they can be asked for a response. (The last contact may be by telephone.)

When prospects indicate they are willing to commit themselves to a position, let them observe an experienced and competent leader in action. Show them where to find the resources they need. Give them the help they need to begin to feel confident in performing their ministry.

A procedure like the one described here takes time, but it is productive. People join the ministry team because they want to. They understand what they are to do. They will continue to need help and encouragement, of course, but they are informed and far more committed than if we begged them to take the ministry without appropriate information and understanding.

Training Leaders

Those recruited to ministry need education to carry out their tasks. Teacher training is perhaps one of the most overlooked aspects of staffing. Training may be of two kinds: preservice and in-service. Preservice training is that provided prior to service; in-service refers to training that occurs while the person is performing the ministry.

Preservice preparation is important. A regular Bible survey class should be offered as an elective in the adult education program. Those who are prospects for teaching could be urged to enroll in the class as preparation for teaching (or a help if they are teaching).

Many churches offer occasional short classes entitled "Understanding the Ministry of Teaching," or "Understanding Children," or "Understanding Teens." These are helpful both to prospective teachers and to parents.

Though preservice training serves a useful purpose to help prospective ministry leaders understand what is involved, the most effective training is usually *in-service*. Seminars, teachers' meetings, conferences, library resources, and video materials should be made available and offered at convenient times to help teachers learn specific skills and techniques for teaching: lesson planning, methods of presentation, classroom management, and much more.

The most effective training is usually in-service.

Many years ago teachers were expected to meet monthly, teachers of all ages together, for training and planning. But that is not the most effective way to encourage and train staff except, perhaps, in the smallest of churches. It is usually far more productive to have teachers of children, youth, or adults of all programs meet together to plan and learn. Even if this occurs only quarterly, the net result is better, more focused training than a monthly meeting of all of the staff. Now and then a large event can be planned for all teachers and leaders.

Effective training programs are marked by five criteria:

❶ Continual. Good training occurs regularly. Several smaller events planned and conducted consistently are far more useful than only an occasional large event.

❷ Age-related. The topics of interest to teachers of children are not those relevant to adults or youth, and vice versa.

❸ Experiential. Every training session should include a time of doing, of hands-on experience in using the method or principle presented.

❹ Curriculum-related. The best training is linked to the curriculum materials used in the teaching program. Show the participants skills needed to teach the materials.

❺ Practical. What is taught should be based on good theory, but never merely theoretical. It should provide skills that can be used the next time the teacher enters the classroom.

Every training program should be measured by these principles.

Retaining Volunteers

It does little good to recruit and train volunteers if they are not nurtured and retained. Constant staff turnover is hard on students. But it is a certain way to assure that few of those who drop out of their ministry ever return to it. It is important, then, to encourage those who are involved in leadership in Christian education. How can this be achieved?

Effective leaders in Christian education are alert to the praiseworthy efforts of volunteers and find ways to express their appreciation. Most volunteers do not choose to perform their ministries for the praise they can receive. But at the same time, they find it encouraging to know that supervisors are alert to the positive efforts and outcomes in their area of service. A gesture as simple as a thank you note encourages volunteers to continue in their ministries and develop their skills even further. Bulletin boards and feature articles in church publications are also useful ways to express appreciation.

It is also important to provide feedback to volunteers. They want to know what they are doing well. Though they should never be inundated with too many points to improve at one time, they usually appreciate the leader who gives helpful information on how to improve a specific skill. It is a worthwhile practice to spend a few minutes with every worker every year to provide formal feedback. Such sessions are most productive if they begin with citing something they do well, a specific suggestion for improvement, and another positive aspect of their work. It provides needed evaluation, but in a context of encouragement.

Almost every volunteer worker will at one time or another need to take a break from his or her chosen place of service.

Almost every volunteer worker will at one time or another need to take a break from his or her chosen place of service. When that occurs, accept the decision graciously. Yet keep the door open for a subsequent return to the volunteer staff. That is far more likely to result in long-term retention than ignoring, ridiculing, or rejecting the request. It is far better to give a volunteer a year or two off when they need it than to quench their desire to serve at any time in the future.

Leaders are more likely to stay involved in ministry if they have access to appropriate resources to help them carry out their ministries. If they have to buy the crayons and glue and construction paper and overhead transparencies and any other needed materials, they find it hard to believe that congregational leaders value their ministry in Christian education. But if they have access to what they need, it indicates support and value for the ministry in which they are involved. Of course, church leaders have limitations to what they can provide to support ministry, but they should develop a strategy to supply as much as they can.

One or two large, carefully planned appreciation events each year signal volunteer leaders that their work is valued. This often takes the form of an appreciation dinner. These events are valuable support events for volunteers.

Conclusion

Recruitment of volunteer workers is at the heart of educational ministry. But recruitment is more than merely convincing people to join the ministry team. It should be based on sound principles, followed by training, and supported by appreciation for the work of those who minister. Recruiting, training, and keeping volunteer workers is work—but work that results in great satisfaction as additional Christians join in ministry in the name of Christ.

p r o j e c t s

★ Write a position description for a Sunday school teacher for juniors and one for a high school youth coach. ★

★ Make a list of your church's available resources for educators. In what areas is it exemplary? Lacking? ★

For Further Reading

David Arthur Bickmier
Leadership in Religious Education. Birmingham, AL: Religious Education Press, n.d.

Kenneth O. Gangel
Building Leaders for Christian Education. Chicago: Moody Press, 1970.
Leadership for Church Education. Chicago: Moody Press, 1970.

Ellen Larson
Recruiting: Help and Hope for Finding Volunteers. Cincinnati: Standard Publishing, 1994.

Reginald M. McDonough
Working with Volunteer Leaders in the Church. Nashville: Broadman, 1976.

Mark Senter
Recruiting Volunteers in the Church. Chicago: Victor Books, 1990.

Dennis E. Williams and Kenneth O. Gangel
Volunteers for Today's Church: How to Recruit and Retain Workers. Grand Rapids: Baker, 1993.

CHAPTER 17
LEGAL ISSUES
RELATED TO CHRISTIAN EDUCATION

Chapter Seventeen Summary
- ☑ Historical factors contributing to church legal problems
- ☑ Various areas of church liability
- ☑ Copyright guidelines
- ☑ Prevention of abuse
- ☑ Dealing with abuse problems
- ☑ Religion in the public schools

The word *law* is used scores of times in the Old Testament. On Mount Sinai, God gave the Ten Commandments, the divine framework for all the laws that He later revealed to His people. These later laws, dealing with religious and social activities, fleshed out and made more specific the issues covered in the Ten Commandments. But the Israelites were not able to live up to these laws and often rebelled against God. As a result God allowed their neighbors to conquer them again and again. Yet even as they were forced to live under these foreign conquerors, the Israelites never lost their concern about law.

"In the fullness of time," while the Jewish people were subject to the Romans, God sent His Son, Jesus Christ into the world. During His ministry Jesus showed respect for the Roman laws that had been imposed upon His people, yet He did not hesitate to challenge the numerous interpretations that Jewish leaders of His day had added to God's laws. The church, which Jesus came to found, received new revelation through the Apostles and other inspired men. The new message brought by the church was salvation by grace, not by law, but this did not mean a rejection of God's law. The church was soon engaged in a life and death struggle for its very existence, first with the Jews and then later with the Roman government. The early Christians attempted to be law-abiding citizens in the Roman Empire, but if the demands of the Empire conflicted with the demands of God, they were willing to die rather than submit to Rome.

In the centuries that followed, Christianity finally triumphed in the West. Although Christians often fell far short of living up to the high standards our Lord had set for His followers, yet through the Middle Ages and into Modern times Christianity enjoyed the status of the established religion. Because of this, the legal systems of most European states reflected, however imperfectly, the solid core of God's law.

The settlers who came to the New World, whether they be Spanish, Portuguese, French, or English, brought with them law codes that reflected their Christian heritage. The English colonists were mostly Protestant, and their laws in America reflected this. The colonial period ended with the American Revolution, resulting in a new political entity, the United States of America, whose political and religious life were to be governed by the Constitution. The First Amendment sums up in one brief sentence the important guarantee of religious freedom that we have come to take for granted: "Congress shall make no law respecting an establishment of religion, or prohibiting the free exercise thereof." For a hundred years or so after the adoption of the Constitution, Protestantism in its various denominational forms was dominant in America with very few legal problems.

Settlers to the New World brought with them law codes that reflected their Christian heritage.

However, by the end of the nineteenth century, this situation began to change. At least three factors contributed to this change. The first factor was immigration. Millions of people from Europe and other parts of the world made their way to the American shores, bringing with them their differing cultures, including different religions. Among the most significant of these numerically were Roman Catholicism, Eastern Orthodoxy, and Judaism. Later in the twentieth century Muslims, Buddhists, Hindus, and others came in great numbers. This diversity of religious faith led to challenges to the entrenched Protestantism and eventually led to legal conflicts.

The second factor that has greatly impacted Christianity in the twentieth century is the growing secularism of our culture. This present world and all the pleasures it offers has become more important to most people than any concern about Christianity and the promise of a future life that it offers. As a result, people are much more likely to challenge the church and the privileges it enjoyed for so long. The third factor, which in the last three or four decades has increasingly influenced the way people think and act, is a self-centered individualism that makes demands for itself with little regard as to how these demands may influence anyone else. And there is no shortage of lawyers who are willing to press these demands in the courts.

This present world and all the pleasures it offers has become more important to most people than any concern about Christianity and the promise of a future life that it offers.

Liability

A generation ago a lawsuit against a church was almost unheard of. Today they are commonplace, with plaintiffs winning many of them resulting in courts granting sizeable awards to the winners. As a result every church should carry comprehensive liability insurance. If the church has borrowed money for a building program, the lending agency will usually require this type of coverage to protect its own interests. This coverage will provide protection to the church in case anyone is injured on church property. But a church should be concerned about more than just financial protection of its property. Since educational programs involve many people, especially children, in a variety of activities, increased insurance protection may be wise. If a person is injured on church property, the congregation should feel a moral responsibility to provide coverage for medical expenses and any other losses that might be incurred.

A church should be concerned about more than just financial protection of its property.

A church often sponsors educational activities such as recreation or field trips that occur away from church property. Motor vehicle insurance may cover injuries while persons are traveling in church vehicles, but to cover other activities, many insurance companies offer "riders." While the cost of some of these riders may be prohibitive for small congregations, yet every church ought to investigate what might be available. A less expensive form of insurance is co-insurance. Since many families now have health and accident coverage provided by their employers, co-insurance pays only that covered by the primary insurer. In purchasing insurance, the church should be aware of exclusionary clauses that exclude some activities that are considered especially hazardous such as skiing, water skiing, and rappelling. Some vehicle insurance also requires that the driver be at least twenty-one and have a good driving record. In an increasing number of churches, church members including young people are taking mission trips beyond the borders of the United States. Churches need to investigate insurance coverage for these people if they are not covered by their own policies.

Special provisions need to be made for persons under eighteen years old who are involved in Christian education programs. Physicians and hospitals often require releases from parents or guardians before they can provide medical services. In an emergency situation parents are not always readily available to give permission for such services. While the requirements vary from state to state, this situation can usually be handled by having the parent or guardian sign a release form before the activity takes places. Because educational programs in these days include parents who have no connection with the church, it is wise to keep release forms permanently on file. Churches also should be very careful that the person picking up children at the conclusion of the activity is properly identified. Many divorce cases these days end up in bitter custody battles, and some parents are desperate to resort to what amounts to kidnapping to gain control of their children. Taking a few simple precautions can protect the church from being caught in the middle of such a battle.

Church Property

Christians should not resent equal access laws.

For centuries Christians built buildings with little thought about those who are physically challenged. Now state and federal laws have changed all this. Regulations covering new construction require that the building be accessible to persons in wheelchairs, requiring ramps, special restroom facilities, and elevators. While churches are not required to retrofit older buildings, they may be required to do so when they remodel an older building. While these regulations often place a heavy financial burden on a congregation, Christians should not resent these laws. Since a part of our Christian education philosophy is that every person is a child of God and deserves an opportunity to learn about Him and the wonderful salvation He offers through His Son, we should rejoice that the government is requiring us to do what we should have been doing all along. New buildings or remodeled older buildings will need to conform to state and local fire codes. Exits properly marked and located are governed by these codes, as well as fire retardant building materials. Sprinkling systems are now mandated by many codes. While these items add to the cost of construction, they do provide protection for those who use the buildings and may protect the buildings against disastrous fires. Church schools, which are used more frequently than Sunday school rooms, must conform to more stringent regulations.

Copyright Laws

Workers in Christian education and other areas of church work have, in recent years, more often been guilty of violating copyright laws than any of the other regulations thus far discussed in this chapter. There are at least two reasons for this. For one thing, the copyright laws were extensively revised more than two decades ago. Many people apparently are not aware of these changes which were put into effect by the Copyright Act of 1976. The second reason that violations are so frequent is the ready availability of photocopying machines.

When a writer, musician, or artist produces a work and copyrights it, that property belongs to him or her. In this respect a copyrighted work is no different from a house, a piece of land, or an automobile that one may own. The producer may sell it, give it away, or charge a fee for its use. Some Christians feel that such a work ought to be available free of charge so long as it is used in the work of the Lord's kingdom. Few people would hold such a view about other types of property, and to take such property without compensating the owner is stealing. Exactly the same rule applies to copyrighted works. To use them without permission or without compensating the owner is stealing.

We hear of a few authors who write best-sellers and become quite rich. But few writers, especially those who write materials used in Christian work, have the good fortune to join this elite group. Writers and composers spend countless hours, even years, writing something that is copyrighted and published. Few of them are able to make a living doing this alone and must hold other jobs. Further, if their works are not protected by copyrights, many would lack the incentive to create them, and publishers, without an opportunity to make a profit on what they sell, could not stay in business long.

Under the old regulations, a copyrighted work was protected for twenty-eight years and the copyright could be renewed for another twenty-eight years. This gave the author or his heirs or the company to which the work might be assigned a total of fifty-six years of protection. After the expiration of the copyright, the item was in "public domain" and could be used freely without permission or paying any royalty. Under the Act of 1976, a copyrighted work is protected for the life of the author plus fifty additional years. Suppose an author copyrighted a work in 1990 and lives twenty-five more years. Since the author dies in 2015, the copyright will be in force until 2065. The new regulations thus treat authors more generously than did the old regulations. These new regulations may create some confusion in the future unless careful records are kept of the deaths of authors.

The most frequent copyright violation involves the copying of music.

Violating a copyright is a serious matter. Penalties for violating the law can result in fines up to $10,000 and/or one year in prison. In addition the court may require the violator to pay damages and legal fees. A person who willfully and knowingly violates a copyright may be assessed statutory damages up to $50,000. Churches have been known to buy one copy of a Sunday school quarterly or a vacation Bible school booklet and then photocopy enough copies for their whole program. Probably the most frequent violation involves the copying of music. Churches have on occasion photocopied music for the choir rather than buy choir books for the whole group. Or churches have printed the words and music on song sheets to use in a worship service. Publishers have been rather reluctant to use the courts to punish violators, but their policy of benign neglect in this matter may not last forever.

While the copyright laws protect the rights of the owner of the copyrighted material, they are not intended to prevent teachers and others from using that material in teaching situations. A work on which the copyright has expired (this would include a great number of our old favorite hymns) is considered to be in the public domain, and may be used without permission or paying a royalty to the owner. Persons who desire to use material still protected by copyright law may do so by obtaining permission from the owner. There may be a charge for such usage if the owner feels that the value of his material will be lessened by allowing others to use it. However, in many cases there will be no charge because the owner views such usage as a promotion or advertisement for his work. Several organizations have drawn up widely accepted guidelines that define "fair use" of copyrighted material. These guidelines are too detailed to include in this discussion, but these may be summarized briefly here.

✎ One may quote brief passages from a work for the purpose of comment, criticism, or teaching. This would cover the use of many of the new versions of the Bible. However, older versions such as the King James and American Standard are in the public domain and may be quoted freely.

✎ A teacher may photocopy materials for his own study, research, or class preparation. Under some circumstances a teacher may photocopy materials to distribute to students providing it is not done for profit.

✎ Church and religious groups may perform musical works providing admission is not charged. (However, an offering may be taken.) Recordings of such productions may be made and tapes may be made providing they are not sold for profit.

✎ Under some circumstances sheet music or songs in hymnals may be photocopied, but these circumstances are narrowly defined, and one should always obtain written permission from the publisher before photocopying music.

A licensing arrangement has been developed with most of the publishers of religious music. For the payment of an annual fee, a church, Sunday school, camp, college, or other religious organization is granted the right to use copyrighted music under certain specified conditions. (The fee varies depending upon the size of the organization.) The licensee is allowed to print song sheets and insert songs in bulletins and programs. The licensee may also create overheads, slides, or other formats in which songs are projected for congregational usage. All such usages must indicate that the material has been reproduced under the terms of the agreement and must carry the organization's license number. Churches may record their worship services using copyrighted songs, and tapes so produced can be distributed free of charge or for a small fee. Further information about this licensing arrangement may be obtained from Christian Copyright Licensing, Inc., 1720 N. E. Sacramento, Portland, OR 97230.

These and other provisions for fair use may be summed up in the position that anything that denies the owner or publisher of copyrighted works a fair return on his property is illegal, and Christians should never be guilty of literary stealing. A good rule in copyright matters is to contact the owners or publishers when in doubt.

Physical and Sexual Abuse

Almost daily our newspapers headline an account of another case of physical or sexual abuse of a child or children. Undoubtedly, such abuse has been happening for a long time. Whether it is more prevalent now than in years past may be debatable, but there is no question that it has become a matter of growing concern. Of course, Christians should be greatly concerned about any kind of abuse regardless of who the victims are, but the heightened public concern about abuse and its legal ramifications make it imperative that Christians give considerable attention to the matter.

Physical Abuse

For several years workers in health services, law enforcement officials, and teachers in public and Christian schools have been required by law to report all examples of what they believe to be physical abuse of children. Such cases have to be reported to the proper authorities, and anyone who fails to do so is subject to punishment under state laws. At this writing nearly half the states have extended these laws to cover persons working in religious institutions. Thus persons working in Sunday schools, day care centers, and other youth activities need to be aware of these legal requirements. Congregations need to have in place procedures to handle these matters. It is important that this process be kept confidential.

Public school teachers who are required to report suspected cases of abuse are to an extent insulated from the persons or families about which they have to report. This is often not the case in church situations. Teachers and the families of children they teach are involved in a number of church activities together such as worship and educational and fellowship activities. Thus any cases of suspected abuse must be treated very delicately lest the repercussions affect the whole church. This is one of those situations where Jesus' advice is most appropriate: "Be as wise as serpents and as harmless as doves."

Some of the harshest words Jesus ever spoke were against those who mistreated children.

Sexual Abuse

Most Christians have been shocked at recent news stories relating the frequency and extent of the sexual abuse of children and even infants. Even more shocking has been in efforts of some religious organizations either to deny that these things are happening or to attempt to cover them up and thus protect themselves. These efforts have resulted in very sizeable court awards in some cases, and justly so. Some of the harshest words Jesus ever spoke were against those who mistreated children: "And if anyone causes one of these little ones who believe in me to sin, it would be better for him to be thrown into the sea with a large millstone tied around his neck" (Mark 9:42). Our concern should be no less intense.

Dealing with Abuse Problems

The best program for dealing with abuse problems is to take measures that will attempt to avoid them before they arise. Every congregation should have definite policies written out and clearly explained to workers in Christian education programs and other church activities. Here are some items that should be included in such a policy:

✎ The two-adult rule: Two adult supervisors (preferably, one should be a parent of one of the participants) should be present during any church activity. This will reduce the risk of sexual misconduct and also protect against the risk of false accusations. (This second purpose is quite important, because in some cases children have brought false accusations against adults.)

✎ Suspicious behavior: Any apparent inappropriate conduct between adult workers and any youth or child should be dealt with immediately. These situations require considerable discretion. Today hugging, kissing, and touching have become much more a part of our culture than they were a generation ago. Drawing the line between what is acceptable and what is inappropriate is not always easy. When attempting to draw lines, it is always better to err on the side of safety.

Drawing the line between what is acceptable and what is inappropriate is not always easy.

✎ Open doors: Whenever feasible, classrooms where children are taught should have windows. For safety purposes these should be of shatterproof glass or acrylic. When windows are not feasible, classroom doors should be left open during use.

✎ Random visits: The Sunday school superintendent or departmental superintendent should make random visits to classrooms and other areas on the church property that may not at that time be in use. This not only provides protection, it also allows the supervisor to observe the teaching situation.

✎ Adequate personnel: All programs maintained by the church should be adequately staffed. When the class period is over, some personnel should remain until all children and youth have left the room. Small children should be released only to a properly identified or preauthorized adult.

✎ Overnight rule: All leaders and chaperones involved in overnight activities for children should be cleared in advance and all children should have permission slips from parents permitting such activities. Sometimes emergencies arise such as when a young person runs away from home or is expelled from home and seeks a place of shelter for the night. The overnight rule still holds. When such a situation arises, the teacher or leader involved should work for a reconciliation. If this is not possible or the young person seems in danger of physical or emotional harm, church leaders should turn to the appropriate authorities or institutions equipped to handle such emergencies. To take a young person into one's home in such a situation opens that leader or the church to possible legal action.

✎ Identification procedures: In dealing with small children a procedure should be in place for identifying the parent, guardian, or other person who is authorized to pick a child up. This is especially important in larger congregations where one is not likely to know all the persons involved in the church's various programs.

Legal Issues Involving Other Activities

The previous discussion has dealt with many of the ways that a local congregation will be involved with legal issues. But many Christians serve in educational ministries that extend beyond and independently of the local congregation. Some of these will be discussed.

Christian Camping

A Christian camp may be owned and operated by a congregation, but this is an unusual situation. Most camps are controlled by a denomination or are established as separate legal entities, each with its own board. Camps must comply with legal regulations such as those dealing with food service, shelter, personnel, and health and safety requirements. These requirements, which have become increasingly more stringent as camping programs have grown, vary depending on whether the camp is a day camp or a residential camp. They also vary from one area to another, and so a complete discussion of these is beyond the scope of this chapter.

Religion in the Public Schools

During much of our history, the public schools had considerable freedom to teach religion and the Bible in the classrooms. However, following World War II several U. S. Supreme Court decisions changed this drastically. The *McCollum v. Board of Education* (1948) case involved the Board of Education of Champaign, Illinois. The board permitted the local Council on Religious Education to provide classes on religion in the public schools. Parental permission was required for those attending the classes, which met thirty to forty-five minutes each week. Teachers were provided by the Council without any cost to the Board of Education. The Court ruled that this arrangement constituted an establishment of religion, which is prohibited by the First Amendment of the Constitution. Four years later the *Zorach v. Clauson* (1952) decision permitted a somewhat similar situation in New York City schools, where children with parental approval were dismissed from school for one hour each week to attend religious classes. Since these classes were held off school property and the school was not involved with the program in any direct way, these so-called "released time classes" were permitted. Some churches, usually one located near a school, have used this method for providing religious education to their children. In other communities several churches have cooperated to offer Bible teaching. This method of Bible teaching deserves to be used more than it has been because it offers a chance to reach children who might not otherwise receive such teaching.

Released time Bible classes deserve to be used more often.

In the *Engel v. Vitale* (1962) decision the Court ruled that a "nonsectarian" prayer, which the New York State Board of Regents had prepared, could not be displayed, arguing that it violated the no-establishment clause. The following year, the Court ruled in two cases *Abington School District v. Schempp; Murray v. Curlett (1963)*, one arising in Pennsylvania and the other in Maryland, that the reading of the Bible in school classrooms also violated the Constitution. The Court did not rule out studying the Bible as history or literature, but school officials have been so concerned about avoiding controversy that this ruling has for all practical purposes kept Bible study out of public school classrooms. However, these rulings have not eliminated the opportunity for student-led Bible clubs and prayers before or after regular school hours. Also some states now have laws permitting a moment of silence at the beginning of the school day. Thus far, these have not been successfully challenged at the U. S. Supreme Court level.

Christian Schools

The growth of the Christian school movement has been one of the most encouraging activities on the contemporary educational scene and promises to continue its growth into the twenty-first century. In some areas, especially the South, these schools allowed whites to avoid the desegregation of public school in the 1950s and 1960s, but this motive for starting and maintaining private schools is no longer a significant factor. Much more important are the issues of the growing secularization of the public schools, the declining quality of many public schools, and the violence associated with public schools. Very important to many parents willing to sacrifice financially is their desire for their children to have an education that upholds Christian values. The courts and state laws now recognize the right for churches or other groups to establish and maintain religious schools.

The standards set for Christian schools vary from state to state and so it would be impossible in this brief chapter to try to spell them out. These standards include such things as building codes, health standards, curriculum requirements, and standards for teachers and supervisor. Some states require that all teachers be state certified. In some the school is required to be state accredited. School administrators must be aware of the Americans with Disabilities Act, which embodies many regulations concerning persons who have some form of disability. The courts are still in the process of defining many of the provisions of this act, and so schools must be alert to new rulings that may affect them.

The Christian school movement has been one of the most encouraging activities on the contemporary educational scene.

Several state and national Christian school organizations have been formed. One of these, the Association of Christian Schools International, issues a periodical, *Legal Legislative Update,* that seeks to keep its members abreast of legal matters that affect Christian schools.

An interesting new possibility, vouchers for parents of school children, is now developing. According to this arrangement, a parent is issued a voucher worth a certain set sum for each school-age child. This voucher may be used in a public school, a private school, or a religious school. A few states are currently experimenting with this program. Many public school officials and others supporting a strict separation of church and state have voiced strong opposition to the voucher system. Undoubtedly the voucher program will be challenged in the courts right up to the United States Supreme Court. If the courts do not reject the voucher system, Christians will be in a position to enjoy some exciting new possibilities for Christian education. But any system of vouchers will bring with it more regulations and the possibility of new types of legal conflicts.

Home Schooling

Another area enjoying considerable growth is home schooling. Under this arrangement parents are allowed to educate children in their own home without sending them to public or private schools. As is the case with Christian schools, laws governing home schooling vary widely from state to state. Some states require the teacher, if not a parent, to be certified. Many require a standard curriculum and regular testing of the students with standardized tests. Most require the parents to register with the local school board or the state board of education and to keep attendance and progress records. Several organizations for home schoolers at the state and local level have been formed. A few publishers now have curriculum materials available. Parents contemplating home schooling should make a thorough investigation of the legal requirements in their state in order that they not violate truancy laws, which sometimes carry substantial penalties.

p r o j e c t

★ Find out how your congregation is assuring legal and security responsibility. Check regarding each liability topic in this chapter. ★

For Further Reading

Michael J. Anthony, ed.
Foundations of Ministry. Grand Rapids: Baker Books, 1997.

Robert E. Clark, Lin Johnson, and Allyn K. Sloat
Christian Education: Foundations for the Future. Chicago: Moody Press, 1991.

John Eidsmoe
The Christian Legal Advisor. Milford, MI: Mott Media, 1984.

Edwin Scott Gaustad
A Religious History of America. San Francisco: Harper and Row, 1990.

Anson Phelps Stokes and Leo Pfeffer
Church and State in the United States. New York: Harper and Row, 1964.

Sources of Information

Association of Christian Schools, International
P. O. Box 35097, Colorado Springs, CO 89035-3509.

Bob Jones University Press
Greenville, SC 29614-0062.

Christian Copyright Licensing, Inc.
17201 N. E. Sacramento, Portland, OR 37230.

Home School Legal Defense Association
P. O. Box 159, Paeonian Springs, VA 20129.

The Moore Foundation
Box I, Camas, WA 98607.

CHAPTER 18
EVALUATING
THE EFFECTIVENESS OF CHRISTIAN EDUCATION

Chapter Eighteen Summary
- ☑ Basis for evaluating Christian Education
- ☑ Congregational objectives
- ☑ The necessity of performing evaluations
- ☑ Setting and measuring goals
- ☑ *How* to evaluate
- ☑ *What* to evaluate
- ☑ *When* to evaluate
- ☑ Sample evaluation questionnaire

We receive a statement from the bank and then compare it with our checkbook—that's evaluation. We step on the bathroom scales and then, sometimes painfully, compare the numbers registered to those that registered the last time we checked our weight—that's evaluation. A teacher scores a student's test paper and then marks a grade on it—that's evaluation. A pilot of a plane carefully observes the dials on the instrument panel before him and makes necessary adjustments in his controls so that the aircraft lands safely—that's evaluation.

Every day we make numerous decisions based on evaluations. Often these decisions concern relatively trivial matters, but on occasions our evaluations and resultant decisions are matters of life and death. It should not surprise us, then, that Christian education programs in our churches must regularly be evaluated. The actions that stem from these evaluations may seem relatively unimportant, but sometimes they deal with matters of life and death—eternal life and death.

Christian education programs in our churches must regularly be evaluated.

Establishing a Basis for Evaluation

If an evaluation is to be meaningful, it must be based upon an established or recognized standard or measuring rod. For example, one might be driving down the highway and glance at the speedometer and be shocked to realize that it registered 100. But a second look brings a sigh of relief. The speedometers of many modern automobiles are marked in both kilometers per hour and miles per hour. The 100 on the kilometer scale is a much safer 63 on the mile scale. Thus numbers alone are meaningless unless we know what scale is being used. Any attempt to evaluate the Christian education program of a local church must begin with foundational matters. These issues are dealt with in some detail in Part I, and so need not be discussed in detail here.

Objectives Come from Philosophy

At the heart of the foundational matters in any organization whether it is a local congregation, a parachurch organization, a camp, a college, or a business corporation is its philosophy. An organization's philosophy will determine its goals or objectives, and these in turn will determine how the organization is evaluated. A business corporation, for example, may have several reasons for existing, but its most obvious objective is to make a profit. Thus the bottom line of its financial report is the best measuring rod of how well it met its major objective. An athletic team may exist for several reasons—providing physical development for its members, creating attitudes of good sportsmanship, building a spirit of cooperation among its members—but still the most frequently used measurement of a team's success is its record of games won and lost.

**At the heart of the foundational matters
in any organization is its philosophy.**

Congregational Objectives

The church, the Body of Christ (specifically in its local manifestation), is called into at least five distinct ministries: evangelism (including missions), worship, fellowship, service (including benevolence), and education. Because of the limitations of this chapter, this discussion will be confined to the educational ministry of the church. In an effort to evaluate the educational ministry of the church, one could develop literally scores of specific objectives. A congregation in developing its objectives would share many of these in common with all local congregations. Yet each congregation is unique because of such things as its geographical location, ethnic composition, socioeconomic status of its members, and general cultural milieu. Thus each congregation must give serious and prayerful thought to these and other factors as it attempts to establish measuring rods to evaluate the effectiveness of its educational ministry. Normally, a congregation should begin this process by establishing objectives for its whole educational ministry. Obviously, these objectives will be rather general and must begin with the congregation's overall philosophy. Within the framework of that philosophy, the congregation must then determine how it will apply its philosophy within its unique situation. For example, a congregation located in a retirement community in Florida is likely to emphasize those objectives that seek to meet the needs of older adults with little attention given to meeting the needs of the nursery department. An inner city congregation with few adult members, in contrast, would give little attention to the needs of older adults and concentrate on meeting the needs of children and youth.

Departmental and Class Objectives

Once the congregational objectives have been established, attention should be given to preparing departmental objectives. A very small church may have only three departments: nursery, children, and adults. Larger congregations may have nursery, preschool, children, youth, adult, and other special areas such as teacher development or for persons with special physical and mental needs. Further, in a larger church these main departments may be further divided so as to necessitate additional objectives for each. But the process of developing objectives does not stop here. Each class in turn should have objectives that address its special contribution to the overall congregational objective. These should include objectives for both teachers and students.

Objectives must be expressed in terms that can be measured with some degree of accuracy.

When objectives are developed, they must be expressed in terms that can be measured with some degree of accuracy. For instance, one objective for a children's class might be that each student will be able to name the books of the Bible in order. Such an objective can be readily measured by an oral or written test. However, many objectives, even some of the most important objectives, a church may write for its educational program cannot be so easily or quickly measured. Leading persons into a mature relationship with Jesus Christ is at the very heart of what every congregation should be striving to achieve. But since this is a goal of an entire lifetime, it cannot be measured after only a few weeks or months of teaching. Nor can Christian maturity be accurately measured with an oral or written test.

In writing objectives, it is a common practice to divide these into three major categories: cognitive, affective, and conative. Cognitive goals deal with what the student comes to know or understand. Affective goals deal with what the student feels or his emotional commitment to accepted ideas. Conative goals deal with what a student is able to do either physically or mentally.

Why Evaluate?

Evaluation is necessary in order to determine whether the objectives for the congregation, each department, each class, each teacher, and each student are being met. Objectives are sometimes classified in terms of the time frame within which they are expected to be reached: short-range goals within a year, midrange goals from one to five years, and long-range goals in ten years or more. Of course, these classifications are rather arbitrary and should not be imposed rigidly. Some insist with some justification that our society is changing so rapidly that any goal beyond a year should be considered a long-range goal. Further, we need to recognize that in evaluating changes in students, any arbitrary time frame for change simply does not deal adequately with the differing rates at which students move toward spiritual maturity.

Measurable Goals

Whenever possible, an organization should establish goals that can be measured and compared. Thus leaders should attempt to define goals in the most precise terms possible. Efforts to determine if goals are being met are likely to be futile unless appropriate standards have been stated when the goals were designed. For instance, a Sunday school may have as its goal an increase in attendance. But unless specific numbers are a part of the objective and a part of the evaluation, there would be no way of knowing whether that objective has been met.

To Revise Goals

Another reason for evaluation is to revise goals. A Sunday school with an average attendance of 200 each week might set a goal of averaging 1,000 within one year. Under anything but the most unusual circumstances this would be a most unlikely goal and should be revised to a more realistic figure. To set such extreme goals can create discouragement when they are not reached. So one should not hesitate to change goals when they are unrealistic. On the other hand, leaders should not set objectives that are too easy to attain because this can lead to complacency.

To Discover Weaknesses

An organization evaluates its program in order to discover weaknesses. A sudden drop in the average attendance of a class should raise a red flag, and the evaluation process should begin immediately to find the cause. Is the problem the teacher, the curriculum materials, the location of the room, or did several key members move away? A careful study of all the factors involved in the situation will often suggest a solution.

To Discover Strengths

Evaluation may also help discover strengths in a program. A class may be growing very rapidly, and by evaluating the situation leaders may discover ideas that can be used in other classes. When objectives are clearly spelled out, it is much easier to isolate the factors that have contributed to the growth of a class or the success of a program. When these factors have been isolated, they can be more readily applied to other situations.

To Provide Motivation

Evaluation is also important because it provides motivation for leaders, teachers, and students. Most of us do a better job when we understand what is expected of us, and the more clearly these expectations are spelled out the more likely we are to measure up to them. Without specific objectives, leaders are inclined to fall into the rut of doing what has always been done before. Such an attitude may not have had many serious consequences in earlier times when changes came slowly. But we live in times of rapid change, and unless we are willing and able to alter our programs to meet these challenges, the kingdom of God will suffer. We recently saw a church signboard that summed it up this way: "The seven last words of a dying church: '*We have always done it that way.*'" A church that follows this advice is likely to suffer serious decline if not death.

To Motivate Teachers

Studies show that teachers who have clear objectives when they teach a lesson and follow it up with appropriate self-evaluation or evaluation from an observer will be more effective. Experienced teachers have learned to employ various means of self-evaluation. They use the results to improve their teaching, changing the methods that did not seem to work, and enhancing those that proved effective. Few things would improve teaching in Sunday school and other church educational activities more than having teachers who regularly evaluated their teaching methods and the results they obtained with these methods.

To Motivate Students

In the same way students are more highly motivated when they realize that they will be evaluated. Many people are so apprehensive about taking tests that we hesitate even to talk about testing in church educational activities. We fear that students will feel so threatened that they may even hesitate to come to class. Yet this need not be the case, and studies show that students learn more and retain it longer when they understand the lesson objectives and know that they will be tested over the material that has been studied. Adults especially are apprehensive about tests. Perhaps this attitude stems from earlier experiences in school. But these attitudes can be changed. A teacher of one adult class regularly gives a test provided by the lesson commentary at the beginning of each quarter. Since students grade their own papers, they are spared the embarrassment that accompanies low grades (and most of them make low grades on such a test of Bible knowledge). Then the teacher gives the same test at the end of the quarter. The students all make better grades on this second test, and so they feel good about themselves because this kind of evaluation gives them definite evidence that they have learned a great deal during the quarter's study.

Students are more highly motivated when they realize that they will be evaluated.

How to Evaluate

Once we establish the reasons for evaluating the church's educational ministry, we turn our attention to how this evaluation is to be carried out. Without a clear idea of what is to be done and how it is to be accomplished, efforts to achieve a useful evaluation are likely to be wasted. Our efforts may be confined to two different approaches to evaluation: processes and results.

Evaluating Processes

In process evaluation we are concerned with how the congregation's educational objectives are to be achieved. Since one major objective should be leading the students to a mature understanding of the Scriptures, we need to ask how this is to be accomplished. We can ask questions about how each teacher prepares his or her lesson, how the lesson is introduced, how the students are led into the Bible. Further, we need to ask how the specific Scripture used in the lesson is made meaningful to the students, how they are challenged to apply it to their lives. We also need to ask about efforts made to follow up on the lesson to ensure that biblical truths are made applicable in life situations not specifically discussed in the classroom.

We need to evaluate the process by which new members are brought into the educational programs of the church.

Since a major ministry of every congregation should be to reach unsaved persons in its community, we need to evaluate the process by which new members are brought into the educational programs of the church and how they are encouraged to become seriously involved in these efforts. Does the church or the individual teacher contact visitors and new members on a regular basis? Does the church show a concern for each person by noting such events as birthdays, anniversaries, or outstanding accomplishments? Has the congregation ever taken a religious census of the community that it serves? Is the census up to date? While the membership of some congregations is so scattered geographically that a census of the area they serve would be impractical, in other situations a census may be an effective tool in finding persons and families that are outside of Christ or who are not actively involved in any church. These and many other questions need to be asked about how the church goes through the process of carrying out its ministries. Are these efforts planned and conscientiously carried out or are they conducted in a haphazard, slipshod manner? Careful evaluation will answer some of these questions.

Evaluating Results

We must be concerned about the process of carrying out the educational ministry, but we should not become so involved in the process that we fail to measure the results. A church may have an excellent process of selecting its worship leaders. The instrumentalists have the necessary skills and the song leaders have appropriate backgrounds in music education and experience. But even if the process of selecting worship leaders and programs is properly done, we must still ask if the students are really involved in the singing. Do they join enthusiastically in the singing and does their participation prepare them for the lesson or sermon that follows? Do the participants leave the worship service cleansed and prepared to serve? When we ask questions like this, we are attempting to measure results.

Use Measurable Objectives

Meaningful evaluation must begin with objectives that provide a basis for objective comparisons. Some objectives lend themselves readily to statistical comparisons (attendance, offerings, baptisms). If the goal for the average attendance in a class was 10 and the class averaged 12, we can state that the class exceeded its goal by 20 per cent. If, on the other hand, the average attendance was only 9, we can state that the class attendance fell 10 per cent below its goal.

Keep Accurate Records

Since statistics play such an important part in this kind of evaluation, it is important to keep accurate records. In the Sunday school, normally record-keeping duties fall upon the Sunday school secretary or some other person who might be appointed by the Sunday school superintendent or the church's board of Christian education. Christian publishing companies make available record-keeping books and other tools to facilitate record keeping. The advantage of such tools is that the records will be consistent from year to year. Today most churches have computers and software that make record keeping relatively easy. Further, data saved this way keeps records that make statistical comparisons quite easy, and the information can be printed out and made available to teachers and other leaders.

Keep Appropriate Records

Not only must records be accurate, they must be appropriate. For example, we would not get a very useful evaluation of Sunday school attendance if we compared attendance in April (which in one particular year included Easter) and attendance in July. For that matter if we compared April attendance this year with April of last year (when Easter occurred in March), the results might be statistically skewed. In this day when worship attendance in most congregations is substantially larger than Sunday school attendance, comparing the two would not be particularly meaningful unless we wanted to show the need for greater emphasis on the importance of Sunday school in the total program of the church.

Use Questionnaires

We have already mentioned the fact that not all of the objectives in a church's educational program can be measured with statistical accuracy. We cannot plug a student into a computer and by pushing the right buttons determine what he believes about God, or Christ, or the church, or about how to apply the Bible to life situations. Yet at times questionnaires may give us some clues about a student's spiritual development.

We need to be aware that when students are questioned about values or attitudes, many of them will give the answers that they think their parents and teachers want. Of course, we need also to recognize that some students are nonconformists and will deliberately give answers contrary to what they are expected to give. For these reasons, these questionnaires must be carefully designed if they are to produce useful results.

At times questionnaires may give us some clues about a student's spiritual development.

Use Feedback from People Involved

While organizations, facilities, and curriculum materials are certainly important, yet the teachers and leaders involved and those whom they seek to reach and serve are most important. For that reason, we must seek frequent and regular feedback from those who are involved in our educational programs.

From Teachers

Teachers' meetings provide a good opportunity for feedback from teachers, helpers, and other workers. Those who lead these meetings should create an atmosphere that encourages a free exchange of ideas and criticisms. It is a good idea for the secretary to record these ideas. For one thing, writing down an idea helps to clarify it. It is also important to have a record of these so that they can be evaluated and acted upon at a later date. Relying on faulty memories for such information can result in misunderstanding. An effective leader will utilize many different techniques such as "brainstorming" to elicit these ideas. In evaluating a vacation Bible school or camping program, it is a good idea for the leaders and teachers to meet as soon as possible after the conclusion of the program. Otherwise, time is likely to erase some of the good ideas or criticisms that grew out of the program. These suggestions ought to be written down and filed for the benefit of those who will lead the programs in the future.

From Students

Students, especially youth and adults, are constantly evaluating our religious education programs. If they are not satisfied with what they are receiving, they will let us know with their feet—their attendance becomes infrequent or they quit coming at all. It is far better to seek out problems and to correct shortcomings before they become major sources of trouble. For example, adults and youth may be dissatisfied with the Sunday school curriculum developed by the leaders. It is often a good idea to get them involved in choosing the topics they study. There are today available a whole range of elective studies that may for some be more interesting and useful than the usual lessons. When students express these concerns, good leaders will quickly respond to them. Every good church program will have methods of evaluating the effectiveness of personnel involved in the program. But we need to recognize that students also evaluate teachers and other leaders. A teacher, for example, may be judged an excellent teacher by formal standards, and yet not be effective in a classroom situation. Sometimes the problem can be solved by moving the teacher to a different age group where his or her skills can be better utilized. In making decisions like this, student feedback is quite helpful. However, church leaders must use caution in seeking and using student feedback. In a public school or a college situation where personal relationships between teachers and students are not extensive, a questionnaire may be used effectively. But in a church setting where there are all kinds of personal relationships, having students evaluate a teacher by using a questionnaire can create problems. For this reason, leaders in the Christian education program are more likely to rely upon informal comments and observations as a basis for their evaluation.

If students are not satisfied with what they are receiving in our religious education programs, they will let us know with their feet.

What to Evaluate

In the education program of a typical congregation there are a number of elements that should undergo regular scrutiny. The following items are intended as examples of things that should be evaluated, but the list is not intended to be exhaustive.

Organizational Structures

There is no one set pattern for the structure and interrelationship of the various organizations that may be involved in a congregation's education program. These may vary depending upon the size of the congregation and its denominational affiliation. Most congregations will have a governing body that may be called a board of elders, a board of deacons, or some other designation. The committee or department of Christian education will be responsible to this board. The important issue is not how these boards and committees are organized or what names they bear but whether or not they function efficiently in carrying out the program of Christian education. An organizational chart on the wall may be impressive, but unless the chart facilitates the education program, it is nothing but an interesting wall hanging. In evaluating the organizational structures, several questions need to be asked. First, of course, is the arrangement getting the job done? Are the channels of responsibility clearly understood? Who is responsible for what and to whom? Are there overlapping responsibilities? Is the person to whom responsibility has been delegated given the authority and resources to fulfill the responsibility? Are the persons actually doing the necessary tasks given some voice in the decision-making process? Asking these and similar questions will keep the organization functioning effectively and prevent it from becoming a bureaucratic fossil.

Agencies within the Education Program

Most congregations will have several educational agencies. The largest and most obvious in most congregations is the weekly Sunday school, or church school, or Bible school, as it may be variously called. Youth groups, midweek programs, after-school programs, vacation Bible school, day camping, and resident camping are others. Each of these agencies should have clearly written out objectives, which provide a basis for evaluation. We need to ask how resources are allocated to each agency and how personnel is recruited and trained. The most important issue is whether each agency is attaining the objectives it has set for itself.

Programs

Most congregations develop programs to meet the needs of the congregation. These programs may be for specific ministries such as missions, evangelism, stewardship, or shepherding or for special groups such as older adults, youth, shut-ins, or singles. The success of these programs depends upon the involvement of the various agencies within the congregation, including the educational agencies. A missions program, for example, should involve the Sunday school and youth groups with emphases appropriate to each age group. Evaluation of such a program should reveal its strengths and weaknesses and provide help for future programs.

Facilities

The use of facilities such as buildings, equipment, and other resources has been treated in a previous chapter. Any evaluation of these matters must begin with the acknowledgment that no congregation is able to meet its educational needs perfectly. (Even if a situation seems perfect, it is certain to change in a few weeks or months as the congregation grows, shrinks, or its membership changes.) Thus evaluation must be an ongoing process. As class sizes in Sunday school change, room assignments must be changed. As a congregation grows, it must resort to creative scheduling to best utilize its facilities.

Curriculum

The curriculum of a congregation's educational program must be evaluated on a regular basis. The curriculum is treated in a previous chapter and need not be discussed at length here.

We need to keep in mind that the curriculum is not just the printed materials that a congregation uses in its various programs, but must include all the learning activities, either formal or informal, that a congregation uses to achieve its educational objectives. For the purpose of evaluation, it is a good idea to keep written records of all of these activities in order to provide a solid basis for evaluation.

The various personnel involved in a church education program comprise its most important element.

Personnel

The leaders, teachers, assistants, musicians, and other persons involved in a church education program comprise its most important element. For that reason the personnel must be evaluated. But the fact that most of these workers are volunteers poses a delicate problem when it comes to evaluation. Public school teachers, who are paid for their services, expect to be evaluated as a part of their employment contract. But volunteer Sunday school workers are not accustomed to this, and many of them would resent it. Yet if a church is to do an effective job of carrying out its educational mandate, it must have competent people involved, and so evaluation of personnel becomes essential. It is not wise to begin with a complete formal evaluation of teachers. It is better to begin with an occasional classroom visit by the Sunday school superintendent, departmental superintendent, or other supervisory persons. On occasion, it is a good idea to have a teacher do a self-evaluation with a form that he or she can fill out.

Students

Students in schools from kindergarten through college are subject to frequent and regular evaluation—tests of every conceivable shape and form. The results of these tests provide ammunition for critics of our public education systems. Yet few indeed are the voices demanding that students involved in religious education be tested. Why? Is it because we aren't really all that concerned or is it that we don't know how to design tests that help us evaluate the spiritual growth of our students? Perhaps a bit of both. We have a feeling that if a person attends religious programs, he or she will automatically grow spiritually.

In the final analysis, nothing is more important than what happens to the student.

In the final analysis, nothing is more important than what happens to the student in the church's educational program. Unless there is clear evidence of Christian growth, with a student becoming more Christlike in his attitudes and behavior, the program has fallen short of its primary objectives. Testing for cognitive learning is relatively simple and should be done more frequently than it is, especially with many publishers providing tests with their material. While some persons may react negatively to tests, yet they can be administered in such a way that they are not threatening. While testing for evidence of spiritual growth may be more difficult, we should continue to work for ways of evaluating this.

When to Evaluate

Often churches do not become seriously concerned about evaluation until a crisis arises. Then leaders hastily and often with less than ideal results seek to find out what went wrong. Of course, evaluation is essential when a crisis arises, but efforts at evaluation carried on regularly and systematically will usually prevent these crisis situations. Further, when evaluations of various types are built into the program, they will come to be accepted and even welcomed. Some evaluations need to be done on an annual basis, others may be done quarterly, monthly, or even weekly. Teachers should be encouraged to evaluate their own efforts for every lesson, and most will come to see this as a means to more effective and more enjoyable teaching.

Conclusion

Talking about evaluation may seem idealistic, or impractical, or even unimportant. But when we recognize that those who work in Christian education are involved in the most important task in the world, nothing is unimportant that will contribute to carrying out this ministry more effectively. As we have already noted, some kinds of evaluation—at least informally—are going on all the time. Our concern is to make this process more systematic and efficient and useful. The forms that have been included with this chapter may encourage leaders and teachers to start the process.

p r o j e c t

★ Using the evaluation guide attached to this chapter, assess the Christian education program in your local church. ★

For Further Reading

Lowell E. Brown and Bobbie Reed
Grow: Your Sunday School Can Grow. Glendale, CA: International Center for Learning, 1975.

Daryl Eldridge
The Teaching Ministry of the Church. Nashville: Broadman and Holman, 1995.

Kenneth O. Gangel
Building Leaders for Church Education. Chicago: Moody Press, 1981.

Kenneth O. Gangel and Howard G. Hendricks
The Christian Educator's Handbook on Teaching. Grand Rapids: Baker, 1998.

Werner C. Graendorf, ed.
Introduction to Biblical Christian Education. Chicago: Moody Press, 1981.

Thomas H. Groome
Christian Religious Education. San Francisco: Harper & Row, 1980.

Randolph Crump Miller
The Theory of Christian Education Practice. Birmingham, AL: Religious Education Press, 1980.

Bruce P. Powers, ed.
Christian Education Handbook, revised. Nashville: Broadman and Holman, 1996.

Charles A. Tidwell
The Educational Ministry. Nashville: Broadman, 1996.

Elmer Towns
The Successful Sunday School and Teachers Guidebook. Carol Stream, IL: Creation House, 1976.

Evaluation Questionnaire

A. Objectives

1. Does the church have objectives for its total program? ___ Yes ___ No
2. Are these written down and readily available? ___ Yes ___ No
3. By whom were these objectives designed? (Check more than one if appropriate.)

   ___ Minister ___ Church board or other governing body
   ___ Committee chairpersons ___ Members of the congregation

4. Does the church have objectives for its educational program? ___ Yes ___ No
5. Are these written down and readily available? ___ Yes ___ No
6. By whom were these objectives designed? (Check more than one if appropriate.)

   ___ Minister ___ Sunday school superintendent ___ Teachers
   ___ Students ___ Church board or other governing body
   ___ Committee chairpersons

7. Have objectives been established for each department? ___ Yes ___ No
   For each class? ___ Yes ___ No

8. When were these objectives last evaluated and revised?
   ___ Within the last year? ___ Within the last five years? ___ Never

B. Organization and Administration

1. Does the Sunday school have a superintendent? ___ Yes ___ No
2. Does each department have a superintendent? ___ Yes ___ No
3. How many departments are there in the Sunday school? ____
4. How many classes? ____
5. How many teachers? ____ Assistant teachers or helpers? ____
6. Do you have regular meetings of the teachers?
   ___ Annually ___ Quarterly ___ Monthly
7. Does the church have a regular leadership training program? ___ Yes ___ No
   How frequently do they meet? ___ Annually? ___ Quarterly? ___ Monthly?
8. In addition to the Sunday school, what other regular agencies does the church use in its educational program?
   ___ Sunday evening classes ___ Camp ___ Youth meetings

__ Retreats __ Children's church or extended Sunday school sessions
__ Kindergarten __ Weekday classes __ Midweek classes
__Vacation Bible school __ Other

C. Records

1. Are attendance records kept for various church activities?
   __ Worship __ Midweek service __ Sunday school __ Other
   __ Sunday evening service

2. Are these records kept in such a way that comparisons can easily be made
   with last year's figures? __ Yes __ No
   Figures from five years ago? __ Yes __ No

3. Are these records kept in a convenient location? __ Yes __ No

4. Are these records regularly used to evaluate the progress of the church's
   educational program? __ Yes __ No

5. Are more or less detailed records kept on individual students?__ Yes __ No

D. Facilities and Equipment

1. Do the educational facilities allow for easy departmentalization of the
   Sunday school? __ Yes __ No

2. Are classrooms assigned in such a way as to allow for easy movement of
   students? __ Yes __ No

3. How many square feet of floor space per student are provided in each
   department? Nursery ____ Beginner ____ Primary ____
   Middler ____ Junior ____ Junior High ____ Senior High ____
   Adult ____

4. Indicate which of the following are located in classrooms:
   __ Chalkboards __ Pictures __ Bulletin boards __ Maps and charts

5. Indicate which of the following are available to teachers:
   __ Flannel boards __ Filmstrip projectors __ Flannel board materials
   __ Overhead projectors __ Overhead transparencies __ Slide projectors
   __ VCR equipment

E. Curriculum

1. Has the church attempted to correlate all of its learning activities in relation to one another and to its educational objectives? __ Yes __ No

2. Does the curriculum provide for both student needs and student learning readiness?   __ Yes __ No

3. Who selects the printed curriculum materials?
   __ Minister   __ Superintendent   __ Committee   __ Teachers
   __ Other persons

4. Do the curriculum materials present the Scriptures as the infallible, divinely inspired Word of God?   __ Yes __ No

5. Are the materials true to the Bible in terms of emphasis?   __ Yes __ No

6. Are the materials attractive and up-to-date in appearance?   __ Yes __ No

7. Do the materials encourage students to apply the Bible to life situations?
                                                              __ Yes __ No

8. Do the materials provide sufficient help for the teachers?   __ Yes __ No

9. Do the materials give a strong emphasis to evangelism?   __ Yes __ No

10. Are the materials accurately graded to meet the needs of students at each age level?   __ Yes __ No

CHAPTER 19
THE MINISTER
AND CHRISTIAN EDUCATION

Chapter Nineteen Summary
- ☑ Reasons for involving the minister in Christian Education
- ☑ The role of the minister in Christian education
- ☑ Ways a minister may support the Christian education programs

---

You can call it Sunday school, church school, Bible school, Bible studies or Bible fellowship, but whatever you call it, ministers should be actively involved. They should be involved because it is good for their people. What other program in the church allows people to get to know each other better while also helping them get to know the Bible better? Ministers often decry the biblical ignorance and lack of commitment seen in many church members. It is doubtful that those problems can be adequately addressed from the pulpit alone. For Christians to grow, they need exactly what the Christian education program offers. The give and take of the class along with the extra biblical input and opportunity for feedback gives both long-time and new believers opportunities for growth. So the Christian education program touches all ages, all levels of spiritual maturity, and addresses several of the key needs of the church.

It is doubtful that biblical ignorance and lack of commitment can be adequately addressed from the pulpit alone.

Even if ministers look at Christian education from a purely mercenary point of view, they will want to befriend the program. No one minister can meet all the pastoral needs of the congregation. There are too many hospitals to visit, too many shut-ins to see, and too many members who need counseling. But through the pastoral care of a Bible study group or Sunday school class, ministers may find a whole new avenue of opportunity for assistance. When a class member has a need, the class can go into action. The class can provide practical needs for the time of crisis, a listening ear in the time of despair. No one minister can meet all the evangelistic needs of a church, but he or she may be greatly aided by a class that is focused on outreach. If a class takes evangelism seriously, class members will invite and bond with guests to the church. By the time visitors decide to join a church, they already have a peer support group. So the class assists the minister in identifying those who need the gospel or the church and assists in evangelism and discipleship.

**No one minister can meet all the pastoral needs
of the congregation.**

Rightly approached, support of the Christian education program maximizes efficiency; it does not steal time from an already busy schedule. Undergirding the Christian education program is one of the best investments a minister will ever make.

Ministers can relate to the Christian education program of a local church in three distinct ways. The first applies to a solo minister, who will actually be the Christian education minister in addition to regular duties. The second applies to all ministers and that is the recognition that every minister is an educator. The third way is distinctive to ministers leading a multiple staff and that is as supporter of the Christian education program.

The Minister as Christian Education Director

If you are a solo minister, you are the Christian education director. It is your duty to manage the Sunday school program, the small groups ministry, and other Christian education opportunities. You may not feel qualified. It may not be your greatest interest and you may not feel you have the gifts or aptitude for it. This book is filled with the very helps you need to be an effective administrator and trainer of teachers for the program.

A few things need to be said about the unique frustrations of the solo minister in relation to the Christian education program. You may often feel as if you are facing the challenges alone, but you don't have to do it alone. You may very well want to work with a Sunday school superintendent or coordinator of small groups. Still, much of the management of the program will fall on your shoulders. The benefit of training a good superintendent is first seen in the timesaving potential. Greater still is the benefit of having a volunteer to help you recruit other volunteers. If the minister asks for help, it is quite different than a volunteer asking, for the minister is a paid employee. When someone who is donating his or her time asks someone else to volunteer, it takes on a new dynamic.

Ministers themselves are Christian educators.

Probably the greatest frustration for the solo minister is lack of qualified teachers. Volunteers are increasingly selective about how they will fit into a program. You will probably be in a constant state of recruiting, training, and replacing workers. Some smaller churches have space difficulties, which can be addressed with off-site locations.

The solo minister should not see the Christian education program as some separate institution, but as an extension of other church labors.

The Minister as an Educator

Ministers themselves are Christian educators. This is the case when they are preaching. The line between a sermon and a lesson is often fuzzy. Preachers continually blur the distinctions. While there are significant differences between a sermon and a lesson, there are also many similarities. Every Christian sermon contains some teaching; every Christian lesson contains some exhortation. Perhaps you have heard a preacher called a "teaching preacher." There would be a great benefit for the preacher to stay abreast of trends in education, particularly pedagogical trends. Techniques that enhance lessons can often be used in sermons. Principles of developing a lesson can be utilized in sermon construction.

Most ministers will teach some kind of class in the church program. One problem that faces many ministers is the tendency to "preach" a lesson or to exclusively use the lecture method. The lecture method does offer some advantages, but it is doubtful that a minister would want to use it in every situation or teaching opportunity. Ministers need more than one weapon in their arsenal. Recognizing their role as an educator and making themselves aware of teaching techniques will pay dividends for those who listen to them teach.

Should the minister teach a Sunday school class? There are valid points to be made on both sides of the issue.

This is as good a point as any to ask the question, "Should the minister teach a Sunday school class?" There are valid points to be made on both sides of the issue. Obviously, some churches have worship and Sunday school schedules that prohibit a minister from even considering the possibility. But assuming it is possible for ministers to teach, should they? Some argue that allowing the minister to teach prohibits the development of other teachers. Surely any church program can offer enough classes to utilize and develop other leaders. In many cases, the preacher is one of the best teachers in the church. Shouldn't that talent be used? This could be said of any ministerial staff member as well. Some churches find that a minister's class can serve as a nice handshake for the church, or even serve as a feeder class for the others. Some churches have this class in the auditorium. The appeal of the class is that those who like the preacher's preaching may also like his or her teaching. If the minister does teach a class, it is particularly important to have class officers, class greeters, and social directors. The minister will be under such time pressure that adequate attention would not be given to these areas. Besides, this is a golden opportunity to develop volunteer leadership.

Even if they don't teach a Sunday school class, ministers may very well teach in an expository method or topical approach for a Sunday evening or midweek service. Many ministers crave to teach an in-depth Bible study. The Sunday morning service will not be the best time for the greatest depth. The Sunday school hour may also require a lighter touch. There is a time for in-depth study as an elective; Sunday evening, Wednesday evening or a home Bible study may be the best time.

Ministers may teach a new members' or inquirers' class or teach at church camp. They may teach a leadership training or teacher training class. In evangelistic work the minister is frequently called upon to teach the basics of God's plan of salvation in the home or office setting. There is no getting around the fact that every preacher is already a Christian educator.

The Minister as Supporter of Christian Education

If ministers choose not to teach, they should at least attend Sunday school if the schedule allows. This demonstrates that the minister supports the Christian education program and considers it valuable. It is tempting, if ministers allow, to let the time between worship services be used to relax or do errands. Even if they must do greeting for the next service, they could surely find a class where they could slip in for part of the hour. Some ministers may suppose that sitting and listening to someone else teach may be boring. Jesus must have been bored to hear others teach in the synagogue, but He supported it with His attendance anyway. While ministers may be the most knowledgeable person in the church about the Bible, they perhaps have much to learn about life or technique from another teacher. Instead of being bored, they can see this as an opportunity to receive a blessing. Ministers must give out cognitive information so much; they need to take some time to receive.

A practical way a minister may assist in the Christian education program is in facilities support. Ministers are often influential in the allocation of space. They can help a class find the right kind of space and, of course, provide guidance in decisions to add or remodel Sunday school space. They can even guide in the extremely difficult decision of asking a class to move.

Ministers can help keep the Sunday school up to date by helping teachers and leaders to utilize the latest equipment. It is important that the church in general and the Sunday school in particular not be the last to use new technologies. This also means ministers must give budgetary support. They are in a position to remind leaders to give the Christian education program the financial resources needed to fulfill its mission.

Ministers may support the Christian education program through preaching by telling interesting stories furnished to him by the teachers. Stories about cute or interesting things said in the class not only make the student feel important, but also highlight the significant ministry of the program.

Ministers may also verbally invite people to Sunday school every single Sunday from the pulpit, offer to help people find a class, or recommend classes in visitor letters and brochures.

It goes without saying that ministers can support the Christian education program by supporting the Christian education professional staff.

Ministers, whether solo or leading a multiple staff, may want to lead in attendance promotion in Sunday school. Some shy away today from attendance promotion as if it is unspiritual. Admittedly some of the methods used years ago seem tacky by today's standards. Still, there are several promotional ideas that can help add interest to the Sunday school. There are programs that add fun without being silly. Others, like the famous "Friend Day," simply encourage people to do what they should be doing all along. If the church does some kind of Sunday school promotion, then the minister must lead and become the flag waver.

It goes without saying that ministers can support the Christian education program by supporting the Christian education professional staff. It is a key duty of the minister to manage staff and help them to be a success. This is true for all church staff. Ministers often struggle with how much to supervise staff. If they supervise too much, it will stifle staff members' ability to make independent decisions. If they supervise too little, staff members may feel unappreciated or even fail to do what is expected. Much of this is determined by the temperaments of individual members of the staff and can be determined only by trial and error. The bottom line is that any staff person wants to feel a part of the team and to feel respected and affirmed. You will know from personal experience how frustrating it is to recruit workers. You will know the additional frustration of finally recruiting workers, then having them fail to show up for their duties. Any encouragement you can bring will be welcome.

The bottom line is that any staff person wants to feel a part of the team and to feel respected and affirmed.

There is no doubt that the Sunday school program has suffered numerically in recent years. A few in your church may remember the day when Sunday school attendance outran worship attendance by a large margin. That is no longer the case. Ministers used to beg people to come to worship service. Now they beg people to come to Sunday school. Some ministers may be tempted to disregard it or de-emphasize the Sunday school. While it may take on different forms or even different names, there will always be a need for some kind of Christian education program. Sunday will probably always be a convenient time to schedule some or even most of those opportunities. Rick Warren tells of his personal experience when he founded Saddleback

Church. Rick was willing to be innovative. After all, he was starting a new church in California. He wasn't going to call his program Sunday school. He was going to use small groups. He surveyed his brand new constituency in southern California to see what times were favored for these groups. Sunday morning was the favorite by far.

Who knows what trends will affect the Sunday school? Who knows whether it will remain static, decline, grow to the heights it enjoyed in its attendance peak, or even grow beyond the high-water mark? Two things are certain. One is that the Sunday school program will not thrive without the enthusiastic support of the minister. Secondly, there will always be a need for a vibrant Christian education program whatever form it takes.

p r o j e c t

★ Interview a minister and find out how he carries out his educational function. Does he teach a class? Prepare a list of interview questions based on ideas presented in this chapter. ★

For Further Reading

Robert L. Browning, ed.
The Pastor as Religious Educator. Birmingham, AL: Religious Education Press, 1989.

Daryl Eldridge, ed.
The Teaching Ministry of the Church. Nashville: Broadman, 1995.

Bill Hull
The Disciple-Making Pastor. Old Tappan, NJ: Fleming H. Revell, 1988.

Richard Allen Olsen
The Pastor's Role in Educational Ministry. Philadelphia: Fortress Press, 1974.

Eugene Roehlkepartain
The Teaching Church. Nashville: Abingdon, 1993.

Earle F. Shelp and Ronald H. Sunderland
The Pastor as Teacher. New York: Pilgrim Press, 1988.

Charles A. Tidwell
The Educational Ministry of the Church. Nashville: Broadman, 1995.

CHAPTER 20
THE PROFESSIONAL
CHRISTIAN EDUCATOR

Chapter Twenty Summary

- ☑ Images of professional Christian educators
- ☑ Necessary preparation for professional Christian educators
- ☑ Responsibilites of professional Christian educators

Quiz: Minister of Christian Education. Youth Minister. Children's Minister. Adult Education Minister. Discipleship Minister. Women's Minister. Family Minister. What do all of these—all found in various churches, sometimes several in one church—have in common?

At first glance, they appear to have little relationship to each other. But look again. All of them are related to the Christian education ministry of the church. They define an age division or a specified group on whom efforts are focused. The person in each position is concerned to lead the teaching program of the church for that designated group so learners can develop into mature disciples.

We once described the professional Christian educator as the Director or Minister of Christian Education. Though some educators still carry that title, many churches have continued to add professional leaders, each with a designated focus group. It has occurred for two reasons: the growth of churches with the need to add staff and the rush toward specialization in society at large.

The title by which a person is described is largely irrelevant. What is important is that the person—regardless of title—

understand the scope and purpose of the ministry to which he or she has been called. The purpose of this chapter is to describe the work of professional Christian educators in general terms—preparation, responsibilities, and relationships—understanding that this may apply to those responsible for the total Christian education program or those responsible for a segment of the total Christian education program.

The title by which a person is described is largely irrelevant.

Images of the Professional Christian Educator

Timothy Lines's helpful book *Functional Images of the Religious Educator* provides insightful metaphors to explain the task of the professional Christian educator, whether that person is responsible for the total educational program or only part of it.

Parent

Parents are first of all providers. They try to decide what is necessary and appropriate for their charges. They make certain that resources are available. But parents are also protectors. They provide a secure environment for growth and development.

The aim of this role is to lead learners to maturity by nurturing them in faith.

Coach

Coaches are supervisors. They delegate, guide, and direct those who perform the work. They are also trainers and motivators and strategists. Professional Christian educators play much the same role as they recruit, train, and supervise personnel who do the work of instruction.

Scientist

Scientists are discoverers. They find new information and develop theories to guide function. They often experiment.

They evaluate. This is descriptive of the functions of Christian educators as they seek to work with local leaders to solve problems and move the educational program forward.

Critic

This sometimes is not a popular word in contemporary society. But it is a good description of a professional Christian educator, for critics analyze the values and assumptions underlying what is being performed. They expose pretensions, exaggerations, and myths that sometimes limit the educational program. Though professional Christian educators should beware of playing this role too loudly, it is indeed one of their functions.

Storyteller

Storytellers function as evangelists, those who bring the good news. They are historians who synthesize historical understandings into understandable narrative. They are mythologists as they share a sacred story. They use stories to teach significant truths. Indeed professional Christian educators understand this role.

Artist

Artists create and design. They imagine new images and communicate them to the viewer in ways that evoke affective response. Much of the work of the Christian educator fits this image.

Visionary

Visionaries are not merely dreamers. Rather, they are able to tell what they have experienced, declare what will come, assert what should be, and attract people to their vision so action can occur. Christian educators often are called to fulfill this role in their ministries.

Revolutionary

Revolutionaries are quick to innovate. They can plan. They agitate until action is taken. They are change agents. This role can too easily be turned into a negative one if the leader has poor people skills. But it is a role that Christian educators should fulfill.

Therapist

Therapists are involved in healing for others. They work as catalysts to bring reconciliation. They facilitate the healing process. The goal is wholeness. As counselors and mentors, Christian educators fulfill this function.

Minister

Ministers sometimes are priests; they are intermediaries leading others to God. They help people celebrate life. They are defenders of the weak and powerless. They are servants. This too describes a role of the professional Christian educator.

Preparation for Christian Education Ministry

Commitment

The primary qualification of a Christian education professional must be a maturing and growing commitment to God and to Jesus Christ. God calls a Christian education professional to ministry as surely as He calls those who preach.

Age and Experience

Christian education professionals tend to be young and relatively inexperienced, although that scenario has begun to change. Sometimes Christian education ministry, especially youth ministry, is seen as the path to preaching ministry. Indeed that may be a valid path for some. But for many, who have the gifts for this kind of ministry, it can be a lifelong commitment, perhaps in fulfilling different educational leadership functions through the years. This writer, for example, began Christian education ministry as a youth minister, then moved to a general Christian education ministry in a medium-sized church, later served as a children's minister in a large congregation, and taught Christian education in college and seminary.

Gender

Both men and women find satisfying ministry in Christian education. A 1998 survey indicated that women are called by churches to any one of the several ministries identified at the beginning of the chapter. They often are called directors of Christian education, children's ministry, youth ministry, or any one of the other areas mentioned, while men are more often called ministers. But both genders can and do serve in Christian education ministry.

Education

Christian education professionals should be as thoroughly prepared as the minister. A good background in Bible and theology is essential so their work will be biblically and theologically informed and so they can teach the Bible, the primary textbook, effectively. A thorough knowledge of educational philosophy, psychology, principles of teaching, and administration are also essential. This can best be achieved with a good undergraduate or seminary program in Christian education.

Leaders in Christian education ministry must continue to grow.

Leaders in Christian education ministry must continue to grow by taking refresher courses, attending seminars and conferences, reading, observing, and other continuing education experiences. Continuing education not only equips them, but also sets an example for the volunteers who work with them.

Skills

Formal education alone does not qualify a person for Christian education ministry. Personal and professional qualifications should be carefully assessed. Many different qualities may be desirable, but some are crucial. Emler (1989) identifies these:

✎ Technical skills involve the ability to use the specialized procedures, methods, and techniques that are basic to the profession. These should be a part of educational preparation, but a changing world makes it imperative that the professional continue to acquire and refine skills.

✎ Human skills involve the ability to work with people at the individual and group level. Conflict management and resolution, communication of values, and negotiation are all necessary skills. The personal touch is critical. This calls for empathy, the ability to accept the values, attitudes, and assumptions of others.

✎ Conceptual skills—the ability to see the overview, the whole organization, to diagnose and understand interrelationships—are essential.

✎ Enabling skills are those that help others to find and succeed in their ministries.

We must add to that list spiritual growth. Professional Christian educators are not finished products of faith, but they must model for those with whom they work a growing faith.

Look again at Ron Oakes' chapter "Planning for Christian Education." The skill areas he outlines in that chapter are essential for successful Christian education ministry.

Responsibilities

Developing the Educational Program

Christian education professionals are primarily responsible for the development and effectiveness of the church's educational program, or a segment of it. This includes:

✎ Helping the staff to articulate an operational definition of Christian education.

✎ Developing a philosophy of Christian education.

✎ Articulating educational objectives.

✎ Determining how various programs work together to achieve the stated objectives.

✎ Building and implementing a curriculum to meet the needs of the learners.

✎ Administering the program budget.

✎ Purchasing and managing educational equipment.

✎ Evaluating the current educational program. See the chapter "Evaluating Christian Education" for further development.

✎ Recruiting and training leaders.

✎ Keeping records.

✎ Serving as a resource person for the volunteers.

Wise professional Christian educators never attempt to do all these tasks by themselves. They form a leadership team to work with them to develop the program. With the leadership team, they analyze, plan, and strategize for effective Christian education.

Wise professional Christian educators never attempt to do all these tasks by themselves.

A Christian education professional responsible for all ages develops an educational program for all ages. Others, however, may develop an educational program only for the targeted group for which they are responsible.

Educational Consultant

Christian education professionals should be the resident teaching-learning experts for the age levels for which they are responsible. This requires continuing growth in an understanding of trends in education, changes in curriculum, and available resources for the volunteer staff. This is carried out in teacher development, curriculum planning and selection, and media development.

Faith Interpreter

Modeling faith is a unique opportunity for those who lead Christian education programs. But these leaders also have opportunity to mentor others and provide direction in their spiritual journey. Sometimes this leads to counseling those with special needs—children, young people, individual adults, or families.

Selecting, Enlisting, and Training Leaders

The church's educational program is dependent on volunteer leadership, even if a professional Christian educator directs the work. Finding, enlisting, developing, and retaining volunteer leaders is a major task for Christian education leaders.

Effective Christian educators keep a list of potential leaders and teachers who could, if trained and challenged, be effective leaders. They may have a team who assists in recruitment and training. But in the end, those who lead the Christian education program are responsible. The chapter "Recruiting, Training, and Keeping Volunteer Leaders" provides detailed help for this important task.

Planning for Visitation

Good visitation programs are essential if the Christian education program is to accomplish what it can and should. Visitation includes personal visits, phone calls, and mailings to those who are newcomers as well as absentees. Christian education professionals are responsible for planning and developing an effective program of visitation.

Interpersonal Relationships
With the Professional Staff

Much of the work of Christian education professionals must be done behind the scenes. Few will notice or give credit for what they do. They rarely are center stage, making it essential that they be constantly alert to the temptation of jealousy of those who do have the more visible positions. They must respect the authority of their supervisors—often the senior minister or a church administrator—and value the team relationship they have with the other staff members. Disagreements among staff members may develop—they almost certainly will—but these must be used as creative opportunities for Christian growth and team development.

Much of the work of Christian education professionals must be done behind the scenes.

Staff relationships have the potential of being one of the most valued aspects of ministry; they also can become one of the worst experiences a person can suffer. Surveys indicate that over half of Christian educators rate their staff relationships as good or excellent.

With Church Leaders

Christian education professionals must take care to develop open lines of communication with key church leaders—elders, church board, Christian education leadership team, finance committee, and facilities and maintenance committee.

With Volunteers

Working with the volunteer staff is essential if Christian education professionals are to be successful. The average volunteer has a greater desire to serve meaningfully than church leaders often recognize. It is this role of identifying, recruiting, training, and working with volunteers that many Christian education professionals find most satisfying about their ministries.

Summary

Christian education professionals are men or women called by a local congregation to lead its Christian education program—or some part of the program such as children's, youth, or adult education. They are called to ministry, as surely as those in other positions, and must seek adequate preparation for the task. They are responsible for leading programs and personnel to achieve the goal of leading people to the standards of Christlikeness. They are key people in their congregation.

---

p r o j e c t

★ Interview three or four Christian education professionals. If possible, select them from various specialties within the Christian education area. Find out what each person does. Learn what advice each would give you if you were to choose to become a Christian education professional. ★

For Further Reading

Donald Emler
Revisioning the DRE. Birmingham, AL: Religious Education Press, 1989.

Charles R. Foster
Equipping Congregations. Nashville: Abingdon Press, 1994.

Timothy Arthur Lines
Functional Images of the Religious Educator. Birmingham, AL: Religious Education Press, 1992.

Systemic Religious Education. Birmingham, AL: Religious Education Press, 1987.

APPENDIX

RESOURCES

APPENDIX
RESOURCES
FOR CHRISTIAN EDUCATORS

Christian educators are always alert to useful resources to meet the needs of a constantly changing field. The following list of resources, curriculum companies, and organizations are helpful to persons interested in Christian educational ministry. Many of these companies and organizations also reflect particular theological perspectives. The reader is encouraged to do further research to determine the suitability of materials for their needs. Neither College Press nor the authors necessarily endorse all the companies, organizations, or resources listed. Please note that addresses, web sites, and telephone numbers may have changed since publication date.

Curriculum Companies

* Augsburg Fortress Publishers: P.O. Box 1209, Minneapolis, MN 55402. 1-800-328-4648.
* Awana Clubs International: One E. Bode Road, Streamwood, IL 60107-6658. 1-800-AWANA-4U. Website: www.awana.org
* CharismaLife Publishers: 600 Rinehart Road, Lake Mary, FL 32746. 1-800-451-4598. Website: www.charismalife.com
* Christian Ed Publishers: P.O. Box 26639, San Diego, CA 92196. 1-800-854-1531.
* College Press: P.O. Box 1132, Joplin, MO 64802. 1-800-289-3300. Website: www.collegepress.com
* Cokesbury: 201 Eighth Avenue South, Nashville, TN 37202. 1-800-672-1789.
* Concordia Publishing House: 3558 S. Jefferson Avenue, St. Louis, MO 63118. 1-800-325-3040.

✦ Cook Communications Ministries: 4050 Lee Vance View, Colorado Springs, CO 80918-7100. 1-800-323-7543. Website: www.cookministries.com

✦ Gospel Advocate Publishers: 1006 Elm Hill Pike, Nashville, TN 37210.

✦ Gospel Light: 2300 Knoll Drive, Ventura, CA 93003. 1-800-4-GOSPEL.

✦ Gospel Publishing House/Radiant Life: 1445 Boonville, Springfield, MO 65802-1894.

✦ Group Publishing: 1515 Cascade Avenue, Box 481, Loveland, CO, 80538-8681. 1-800-447-1070. Website: www.grouppublishing.com

✦ NavPress. 7899 Lexington Drive, Colorado Springs, CO 80920. 1-800-366-7788. Website: www.navpress.com

✦ Pioneer Clubs: P.O. Box 788, Wheaton, IL 60189. 1-800-694-2582. Website: www.pioneerclubs.org

✦ Regular Baptist Press: 1300 North Meacham Road, Schaumburg, IL 60173. 1-800-727-4440. Website: www.garbc.org/rbp

✦ Scripture Press: See Cook Communications Ministries.

✦ Serendipity House: Box 1012, Littleton, CO 80160. 1-800-525-9563. Website: www.serendipityhouse.com

✦ Standard Publishing: 8121 Hamilton Avenue, Cincinnati, OH 45231. 1-800-543-1353.

✦ Sweet Publishing: 3950 Fossil Creek Blvd., Suite 201, Fort Worth, TX 76137.

✦ 21st Century Christian: 2809 Granny White Pike, Nashville, TN 37204.

✦ Wesleyan Publishing House: 8050 Casteway Drive, Indianapolis, IN 46250. 1-800-4-WESLEY.

✦ Word Action Publications: Box 419527, Kansas City, MO 64141. 1-800-877-0700.

Businesses/Organizations/Ministries

■ Answers in Genesis: P.O. Box 6330, Florence, KY 41022. 1-800-778-3390. Website: www.answersingenesis.org

■ Adventures in Missions: R.R. 5, Box 106, Bloomfield, IN 47424.

■ Badge-A-Minit: Dept. CEM798, Box 800, LaSalle, IL 61301. 1-800-223-4103.

■ Campus Crusade for Christ, International: 100 Sunport Lane, Orlando, FL 32809. 1-407-326-2000. Website: www.ccci.org

■ Christian Research Institute: Box 500, San Juan Capistrano, CA 92693.

- Christ In Youth, Inc. Box B, Joplin, MO 64802. 1-417-781-2273.
- Church Art Works/One Way Out: 890 Promontory Pl., SE, Salem, OR 97302. 1-503-370-9377.
- Church Growth Institute: P.O. Box 7000, Forest, VA 24551. 1-800-553-GROW.
- Clean Comedians: P.O. Box 326, La Mirada, CA 90637-0326. 1-800-354-GLAD.
- Evangelical Training Association: P.O. Box 327, Wheaton, IL 60189. 1-800-369-8291.
- The Fellowship of Christian Magicians: 47 Ellwood Place, Buffalo, NY 14225. 1-716-895-0311.
- Fellowship of Christian Athletes: 8701 Leeds Road, Kansas City, MO 64129-1680. 1-800-289-0909.
- Focus On The Family: 8605 Explorer Drive, Colorado Springs, CO 80920-1051. 1-719-531-5181.
- Fowler Productions (video projection): 2800 Boardwalk, Norman, OK 73069. 1-800-729-0163.
- Good News Productions International: P.O. Box 222, Joplin, MO 64802. Website: www.gnpi.com
- Integrity Music: 1000 Cody Road, Mobile, AL 36695. 1-800-239-7000.
- Interlinc (Youth Leader's Only Music Service): P.O. Box 680848, Franklin, TN 37068-0848. 1-800-725-3300.
- International Disaster Emergency Services, Inc.: P.O. Box 60, Kempton, IN 46049. 1-317-947-5100.
- Kingdom Computers: P.O. Box 506, Mansfield, PA 16933. 1-800-488-1122.
- Lay Renewal Ministries (discounted resources): 3101 Bartold Avenue, St. Louis, MO 63143. 1-800-747-0815.
- Mothers of Preschoolers (MOPS): 1311 South Clarkson Street, Denver, CO 80210. 1-303-733-5353.
- The Navigators: 7899 Lexington Drive, Colorado Springs, CO 80920. 1-800-366-7788.
- The Search Institute: Thresher Square West, Suite 210, 700 South Third Street, Minneapolis, MN 55415. 1-800-888-7828. Website: www.searchinstitute.org
- Shepherd Ministries (youth resources): 2221 Walnut Hill, Irving, TX 75038-4410. 1-214-580-8000.

■ Walk Thru The Bible: 4201 North Peachtree Road, Atlanta, GA 30341. 1-800-868-9300. Website: www.walkthru.org

■ Teen Mission, USA: P.O. Box 24336, Lexington, KY 40524.

■ Youth For Christ, International: P.O. Box 228822, Denver, CO 80222. 1-303-843-9000.

■ Youth Ministry Stuff, Ltd.: 1-888-YM-STUFF or FAX 1-502-451-1936.

■ Youth Specialties: 1224 Greenfield Drive, El Cajon, CA 92021-3399. Website: www.youthspecialties.com

Conventions/Workshops/Seminars

↻ International Network of Children's Ministry: 1-800-324-4543.

↻ Children's Ministries University: P.O. Box 5077, Englewood, CO 80155-5077. 1-303-799-6751.

↻ Children's Ministry Workshop (Group Publishing): P.O. Box 485, Loveland, CO 80539. 1-800-774-3838.

↻ National Missionary Convention: P.O. Box 11, Copeland, KS 67837.

↻ National Resource Seminar for Youth Workers (Youth Specialties): 1-619-440-2333.

↻ National Youth and Children's Ministry Convention (Group Publishing): P.O. Box 485, Loveland, CO 80539. 1-800-774-3838.

↻ National Youth Leaders Convention (C.I.Y.): Box B, Joplin, MO 64802. 1-417-781-2273.

↻ National Youth Workers Convention (Youth Specialties): 1-619-440-2333.

↻ North American Christian Convention: P.O. Box 11326, Cincinnati, OH 45211. 1-513-598-6222.

↻ Pilgrimage/Navpress Small Group Training Seminar. 1-800-447-7787.

↻ World Convention of Churches of Christ: 1101 19th Avenue South, Nashville, TN 37212.

Periodicals

☞ *Children's Ministry* ($19.95/year): 1-800-447-1070.

☞ *Christian Standard* ($23.50/year): 1-800-521-0600.

☞ *Christianity Today* ($24.95/year): 1-800-999-1704.

☞ *Discipleship Journal* ($21.97/year): 1-800-877-1811.

☞ *Evangelizing Today's Child* ($20/year): 1-800-748-7710.

☞ *Group* ($21.95/year): 1-800-447-1070.

☞ *Leadership Journal* ($24.95/year): 1-800-777-3136.

☞ *Lookout* ($23.50/year): 1-800-543-1353.

☞ *Syllabus* ($24/year): 1-408-261-7200.

☞ *Teachers In Focus* ($20/year): 1-800-232-6459.

☞ *Vital Ministry* ($21.95/year): 1-800-447-1070.

☞ *Youthworker Journal* ($39.95/year): 1-800-769-7624.

Websites for Ideas, Helps, and Resources

💻 www.christianity.net (a starting point for hundreds of websites pertinent to Christianity).

💻 www.iclnet.org (includes an entire directory of Internet resources)

💻 www.leadnet.org (wonderful archived articles from Leadership Network)

💻 www.prrc.com (George Gallup, Jr.'s site)

💻 www.joshhunt.com (a gold mine for Christian educators, especially adult teachers)

💻 www.goshen.net

💻 www.christcom.net

💻 www.gospelcom.net

💻 www.ministrysearch.com

💻 www.youthspecialties.com (the ultimate youth ministry web site).

Recommended Books to Build Your Library

A survey of Christian educators—including professors, youth ministry specialists, and curriculum experts—helped to develop the following listing of recommended books for individuals who want to build a quality Christian education library.

These Christian educators represented a broad scope of interests, from children through adult ministries, in both parachurch and local congregations. Because the book market can change rapidly, it is possible for many of these books to go out of print. (A few listed are already out of print). However, most can still be purchased through individual bookstores, publishing houses, and wholesale booksellers. The books are listed in order of preference, the first being the most recommended books of all.

Survey participants include:

Virginia Beddow (Manhattan Christian College)
Les Christie (San Jose Christian College)

Rick Chromey (St. Louis Christian College)
Dan Cravatt (Nebraska Christian College)
Dr. Eleanor Daniel (Emmanuel School of Religion)
Dr. James Estep (Great Lakes Christian College)
Dick Gibson (Christ In Youth, Inc.)
Ken Greene (Minnesota Bible College)
Dr. Alvin Kuest (Great Lakes Christian College)
Charles Lee (Southeast Christian Church, Louisville, KY)
Marlene LeFever (David C. Cook Ministries)
Dr. Ron Oakes (St. Louis Christian College)
Sherry Parrott (Ozark Christian College)
Ruth Picker (Minnesota Bible College)
Dan Schantz (Central Christian College)
Thom Schultz (Group Publishing)
John Wade (Atlanta Christian College)
Gordon & Becki West (Kids At Heart, Int'l)
David Wheeler (Johnson Bible College)
Dr. Myron Williams (Cincinnati Bible Seminary)
Dr. Gary Zustiak (Ozark Christian College).

Most Highly Recommended (receiving 10 votes or more):

Creative Teaching Methods by Marlene LeFever (DC Cook,1985)

Teaching to Change Lives by Howard Hendricks (Multnomah, 1987)

Creative Bible Teaching by Lawrence Richards (Moody, 1970)

Purpose Driven Youth Ministry by Doug Fields (Zondervan, 1998)

The Seven Laws of the Learner by Bruce Wilkinson (Multnomah, 1992)

Purpose Driven Church by Rick Warren (Zondervan, 1995)

Family-Based Youth Ministry by Mark DeVries (IVP, 1994)

Christian Educator's Handbook on Adult Education by Kenneth Gangel and James Wilhoit (Victor, 1993)

Education That Is Christian by Lois LeBar, revised by James Plueddemann (Victor,1989)

Christian Educator's Handbook on Teaching by Kenneth Gangel and Howard Hendricks (Victor, 1989)

Learning Styles by Marlene LeFever (DC Cook, 1995)

Teaching for Results by Findley Edge (Broadman, 1956)

A Theology of Christian Education by Lawrence Richards (Zondervan, 1975)

🕮 *Childhood Education in the Church* by Roy Zuck and Robert Clark (Moody, 1975)

🕮 *Why Nobody Learns Much of Anything at Church* by Thom and Joani Schultz (Group, 1993)

🕮 *The Hurried Child* by David Elkind (Addison-Wesley, 1981)

🕮 *Design for Teaching and Training* by LeRoy Ford (Broadman, 1978)

🕮 *Teaching the Bible Creatively* by Bill McNabb and Steven Mabry (Zondervan, 1990)

🕮 *How to Work with Rude, Obnoxious and Apathetic Kids* by Les Christie (Victor, 1994)

🕮 *21st Century Sunday School* by Wes Haystead (Standard, 1995)

🕮 *Christian Education: Its History and Philosophy* by Kenneth Gangel and Warren Benson (Moody, 1983)

Recommended (receiving 7 to 9 votes):

🕮 *Eight Habits of an Effective Youth Worker* by Tim Smith (Victor, 1995)

🕮 *Create in Me a Youth Ministry* by Ridge Burns and Pam Campbell (Victor, 1994)

🕮 *Back to the Heart of Youth Work* by Dewey Bertolini (Victor, 1989)

🕮 *Created to Learn* by William Yount (Broadman, 1996)

🕮 *All Grown Up and No Place to Go* by David Elkind (Addison-Wesley, 1984)

🕮 *The Seven Laws of Teaching* by John Milton Gregory (Baker, 1954)

🕮 *Sunday School Standards* by Lowell Brown (Gospel Light, 1986)

🕮 *The Coming Revolution in Youth Ministry* by Mark Senter III (Victor, 1992)

🕮 *Foundations of Ministry* edited by Michael Anthony (Bridgepoint, 1992)

🕮 *Christian Education: Foundations for the Future* edited by Robert E. Clark, Lin Johnson and Allyn K. Sloat (Moody, 1991)

🕮 *Called to Care* by Doug Stevens (Zondervan, 1985)

Honorable Mention (receiving at least 4 votes):

🕮 *The Fourth Turning* by William Strauss and Neil Howe (Broadway, 1997)

🕮 *Serendipity Encyclopedia* by Lyman Coleman (Serendipity House, 1997)

🕮 *The Next Generation* by Gary Zustiak (College Press, 1996)

🕮 *Student Ministry for the 21st Century* by Bo Boshers (Zondervan, 1997)

🕮 *The Family-Friendly Church* by Ben Freudenberg (Group, 1998)

🕮 *Frames of the Mind* by Howard Gardner (Basic Books, 1983)

🕮 *Why Teenagers Act the Way They Do* by Keith Olson (Group, 1987)

- *The Way They Learn* by Cynthia Ulrich Tobias (Focus On The Family, 1994)
- *Teaching for Moral Growth* by Bonnidell Clouse (Bridgepoint, 1993)
- *Punished by Rewards* by Alfie Kohn (Houghton Mifflin, 1993)
- *Teaching for Spiritual Growth* by Perry Downs (Zondervan, 1994)
- *24 Ways to Improve Your Teaching* by Kenneth Gangel (Victor, 1974)
- *Teach with Success* by Guy Leavitt, revised by Eleanor Daniel (Standard, 1990)
- *Generation Next* by George Barna (Regal, 1995)
- *10 Sunday Schools That Dared to Change* by Elmer Towns (Regal, 1993)
- *A Passion for Learning* by D. Bruce Lockerbie (Moody, 1994)
- *No Youth Worker Is an Island* by Ridge Burns and Pam Campbell (Victor, 1992)
- *Extraordinary Results from Ordinary Teachers* by Michael Warden (Group, 1998)
- *Teaching As Jesus Taught* by Roy B. Zuck (Baker, 1995)

BOOKS FROM COLLEGE PRESS
FOR CHRISTIAN EDUCATION WORKERS

GENERAL REOURCES FOR GROWING YOUR MINISTRY:

Herding Cats by Rusty George and Jeff Krajewski (2001)
Making Your Church a Place to Serve by Don Waddell (2001)
The People-Magnet Church by Darren Walter (2001)
The Prayer-Driven Church: Releasing God's Power to Every Member by Ray Fulenwider
    (2000)
The Servant-Driven Church: Releasing Every Member for Ministry by Ray Fulenwider
    (1997)
Systems-Sensitive Leadership: Empowering Diversity without Polarizing the Church by
    Mike Armour (1995)

RESOURCES FOR LESSON PREPARATION:

Building Blocks for Bible Study by Peter Verkruyse (1997)
The Chronological Life of Christ in 2 volumes by Mark E. Moore (1997)
The College Press NIV Commentary Series
    Includes commentaries on all New Testament books.
        Entire NT also available on CD in 2002.
    Old Testament volumes available as of June, 2002:

Deuteronomy (2000)	*1&2 Samuel* (2000)
1&2 Chronicles (2001)	*Ezra–Nehemiah* (2001)
Esther/Daniel (2001)	*Psalms Vol. 1* [1–72] (1999)
Isaiah Vol. 1 [1–27] (2000)	*Jeremiah–Lamentations* (2002)
Ezekiel (2002)	*Minor Prophets Vol. 1* [Hos–Mic] (2001)

Old Testament History: An Overview of Sacred History and Truth by Wilbur Fields
    (1998)
The Old Testament Survey Series (5 volumes) by James E. Smith

RESOURCES FOR YOUTH WORKERS:

Creative to the Max I by Todd Clark (1996)
Creative to the Max II by Todd and Toby Clark (1999)
Things They Never Taught You about Youth Ministry That You Really Need to Know
    by Todd Clark (1996)

SUPPLEMENTAL STUDIES FOR CHILDREN:

Basic Bible Studies for Children (Grades 1-6) by Gary Olsby (1999)
Thirteen Lessons in Christian Doctrine, Youth Edition by Denver Sizemore and
    John Hunter (1994)
Good As New (Leader's Guide and Student Workbook) by Doug Gibson (2000)

SUPPLEMENTAL STUDIES FOR ADULTS:

Bible History Overview: New Testament (Student Book and Teacher's Guide) by Gary Olsby (1990)

Bible History Overview: Old Testament (Student Book and Teacher's Guide) by Gary Olsby (1990)

College Press Studies for Small Groups

Abortion and the Sanctity of Human Life by Frances J. Beckwith (2000)

Anchors for the Soul by John Mark Hicks (2001)

Characters of Calvary by Kenn Filkins (1997)

Christ and Islam: Understanding the Faith of Muslims by James A. Beverley (1997)

The Family of God: The Meaning of Church Membership by LeRoy Lawson (1995)

For Theirs Is the Kingdom by Scott Gleaves (1997)

Heart, Soul, and Money: A Christian View of Possessions by Craig L. Blomberg (2000)

Heaven, What a Wonderful Place! by Kenny Boles (1999)

How to Dodge a Dragon: A Devotional Reading of Revelation by Mark E. Moore (1998)

How to Love Someone You Can't Stand by Milton Jones (1997)

The Jehovah's Witnesses by Michael C. McKenzie (1999)

Love in Action: A Practical Study of Christian Ethics by Michael C. Armour (1997)

Marriage Is a Covenant, Not a Contract by Glover Shipp (1995)

Payday: Treasures for Stay-at-Home Moms by Cindy Dagnan (1999)

Pick the Brighter TULIP: There Is an Alternative to Calvinism by Alger Fitch (1997)

The Resurrection: Heart of New Testament Doctrine by Gary R. Habermas (2000)

The Resurrection: Heart of the Christian Life by Gary R. Habermas (2000)

Romans for Regular People by Charlie W. Starr (due September 2002)

Scribbles: Sketches for Stressed-Out Moms by Cindy Dagnan (1997)

Slaying the Dragon of Evolution by Isaac Manly (1999)

Sweet Hour of Prayer by Don DeWelt (1999)

Ten Commandments for Couples by Glover Shipp (due August 2002)

What Men Need to Hear: Becoming God's Spiritual Leader through Moral Strength by Rick Atchley (1999)

You Are Not Your Own: Becoming God's Steward by Mike Armour (1995)

Your Way or God's Way? Developing Christian Character When No One Else Cares by LeRoy Lawson (1998)

Encounters with Christ by Mark E. Moore (2001)
The Faces of Our Lives: A Journey of Discovery for Women by Vickie Hull (1998)
Faith under Fire: Studies from 1&2 Peter by David Faust (2002)
Falling in Love with Jesus: Studies in the Book of Luke by Rubel Shelly (1998)
Falling in Love with Jesus' People: Studies in the Book of Acts by Rubel Shelly (1998)
Genesis: The Beginnings of Faith by Rubel Shelly (1997)
I'd Rather See a Sermon: Showing Your Friends the Way to Heaven by Dave Stone
    (1996)
A Life Worth Living Series by Ross Brodfuehrer
        Charting Your Course: Directions for Real Life (1999)
        Controlling Your Pests: Ridding Your Life of Bad Habits (2000)
        Taking out the Garbage: Leaving Your Past (2000)
A Newcomer's Guide to the Bible by Mike Armour (1999)
A Newcomer's Guide to the Bible Personal Workbook by Mike Armour (2002)
Thirteen Lessons in Christian Doctrine by Denver Sizemore (1997)
Twelve More Lessons in Christian Doctrine by Denver Sizemore (1997)
A Year in the Life of Christ by Mark Moore and Jon Weece (2002)
        1. *The Person of Jesus*   2. *The Power of Jesus*
        3. *The Preaching of Jesus*   4. *The Passion of Jesus* (due out in October)

TOPICAL INDEX

Abstract reasoning   68, 165, 168, 238

Abuse, physical and sexual   329-332

Adolescents   65, 70, 72, 76, 178-192

Adults

    Distinctives of adult learners   72-73, 203-204, 205-206

    Divisions of   72-73, 198-203

        Middle adults   73, 199-200

        Older adults   77, 201, 340, 351

        Young adults   72, 77, 198-199, 227

    Goals for   72-73, 77

    Lesson plan for   208-210

    Lifelong learning   77, 88-89, 203

    Single adults   81-82, 202-203, 295, 303, 351

Application of Bible learning   16, 45-46, 73, 109, 123, 154-155, 157, 161, 167, 208

Art, as teaching method   127, 129, 141, 154, 157, 169, 172, 186, 210

Audiovisual methods   129, 234-237, 240-241

Autism   218, 231

Axiology   36, 39, 42

Bible clubs   301-302, 334

Bible studies   111, 300, 302

Camping   175, 301, 303-304, 332-333, 348, 351

Cerebral palsy   217, 231

Children's church   99-100, 175, 281, 295-296

Christian education professional   9, 364-376

Christian preschool   100, 138-158, 175, 315

Christian schools   329, 334-336

Church library   207, 304-305

Closely graded curriculum   102

Cognitive development   141-146, 180-181

Communication disorders   217, 226

Concrete operation stage   67, 76, 144, 164-165, 224

Conservation, principle of   144-145

Contemporary family   251-252

Context, principle of   99

Coordination of programs   274, 276, 284

Copyright laws   326-329

Cross-cultural communication   273

Curriculum

    Definition   96-97

    Evaluation   37-38, 104-107, 242, 284, 351-352, 357-358

    Grading   101-102

    Materials   103-104, 107-108, 170, 172-173, 336, 343, 358

    Selection   103-104

Day camp   175, 291-292, 333

Day care   157-158, 300, 315, 330

Demographics   80-81

Design, principle of   101-103

Developmental stages

    Preschool   9, 65-67, 71-72, 75-76, 138-152

    Elementary children   9, 67-72, 76, 161-165

    Youth   9, 72, 76-77, 180-182

    Adults   9, 72-73, 77, 198-203

Disabilities   89, 213-232, 335

Discipline   35, 72, 74-75, 118, 145, 150, 191, 226, 254

Distance learning   90-91, 243

Divorced adults   202-203

Drama   127, 172, 186, 189-190, 210, 227, 235

Electives   90, 102, 297

Elementary children

    Goals for   170-171

    Cognitive development   67-68, 166-169

Moral/spiritual development 73-76, 161-163

Psychosocial development 70-72, 164-165

Physical development 64, 164-165

Teaching methods 46, 68, 166-169, 172-175

Emotional disorders 217-218, 226

Epistemology 36, 39-42

Essentialism 36-37, 55

Evaluation
Of Christian education 338-354
Of curriculum 98-107
Questionnaire 349, 356-358

Existentialism 36, 38-39

Family 16-17, 83, 101, 160, 179-181, 199, 213-216, 228-232, 250-267, 299-300

Formal operation stage 67-68

Gifted learners 175, 217

Goals 42-43, 68, 107-108, 111, 153, 160, 170-171, 191, 223, 257, 262, 274-275, 277-278, 280-281, 284-285, 339, 341-343

Grading of curriculum 101-102

Hearing disorders 217, 219, 225, 230

Hebrew education 47

History of Christian education 35, 47-57

Home schooling 179, 248, 335-336

Hook, book, look, took
lesson structure 108-111, 208-210

Idealism 36-39, 48

Identity formation 43, 72, 76, 149, 182

Inclusive education 214, 220-228, 229

Intellectual development 50, 65-68, 141-146, 164-165, 180-181

Jesus, as teacher 19, 20-22, 116-120, 214-216

Job analysis 313

Leadership 22, 89, 91, 99-104, 169-170, 259, 263, 273, 278-288, 293, 297-298, 311-320, 356, 363, 371, 374, 376

Learning styles 165-169

Legal and security issues 321-337

Lesson preparation 107-111

Liability, church 323-326,

Liberalism 26, 28, 56

Materials, curriculum 103-104, 107-108, 170, 172-173, 336, 343, 358

Medieval church 47, 50-51

Mental retardation 216-217, 222, 224, 227-228, 230

Metaphysics 36, 38-40

Methods for teaching 116-120, 121-134, 153-157, 172-175, 184-190, 234-238

Minister and Christian education 359-367

Moral/spiritual development 56, 73-78, 149-152, 164-165, 181, 222, 229-230

Mother's Day Out 175

Motor disorders 217, 218, 225

Music, as teaching method 76, 127, 129-130, 153, 155, 173, 186, 189-190, 210, 227, 383

Neoorthodoxy 26-28, 57

Nursery 147, 150-153, 231, 279, 282, 296, 340-341, 357

Objectives 105-106, 108, 110, 156, 170, 190, 208, 257, 275, 282, 338-347, 351-353, 356-357, 373

Off-site ministries 305-307

Older adults 77, 201, 340, 351

Orthopedic disorders 217-218, 225-226

Philosophy of Christian education   39-46, 373

Physical development   138-141, 180, 339

Planning   70, 97-103, 154, 206-207, 239, 246, 261, 271-290, 317, 375

Positivism   36-37

Pragmatism   36, 38-39

Preoperational stage   66-67, 142

Preschoolers   108, 138-158

Process, principle of   44-45, 103

Process theology   27-28, 57

Psychosocial development   71, 146-149

Puberty   65, 180-181

Realism   36-39, 48, 51

Records   283, 327, 336, 347, 352, 357, 373

Recruitment of workers   312-316, 319

Reformation   47, 51-52

Renaissance   51-52

Retreats   207, 304, 357

Sensorimotor stage   66, 142

Sexual development   64-65, 149, 165, 180

Single adults   81-82, 202-203, 295, 303, 351

Small groups   44, 91-92, 127-128, 205-207, 292, 297, 302, 312, 361, 366

Social trends   80, 84-89

Staff relationships   375-376

Storytelling   109, 128, 155, 171

Sunday school   44, 54, 57, 90, 99-100, 103, 121, 175, 185, 206-207, 222-224, 229, 231, 292-297, 309, 313, 327-328, 331, 342, 344, 347, 349-352, 356-358, 359-366

Support groups   160, 163, 175, 207, 257, 299

Synagogue   15, 47-48, 118, 129, 363

Teacher   16-21, 28, 30, 44-46, 60, 62-63, 68, 77, 92, 97-98, 105-108, 115-137, 144-145, 148-150, 155-156, 163, 166-167, 170-171, 173-174, 181, 183-185, 187-189, 191-192, 204, 222, 224, 236, 285, 302, 313, 315-317, 336, 344-345, 349, 364

Teacher training   92, 316-317, 363

Teaching methods   46, 68, 103, 180, 344

Technology, in teaching   233-249

Theology, of Christian education   15-19, 22-32

Thomism   36-39, 51

Traumatic brain injury   218

Uniform lesson plan   101

Vacation Bible School   99, 175, 231, 281-282, 303, 327, 348, 351, 357

Visual disorders   215, 217, 225

Vocabulary development   68, 143-144

Weekday programs   175, 297-305

Writing, as teaching method   21, 119, 129, 166-167, 173-174, 186, 190, 236

Young adults   72, 77, 198-199, 227, 279-280

Youth   70, 77, 85-86, 131, 178-193, 213, 231-232, 244-245, 248, 271, 281-283, 292-298, 300, 303, 307, 311, 313, 317, 330-331, 340-341, 349, 351, 356, 376

INDEX OF PEOPLE

Adler 29

Alcuin 51

Ambrose 49

Anselm 42

Aquinas, Thomas 37, 50-51

Aristotle 37, 48

Augustine 29, 51

Baker, Jason 248, 249

Barna, George 82, 272, 289

Barth, Karl 26

Basil the Great 49

Benedict 51

Benson, Peter 204, 271, 289

Bernstine, Karen Jones 257, 265

Boethius 51

Bower, Bobbie 170

Boys, Mary E. 27, 33

Bultmann, Rudolph 26

Burgess, Harold 56-58

Bushnell, Horace 55-56

Calvin, John 52

Cassiodorus 51

Chafer, Lewis Sperry 31, 33

Chandler, Russell 273, 289

Charlemagne 51

Clement of Alexandria 49

Coe, George Albert 26, 56

Comenius, John Amos 53

Cookston 256, 260, 265

Craig, J.D. 251, 265

Crosby, Fanny 222

Darwin, Charles 54

Deal, R.L. 262, 265

de Feltre 52

Dettoni 62-63

Dewey, John 38, 55

Downs, Perry 163, 176

Dreikers, Rudolf 191

Dunn, Kenneth 165, 238

Dunn, Rita 165, 238

Eklin, Carolyn 204, 271, 289

Elkind, David 70, 169, 182, 193

Elliott, Harrison 26, 56

Emler, Donald 372, 377

Erikson, Erik H. 71, 146, 182

Ferré, Nels F.S. 27-28, 33

Ford, Leroy 112, 123, 136

Fowler, James 75-78, 151, 162-163, 176

Froebel, Friedrich Wilhelm August 53

Gaebelein, Frank E. 27

Gangel, Kenneth O. 27, 57-58, 177, 211, 272, 280, 289, 320, 355

Gardner, Howard 165, 239, 249

Gesell, Arnold 74

Gough 253

Gregorc, Anthony 238-239, 249

Griggs, Donald 292

Groote, Gerhard 52

Habermas, Ronald T. 30, 33, 159

Harris, Maria 29, 33

Havighurst, Robert J. 73, 78

Hayes, Edward L. 20, 33

Herbart, Johann 54

Hill, E.V. 30

Homer 48

Homrighausen, E.G. 27

Houle, Cyril 203, 211

Isocrates 48

Jerome 49

Johnson, Evelyn 170

Josephus 47

Kant, Immanuel 38

Kelly 256, 260, 265

Kevorkian, Jack 86

Kierkegaard, Søren 38

Knight, George   43, 58
Knowles, Malcolm   203, 211
Kohlberg, Lawrence   74, 150
Lazear, D.G.   239, 249
Lee, James Michael   57
Leonard, J.H.   260, 265
Lines, Timothy Arthur   369, 377
Little, Sara   25-26, 32-33, 205
Locke, John   53
Luther, Martin   52
Macauley   73
Malphurs, A.   278, 290
McDonald, Cleveland   252, 254, 265
McDonald, Philip   252, 254, 265
McIntosh, Gary   82
Melanchthon, Phillip   52
Miller, Randolph Crump   27, 57, 355
Norton, M.P.   263, 267
Olson, R.P.   260, 266
Origen   49
Pazmiño, Robert   16, 19, 27, 30, 33, 78, 112
Pestalozzi, Johann   53
Piaget, Jean   55, 65, 67-68, 74, 141-142,
                       144, 164-165, 180
Plato   37, 48
Prevost, Ronnie   50, 58
Price, J.M.   18, 33, 117, 136
Quintillian   48
Rabelais, François   52
Raikes, Robert   54

Reed, James E.   50, 58
Richards, Lawrence O.   27, 112, 137, 159
Robbins, Duffy   308, 310
Roehlkepartain, Eugene   211, 292, 298,
                               310, 367
Rousseau, Jean   53
Sherrill, Lewis Joseph   49, 59
Smith, H. Sheldon   27, 57
Socrates   48
Spencer, Herbert   54
Stein, R.H.   118, 136
Taba   73
Tertullian   49
Thomas, D.M.   256, 266
Thornton, S.   262, 264
Tidwell, Charles A.   18, 355, 367
Tiffin, Gerald   70
Tough, Alan   203, 211
Veith, Paul H.   27
Vogelsang, J.D.   263, 267
Warren, Rick   365-366
Watkins   73
Westerhoff, John   161-163, 177
Whitehead   28
Wilhoit, James   211
Wyckoff, D. Campbell   14, 27, 33
Wynn, J.C.   253, 267
Yancey, Philip   210
Zuck, Roy B.   20, 23, 33, 117, 119,
                          136-137, 159

SCRIPTURE INDEX

Gen	ch. 1	108, 158
	ch. 1–3	30
	ch. 3	61
	1:27	30, 60
	1:27-28	254
	1:28-30	61
	2:15-16	61
	5:1	60
	6:9–7:5	234
	ch. 6–9	156
	9:12-17	234
Exod	3:3	234
	ch. 7–11	234
	12:26-27	17
	13:21-22	235
	18:17	276
	18:20	17
	18:21-23	276
	20:1-7	17
	20:4-12	17
	20:12	254
	20:14	254
	20:17	254
	ch. 20–32	235
	24:12	17
	ch. 35–40	235
	35:34	17
	ch. 39	235
Deut	4:9-10	17
	4:9-11	17
	4:14	17, 18
	6:1	17, 18
	6:1-9	16
	6:4-7	254
	6:4-9	161
	6:6-7	17
	6:6-8	254

	6:6-9	22
	11:19	15
	11:19-20	17
	20:18	15
	ch. 22	18
	26:1ff	18
	29:9	17
	30:11-20	16
	31:9-13	16
	31:9-14	18
	31:12	24
	31:19	17
	31:39	18
Josh	8:30-35	18
Judg	2:10-15	17
	14:12-14	18
1 Sam	10:10	17
	19:20	17
2 Sam	13:1-22	18
1 Kgs	8:41-43	24
	11:29-33	236
	18:16-46	175
2 Kgs	2:3	18
	2:3-5	17
	4:38	17, 18
	5:22	18
	6:1	17
1 Chr	12:32	272
2 Chr	17:7-9	15
	17:7-19	18
	34:29-30	15
Ezra	7:10-11	16, 18
Neh	ch. 8	18
	8:1-9	16
Job	36:22	17
Ps	ch. 8	60
	8:6-8	61
	27:31	18

	37:31	18
	40:8	18
	ch. 78	16
	78:3-6	17
	78:5,6	161
	127:3-5	254
Prov	1:8	17
	1:20	16
	2:17	16
	3:3-11	18
	4:1-4	161
	6:20	17
	8:1-36	16
	9:1	16
	10:8	18
	12:15	18
	13:14	18
	13:24	16
	14:2	18
	15:22	275
	17:20	16
	22:6	161, 165
	22:15	16
	23:13	254
	28:4-9	18
	29:25-27	16
Isa	3:8	17
	8:3-16	17
	8:16	17
	35:4-6	230
	42:21-24	17
Jer	8:8	17, 18
	9:13	17
	16:11	17
	29:7	47
Ezek	ch. 4	236
Dan	ch. 5	236
Hos	1:3-9	17

Micah	6:8	17
Hag	2:11	18
Zech	7:12	17
Mal	2:6-9	18
	3:11	18
Matt	Book of	21
	1:18-25	208-210
	2:28-29	20
	8:5-12	132
	10:25	189
	12:13	237
	14:15-21	133
	15:29-30	215
	18:3	151
	18:3-6	236
	18:5,6	161
	23:10	116
	28:1-8	294
	28:16-20	22
	28:18-20	19, 24, 93
	28:20	21
Mark	Book of	21
	1:17	20
	1:21,22	117
	2:1-5	216
	5:22-43	132
	6:30	21
	9:20-24	215
	9:33-37	161
	9:42	330
	10:1	20
	10:13-16	123, 161
	10:51	215
	16:15	214
Luke	Book of	21
	2:1-20	108
	2:1-21	110
	2:40,52	31

	2:46,47	117
	5:12-14	215
	5:31	94
	10:2	304
	12:12	21
	12:24	237
	14:21-23	215
	17:11-19	133
	18:40	215
	24:13-35	19
John	3:2	117
	5:1-14	215
	5:6	215
	5:14	215
	7:45,46	115
	8:31-59	118
	9:1-3	215
	9:1-12	237
	12:1-3	134
	14:18	255
	21:5,6	133
Acts	Book of	19
	1:1	21
	2:37-42	292
	2:42	19, 21
	2:42-47	21
	5:28	21
	5:42	19
	chs 6, 8, 13	293
	6:1-6	292
	12:1-17	293
	13:2	21
	14:21	21
	ch. 15	293
	17:19	21
Rom	ch. 1–3	40
	1:18-25	40
	3:1-4	40

	5:17,19	61
	8:1-27	20
	12:3-8	21
	15:4	14
	20:7	294
1 Cor	ch. 2	31
	2:6-16	19, 32
	2:10-13	13
	3:1-9	62
	9:22b,23	291
	10:5-11	14
	12:27-31	21
	16:2	294
2 Cor	6:1	20
Gal	4:4-5	111
	5:16-26	20
Eph	2:1-10	31, 61
	4:7-16	20
	4:7-13,29-32	21
	4:11	22
	4:17–5:7	211
	4:26	61
	5:15-20	21
	5:21–6:4	44
	5:25	44
	6:1	44
	6:4	44, 254
Phil	4:8	42
Col	1:28	48, 61
	2:8	36
1 Thess	5:23	42
1 Tim	Book of	20
	2:3-4	20
	3:2	22
	3:4	55
	3:15-17	13
2 Tim	Book of	20
	1:14a	47

	3:15	13		2:11-12	20		4:10-11	21
	3:15-17	14, 29	Heb	5:11–6:3	20	2 Pet	1:20-21	13
Titus	Book of	20		12:2	42		3:2,15-16	13
	1:9	22	1 Pet	1:10-12,21	13		3:9	31
	2:1-15	20		2:2	31			